The Diabetic Cookbook for Beginners

for Beginners

2000+Days of Simple & Healthy Diabetics Diet Recipes with Complete Food List & Meal Planner for Type 1 & 2 Diabetes

Rose J. Heffner

Contents

Welcome to Your Guide to Diabetic-Friendly Cooking

Embarking on a journey with diabetes doesn't mean saying goodbye to delicious food.

Instead, it's about welcoming a new relationship with meals, one that balances indulgence with mindful eating.

Understanding Diabetes in 2024:

The Evolution and Understanding of Diabetes

As we step into 2024, our understanding of diabetes has evolved significantly, reflecting years of research, advancements in medical technology, and an improved understanding of nutrition and lifestyle impact on health. Diabetes, primarily categorised into Type 1, Type 2, and gestational diabetes, affects millions worldwide, posing challenges in healthcare management, personal lifestyle, and global health economies.

Current State of Diabetes

Prevalence: Diabetes continues to be a prevalent chronic disease globally, with a noticeable rise attributed to factors like aging populations, urbanization, and increasing prevalence of obesity and physical inactivity.

Technological Advancements: The year 2024 has seen remarkable advancements in diabetes management, including more sophisticated insulin pumps, continuous glucose monitors (CGMs), and the advent of artificial pancreas systems. These technologies offer better blood sugar control and real-time data to inform daily diabetes management.

Treatment Personalization: There's a growing trend towards personalized medicine.

Health professionals are increasingly focusing on individualized treatment plans, considering the patient's genetic makeup, lifestyle, and specific health needs.

Diet and Lifestyle

Nutritional Understanding: There's a deeper understanding of the role diet plays in managing diabetes. Low-carbohydrate diets, plant-based diets, and the Mediterranean diet are among the recommended eating patterns for managing blood sugar levels. In this cookbook, we will explore different variations of some popular staples of both of these diets.

Lifestyle Interventions: Lifestyle changes, including increased physical activity, stress management, and regular health check-ups, are emphasised more than ever. These are not only seen as supplementary to medication but as foundational to managing diabetes.

Challenges and Opportunities

Global Health Concern: Diabetes remains a significant global health concern. The increasing incidence in younger populations, especially of Type 2 diabetes, poses new challenges in healthcare.

Health Disparities: There's an increased focus on addressing health disparities related to diabetes care, recognizing that access to healthcare, education, and healthy living conditions are not evenly distributed globally.

Future Directions

Research and Innovation: Ongoing research into insulin types, delivery methods, and a potential cure continues to be a priority. The exploration of beta-cell regeneration, immunotherapy for Type 1 Diabetes, or innovative medications for Type 2 Diabetes is at the forefront of scientific inquiry.

Education and Awareness: Efforts to increase diabetes awareness, education, and prevention are amplified, with a focus on early detection and lifestyle modifications to prevent or delay the onset of Type 2 Diabetes.

Integrated Care: There's a move towards more integrated care models, combining nutrition, physical activity, mental health support, and medical care to manage diabetes more effectively and improve the quality of life.

Living with Diabetes in 2024

Living with diabetes in 2024 is marked by more supportive communities, improved healthcare services, and an array of technological tools at one's disposal. Education systems, workplaces, and health insurance models are increasingly accommodating and supportive of individuals with diabetes, reflecting a society more informed and empathetic towards the condition.

As we look at diabetes in 2024, it's evident that while challenges remain, there are more resources, technologies, and information available than ever to manage and live well with diabetes. The future holds promise for continued advancements in treatment, a deeper understanding of the disease, and an ever-growing supportive community for those affected.

This cookbook is a testament to the journey of diabetes management, reflecting on where we've been, where we are, and the hopeful path ahead.

This cookbook is designed to help you navigate your dietary needs without sacrificing flavor or enjoyment. Packed with 320 recipes spread across nine diverse chapters, this collection is your comprehensive guide to diabetic-friendly cooking.

Whether you're looking for a hearty breakfast, a comforting main dish, or a sweet treat, you'll find recipes that satisfy your cravings while keeping your health in check.

Chapter 1: Breakfast recipes

Welcome to the first chapter of your journey toward a healthier, more vibrant start to your day. Breakfast, often hailed as the most important meal, sets the tone for your energy levels, metabolism, and blood sugar control throughout the day.

For those managing diabetes, a thoughtful breakfast is more than a meal—it's an opportunity to nourish your body with balanced nutrients that stabilize blood sugar, provide lasting energy, and keep cravings at bay.

In this chapter, we unveil a collection of carefully crafted recipes designed specifically for the nutritional needs and culinary delight of those with diabetes. Each dish has been thoughtfully created to deliver maximum flavor without compromising blood sugar levels. From wholesome, hearty options to light and refreshing meals, these recipes cater to diverse tastes and lifestyles, ensuring that every morning starts with not just a meal, but a celebration of health and well-being.

We understand the unique challenges that come with managing diabetes, and that's why each recipe is more than just diabetic-friendly—it's a fusion of culinary art and nutritional science. Expect ingredients that are rich in fiber, healthy fats, and proteins, along with low-glycemic fruits and grains that keep your blood sugar in check.

So, let's turn the page and embark on a flavorful journey where each recipe is a step toward embracing a healthier, happier you at the start of each day. Welcome to deliciously diabetic-friendly breakfasts!

Spinach and Mushroom Egg Muffins

Serves: 4

Prep time: 10 minutes / Cook time: 20 minutes

Ingredients:

- 6 large eggs
- 1 cup chopped spinach
- 1/2 cup diced mushrooms
- 1/4 cup diced onions
- 1/4 cup shredded cheese (optional or use a low-fat variety)
- Salt and pepper to taste

Instructions:

1. Preheat the oven to 375°F (190°C) and lightly grease a muffin tin.
2. In a bowl, whisk together eggs, salt, and pepper.
3. Stir in spinach, mushrooms, onions, and cheese until well combined.
4. Pour the mixture into the muffin tins, filling each about 3/4 full.
5. Bake for 20 minutes or until the tops are firm to the touch and eggs are cooked.
6. Allow to cool slightly before removing from the tin.

Benefits for Diabetics:

These egg muffins are high in protein and low in carbs, helping to stabilize blood sugar levels. Spinach and mushrooms provide essential vitamins and minerals, while the optional cheese adds calcium without significant carbs, making it a balanced, nutritious choice for diabetics.

Per Serving:

Calories: 150 | Fat: 10g | Carbs: 3g | Fiber: 1g | Protein: 12g

Avocado and Salmon Lettuce Wrap

Serves: 2

Prep time: 10 minutes / Cook time: 0 minutes

Ingredients:

- 4 large lettuce leaves
- 4 oz smoked salmon
- 1 ripe avocado, sliced
- 1/2 small red onion, thinly sliced
- 1 tbsp capers
- 1 tsp lemon juice
- Fresh dill for garnish
- Salt and pepper to taste

Instructions:

1. Wash and pat dry the lettuce leaves.
2. Place equal amounts of smoked salmon on each lettuce leaf.
3. Top with slices of avocado, red onion, and capers.
4. Sprinkle lemon juice over the top and season with salt and pepper.
5. Garnish with fresh dill and roll the lettuce to form wraps.

Benefits for Diabetics:

Salmon is a great source of omega-3 fatty acids, beneficial for heart health, while avocado provides healthy monounsaturated fats aiding in blood sugar control. The combination of protein, fats, and minimal carbs in this dish makes it ideal for diabetics looking for a satisfying, nutritious breakfast.

Per Serving:

Calories: 220 | Fat: 15g | Carbs: 9g | Fiber: 7g | Protein: 12g

Chia and Coconut Yogurt Parfait

Serves: 2

Prep time: 10 minutes / Cook time: 0 minutes

Ingredients:

- 1 cup unsweetened coconut yogurt
- 3 tbsp chia seeds
- 1/2 cup almond milk
- 1/2 tsp vanilla extract
- 1 cup mixed berries (strawberries, blueberries, raspberries)
- A handful of nuts for topping (almonds or walnuts)

Instructions:

1. In a bowl, mix chia seeds with almond milk and vanilla extract. Let it sit for an hour or overnight until it becomes a gel-like pudding.
2. Begin layering your parfait by spooning a layer of coconut yogurt into two glasses.
3. Add a layer of chia pudding over the yogurt.
4. Top with fresh mixed berries and a sprinkle of nuts.

Benefits for Diabetics:
Chia seeds are a great source of fiber, helping to slow down the digestion of food and the release of sugars into the bloodstream. Coconut yogurt is a dairy-free alternative, lower in carbs than traditional yogurt, making this parfait a healthy, diabetic-friendly breakfast choice.

Per Serving:
Calories: 250 | Fat: 15g | Carbs: 20g | Fiber: 10g | Protein: 8g

Turkey and Veggie Breakfast Skillet

Serves: 4
Prep time: 10 minutes / Cook time: 20 minutes

Ingredients:
- 1 lb ground turkey
- 1 cup chopped bell peppers
- 1/2 cup chopped onions
- 1 cup chopped spinach
- 2 cloves garlic, minced
- 1 tsp olive oil
- Salt and pepper to taste

Instructions:
1. Heat olive oil in a large skillet over medium heat. Add garlic and onions, sautéing until translucent.
2. Add the ground turkey and cook until browned, breaking it apart with a spatula.
3. Mix in bell peppers and continue cooking for a few minutes until they soften.
4. Stir in spinach and cook until wilted.
5. Season with salt and pepper to taste and serve hot.

Benefits for Diabetics:
This breakfast skillet is packed with lean protein and fiber-rich vegetables, making it a filling and balanced meal that helps control blood sugar levels. The combination of turkey and vegetables provides essential vitamins and minerals, while the low-carb content is ideal for diabetes management.

Per Serving:
Calories: 220 | Fat: 12g | Carbs: 6g | Fiber: 2g | Protein: 23g

Blueberry Almond Overnight Oats

Serves: 2
Prep time: 5 minutes / Cook time: 0 minutes

Ingredients:
- 1 cup rolled oats
- 1 cup unsweetened almond milk
- 1/2 cup blueberries
- 2 tbsp almond butter
- 1 tbsp chia seeds
- 1/4 tsp almond extract (optional)
- Sweetener of choice (stevia or erythritol, to taste)

Instructions:
1. In a mason jar or bowl, combine rolled oats, almond milk, chia seeds, and almond extract. Mix well.
2. Stir in almond butter and sweetener to your desired taste.
3. Cover and refrigerate overnight.
4. In the morning, top with fresh blueberries and serve cold.

Benefits for Diabetics:
Overnight oats are a great source of soluble fiber, which can help regulate blood sugar levels. Blueberries add

antioxidants and a natural sweetness without a significant sugar spike. Almond milk and almond butter provide healthy fats, making this a balanced meal for diabetics.

Per Serving:
Calories: 300 | Fat: 14g | Carbs: 34g | Fiber: 8g | Protein: 10g

Cinnamon Flaxseed Pancakes

Serves: 2
Prep time: 10 minutes / Cook time: 10 minutes

Ingredients:
- 1 cup almond flour
- 1/4 cup ground flaxseed
- 1 tsp baking powder
- 1/2 tsp cinnamon
- 2 large eggs
- 1/2 cup unsweetened almond milk
- 1 tsp vanilla extract
- Non-stick cooking spray or butter for cooking
- Sugar-free syrup or fresh berries for topping

Instructions:
1. In a bowl, mix almond flour, ground flaxseed, baking powder, and cinnamon.
2. In another bowl, whisk together eggs, almond milk, and vanilla extract.
3. Combine wet and dry ingredients, stirring until you have a smooth batter.
4. Heat a non-stick pan over medium heat and lightly coat with spray or butter.
5. Pour small ladles of batter onto the hot pan, cooking until bubbles form, then flip and cook until golden.
6. Serve warm with sugar-free syrup or fresh berries.

Benefits for Diabetics:
These pancakes are low in carbs and high in fiber, promoting stable blood sugar levels. Flaxseed provides omega-3 fatty acids, beneficial for heart health, while cinnamon can improve insulin sensitivity.

Conclusion:
Cinnamon Flaxseed Pancakes are a delightful, heart-healthy breakfast option, offering a tasty way to enjoy a classic morning favorite while adhering to a diabetic-friendly diet.

Per Serving:
Calories: 280 | Fat: 20g | Carbs: 12g | Fiber: 6g | Protein: 12g

Greek Yogurt and Nuts Breakfast Bowl

Serves: 2
Prep time: 5 minutes / Cook time: 0 minutes

Ingredients:
- 1 cup Greek yogurt (unsweetened)
- 1/4 cup mixed nuts (almonds, walnuts, pecans), roughly chopped
- 1 tbsp pumpkin seeds
- 1 tbsp sunflower seeds
- 1/2 cup fresh berries of choice
- A drizzle of sugar-free syrup or honey (optional)

Instructions:
1. Spoon Greek yogurt into two bowls.

2. Sprinkle a mix of nuts, pumpkin seeds, and sunflower seeds over the yogurt.
3. Add fresh berries on top for a burst of color and sweetness.
4. Drizzle with a small amount of sugar-free syrup or honey if desired.

Benefits for Diabetics:
Greek yogurt is high in protein and low in carbs, helping to stabilize blood sugar levels. The nuts and seeds add healthy fats and fiber, aiding in satiety and further supporting blood sugar control.

Per Serving:
Calories: 300 | Fat: 18g | Carbs: 15g | Fiber: 4g | Protein: 20g

Savory Quinoa Breakfast Bowl

Serves: 2
Prep time: 5 minutes / Cook time: 15 minutes

Ingredients:
- 1 cup cooked quinoa
- 1 tbsp olive oil
- 1/2 cup diced bell peppers
- 1/2 cup diced tomatoes
- 2 green onions, sliced
- 2 large eggs
- Salt and pepper to taste
- Hot sauce or avocado slices for garnish (optional)

Instructions:
1. Heat olive oil in a pan over medium heat. Add bell peppers and sauté until slightly soft.
2. Stir in cooked quinoa and tomatoes, cooking until heated through.
3. In another pan, cook eggs to your preference (sunny side up recommended).
4. Divide quinoa mixture into two bowls, top each with a cooked egg, and sprinkle with green onions.
5. Season with salt and pepper and add hot sauce or avocado if desired.

Benefits for Diabetics:
Quinoa is a complete protein and a good source of fiber, aiding in blood sugar management. The addition of vegetables and eggs provides vitamins, minerals, and additional protein, making this a well-rounded, nutritious breakfast option for diabetics.

Per Serving:
Calories: 320 | Fat: 15g | Carbs: 30g | Fiber: 5g | Protein: 14g

Tomato Basil Omelet

Serves: 1
Prep time: 5 minutes / Cook time: 5 minutes

Ingredients:
- 2 large eggs
- 1/4 cup chopped fresh tomatoes
- 1 tbsp chopped fresh basil
- 2 tbsp shredded mozzarella cheese (optional or use a low-fat variety)
- Salt and pepper to taste

- 1 tsp olive oil

Instructions:
1. Whisk eggs in a bowl with salt and pepper.
2. Heat olive oil in a non-stick skillet over medium heat.
3. Pour eggs into the skillet, letting them set slightly, then lift the edges to allow uncooked eggs to flow underneath.
4. Sprinkle chopped tomatoes, basil, and mozzarella over one half of the omelet.
5. Carefully fold the other half over the filling and cook until the cheese melts.
6. Slide the omelet onto a plate and serve.

Benefits for Diabetics:
This omelet is high in protein and low in carbs, making it a great choice for blood sugar management. Tomatoes add a good source of vitamins and antioxidants, while the fresh basil provides a fragrant flavor without adding carbs.

Per Serving:
Calories: 220 | Fat: 16g | Carbs: 4g | Fiber: 1g | Protein: 16g

Vegan Tofu Scramble

Serves: 2
Prep time: 10 minutes / Cook time: 10 minutes

Ingredients:
- 1 block firm tofu, drained and crumbled
- 1 tbsp olive oil
- 1/2 cup diced onions
- 1/2 cup diced bell peppers
- 1/2 cup sliced mushrooms
- 1 tsp turmeric
- 1 tsp cumin
- Salt and pepper to taste
- Fresh herbs for garnish (cilantro or parsley)

Instructions:
1. Heat olive oil in a skillet over medium heat. Add onions and bell peppers, sautéing until soft.
2. Stir in mushrooms and cook for a few more minutes.
3. Add crumbled tofu, turmeric, and cumin, cooking and stirring for about 5-7 minutes until everything is heated through and well combined.
4. Season with salt and pepper, and garnish with fresh herbs before serving.

Benefits for Diabetics:
Tofu is a low-carb, high-protein alternative to eggs, making it an excellent choice for diabetics. The turmeric and cumin not only add flavor but also contain anti-inflammatory properties. The mix of vegetables boosts the dish's vitamin and fiber content.

Per Serving:
Calories: 250 | Fat: 15g | Carbs: 10g | Fiber: 3g | Protein: 20g

Spinach and Feta Breakfast Wrap

Serves: 2
Prep time: 5 minutes / Cook time: 10 minutes

Ingredients:
- 2 whole wheat tortillas
- 4 large eggs

- 1 cup fresh spinach, chopped
- 1/4 cup feta cheese, crumbled
- Salt and pepper to taste
- 1 tsp olive oil

Instructions:

1. Whisk eggs in a bowl and season with salt and pepper.
2. Heat olive oil in a skillet over medium heat. Add spinach and sauté until wilted.
3. Pour eggs over spinach, stirring gently until they're set but still moist.
4. Sprinkle feta cheese over the eggs and remove from heat.
5. Divide the egg mixture between the two tortillas, roll them up, and serve.

Benefits for Diabetics:

The combination of eggs and spinach provides a good balance of protein and fiber, helping to control blood sugar levels. Whole wheat tortillas are a better choice than white, offering more nutrients and fiber, and feta adds flavor without too much fat.

Per Serving:

Calories: 280 | Fat: 16g | Carbs: 20g | Fiber: 3g | Protein: 18g

Apple Cinnamon Oatmeal

Serves: 2

Prep time: 5 minutes / Cook time: 15 minutes

Ingredients:

- 1 cup rolled oats
- 2 cups water or unsweetened almond milk
- 1 medium apple, diced
- 1/2 tsp cinnamon
- 1 tbsp chopped nuts (almonds or walnuts)
- Sweetener of choice (stevia or erythritol, to taste)

Instructions:

1. In a saucepan, bring water or almond milk to a boil. Add oats and reduce heat to simmer.
2. Stir in diced apple and cinnamon, cooking until oats are soft and creamy.
3. Serve in bowls, topped with chopped nuts and sweetener to taste.

Benefits for Diabetics:

Oatmeal is a whole grain that's high in fiber, helping to regulate digestion and blood sugar levels. Apples provide natural sweetness and additional fiber, while cinnamon has been shown to improve insulin sensitivity.

Conclusion:

Apple Cinnamon Oatmeal is a warm, nourishing breakfast that's easy to make and endlessly customizable. It's a wholesome way to enjoy the flavors of fall any time of year, while keeping your health in check.

Per Serving:

Calories: 220 | Fat: 4g | Carbs: 38g | Fiber: 6g | Protein: 6g

Berry Smoothie Bowl

Serves: 2

Prep time: 5 minutes / Cook time: 0 minutes

Ingredients:

- 1 cup mixed frozen berries (strawberries, blueberries, raspberries)
- 1/2 cup Greek yogurt (unsweetened)
- 1/2 banana (optional, for texture)
- 1/4 cup unsweetened almond milk
- 1 tbsp chia seeds
- 1 tbsp sliced almonds
- A few mint leaves for garnish

Instructions:

1. Blend the mixed berries, Greek yogurt, banana (if using), and almond milk until smooth.
2. Pour the smoothie mixture into bowls.
3. Top with chia seeds, sliced almonds, and fresh mint leaves.

Benefits for Diabetics:

This smoothie bowl is rich in antioxidants and fiber from the berries and chia seeds, aiding in blood sugar management. Greek yogurt adds a protein boost, while the overall low sugar content makes it suitable for diabetics.

Per Serving:

Calories: 220 | Fat: 6g | Carbs: 30g | Fiber: 7g | Protein: 10g

Southwestern Tofu Scramble

Serves: 2

Prep time: 10 minutes / Cook time: 10 minutes

Ingredients:

- 1 block firm tofu, drained and crumbled
- 1 tbsp olive oil
- 1/2 cup diced bell pepper (mixed colors)
- 1/4 cup diced onion
- 1/2 cup black beans, rinsed and drained
- 1 tsp cumin
- 1/2 tsp chili powder
- Salt and pepper to taste
- Fresh cilantro and avocado for garnish

Instructions:

1. Heat olive oil in a skillet over medium heat. Add onions and bell peppers, cooking until softened.
2. Stir in crumbled tofu, black beans, cumin, chili powder, salt, and pepper. Cook for 5-7 minutes, stirring occasionally, until heated through and flavorful.
3. Serve hot, garnished with fresh cilantro and slices of avocado.

Benefits for Diabetics:

Tofu provides a solid protein base, essential for blood sugar stabilization. The combination of fiber-rich vegetables and beans in this dish aids in digestion and further helps to maintain steady glucose levels.

Per Serving:

Calories: 250 | Fat: 15g | Carbs: 15g | Fiber: 6g | Protein: 18g

Cottage Cheese and Peach Breakfast Bowl

Serves: 2

Prep time: 5 minutes / Cook time: 0 minutes

Ingredients:

- 1 cup cottage cheese (low-fat)

- 1 ripe peach, sliced
- 1 tbsp walnuts, chopped
- A pinch of cinnamon

Instructions:

1. Divide the cottage cheese between two bowls.
2. Arrange the peach slices on top of the cottage cheese.
3. Sprinkle with chopped walnuts and a dash of cinnamon.

Benefits for Diabetics:

Cottage cheese is a great source of protein and calcium, while being relatively low in carbs, making it an excellent choice for blood sugar management. Peaches add natural sweetness and fiber for a well-rounded meal.

Per Serving:

Calories: 180 | Fat: 6g | Carbs: 14g | Fiber: 2g | Protein: 16g

Low-Carb Breakfast Burrito

Serves: 2

Prep time: 10 minutes / Cook time: 10 minutes

Ingredients:

- 2 low-carb whole wheat tortillas
- 4 large eggs
- 1/4 cup shredded cheese (low-fat)
- 1/4 cup bell peppers, diced
- 1/4 cup onions, diced
- Salt and pepper to taste
- Salsa for serving

Instructions:

1. Whisk the eggs in a bowl, season with salt and pepper.
2. Cook the eggs in a non-stick skillet until scrambled to your liking.
3. Warm the tortillas in a separate pan or microwave.
4. Divide the cooked eggs, cheese, bell peppers, and onions between the tortillas.
5. Roll up the tortillas to form burritos.
6. Serve with a side of salsa.

Benefits for Diabetics:

The low-carb tortillas make this a suitable option for those managing blood sugar levels. Eggs are an excellent source of protein, and the added vegetables provide vitamins, minerals, and additional fiber.

Conclusion:

Enjoy a Low-Carb Breakfast Burrito for a filling, flavorful start to your day. It's a versatile meal that can be customized with your favorite fillings and toppings, making it a breakfast favorite you'll come back to again and again.

Per Serving:

Calories: 300 | Fat: 18g | Carbs: 20g | Fiber: 6g | Protein: 20g

Pumpkin Seed and Oat Granola

Serves: Multiple

Prep time: 10 minutes / Cook time: 20 minutes

Ingredients:

- 2 cups rolled oats
- 1/2 cup pumpkin seeds
- 1/4 cup almonds, chopped
- 2 tbsp flaxseed
- 1/4 cup sugar-free maple syrup or honey

- 2 tbsp coconut oil, melted
- 1 tsp vanilla extract
- 1/2 tsp cinnamon
- A pinch of salt

Instructions:

1. Preheat your oven to 300°F (150°C) and line a baking sheet with parchment paper.
2. In a large bowl, mix together oats, pumpkin seeds, almonds, and flaxseed.
3. In a separate bowl, whisk together the maple syrup, coconut oil, vanilla extract, cinnamon, and salt.
4. Pour the wet ingredients over the dry ingredients and mix well until everything is evenly coated.
5. Spread the mixture out on the prepared baking sheet in an even layer.
6. Bake for 20 minutes, stirring halfway through, until golden and crisp.
7. Let it cool completely before storing in an airtight container.

Benefits for Diabetics:

This granola is packed with fiber from the oats and seeds, which helps slow down sugar absorption, aiding in blood sugar control. The nuts provide healthy fats, and the absence of added sugars makes it a diabetic-friendly option.

Per Serving (1/4 cup):

Calories: 150 | Fat: 8g | Carbs: 16g | Fiber: 3g | Protein: 5g

Zucchini and Herb Breakfast Fritters

Serves: 4

Prep time: 10 minutes / Cook time: 15 minutes

Ingredients:

- 2 cups grated zucchini (water squeezed out)
- 2 large eggs
- 1/4 cup almond flour
- 1/4 cup chopped fresh herbs (parsley, chives, or dill)
- 1/2 tsp garlic powder
- Salt and pepper to taste
- Olive oil for frying

Instructions:

1. In a bowl, combine grated zucchini, eggs, almond flour, herbs, garlic powder, salt, and pepper.
2. Heat olive oil in a non-stick skillet over medium heat.
3. Scoop spoonfuls of the zucchini mixture into the skillet, flattening them into fritter shapes.
4. Cook for 3-4 minutes on each side until golden and crispy.
5. Drain on paper towels and serve warm.

Benefits for Diabetics:

Zucchini is low in carbs and calories, making it a great choice for blood sugar management. The eggs and almond flour add protein and healthy fats, while the herbs provide a boost of flavor without additional carbs.

Conclusion:

Zucchini and Herb Breakfast Fritters are a fantastic way to enjoy a vegetable-packed breakfast. They're easy to make, delicious to eat, and beneficial for anyone looking to maintain a healthy, balanced diet.

Per Serving:

Calories: 120 | Fat: 8g | Carbs: 6g | Fiber: 2g | Protein: 7g

Pear and Walnut Baked Oatmeal

Serves: 6

Prep time: 10 minutes / Cook time: 35 minutes

Ingredients:

- 2 cups rolled oats
- 1 tsp baking powder
- 1/2 tsp cinnamon
- 1/4 tsp salt
- 1 cup diced pears
- 1/2 cup walnuts, chopped
- 2 cups unsweetened almond milk
- 1 large egg
- 1 tsp vanilla extract
- Sweetener of choice (stevia or erythritol, to taste)

Instructions:

1. Preheat the oven to 375°F (190°C) and grease a baking dish.
2. In a bowl, mix together oats, baking powder, cinnamon, and salt.
3. Stir in diced pears and chopped walnuts.
4. In another bowl, whisk together almond milk, egg, vanilla extract, and sweetener.
5. Pour the wet ingredients into the dry and stir to combine.
6. Pour the mixture into the prepared baking dish and bake for 35 minutes until set and golden.
7. Let cool slightly before serving.

Benefits for Diabetics:

Baked oatmeal is a great source of soluble fiber, which can help regulate blood sugar levels. Pears add natural sweetness and additional fiber, and walnuts provide healthy fats and a satisfying crunch.

Per Serving:

Calories: 210 | Fat: 9g | Carbs: 28g | Fiber: 5g | Protein: 6g

Mediterranean Veggie Breakfast Skillet

Serves: 2

Prep time: 10 minutes / Cook time: 15 minutes

Ingredients:

- 1 tbsp olive oil
- 1/2 cup diced onions
- 1/2 cup diced bell peppers
- 1 cup chopped spinach
- 1/2 cup cherry tomatoes, halved
- 4 large eggs
- 1/4 cup feta cheese, crumbled
- Salt and pepper to taste
- Fresh basil for garnish

Instructions:

1. Heat olive oil in a skillet over medium heat. Add onions and bell peppers, cooking until softened.
2. Stir in spinach and cherry tomatoes, cooking until the spinach wilts.
3. Make four wells in the vegetables and crack an egg into each.
4. Cover the skillet and cook until the eggs are set to your liking.
5. Sprinkle feta cheese over the top, season with salt and pepper, and garnish with fresh basil.

Benefits for Diabetics:

This skillet meal is rich in vegetables, providing vitamins, minerals, and fiber which are beneficial for blood sugar control. The eggs and feta cheese add protein and healthy fats, making it a balanced, nutritious meal.

Conclusion:

Mediterranean Veggie Breakfast Skillet is a vibrant, tasty dish that's full of flavor and nutrition. It's a wonderful way to incorporate a variety of vegetables into your breakfast, keeping you full and satisfied throughout the morning.

Per Serving:

Calories: 300 | Fat: 20g | Carbs: 12g |18g

Hearty Veggie Breakfast Hash

Serves: 4

Prep time: 15 minutes / Cook time: 20 minutes

Ingredients:

- 1 medium sweet potato, diced
- 1 bell pepper, diced
- 1 zucchini, diced
- 1/2 red onion, diced
- 2 cloves garlic, minced
- 4 eggs
- 1 tsp smoked paprika
- Salt and pepper to taste
- 2 tbsp olive oil

Instructions:

1. Heat olive oil in a large skillet over medium heat. Add sweet potato and cook until nearly tender.
2. Add bell pepper, zucchini, and onion, cooking until vegetables are soft.
3. Stir in garlic, smoked paprika, salt, and pepper, cooking for another minute.
4. Make four wells in the hash and crack an egg into each. Cover and cook until eggs are done to your liking.
5. Serve hot, garnished with fresh herbs if desired.

Benefits for Diabetics:

This vegetable hash is low in carbs and high in fiber, aiding in blood sugar management. The eggs provide a good source of protein, helping to keep you full and satisfied.

Per Serving:

Calories: 250 | Fat: 15g | Carbs: 18g | Fiber: 3g | Protein: 12g

Berry and Nut Greek Yogurt Smoothie

Serves: 2

Prep time: 5 minutes / Cook time: 0 minutes

Ingredients:

- 1 cup Greek yogurt (unsweetened)
- 1 cup mixed berries (fresh or frozen)
- 1/4 cup mixed nuts (almonds, walnuts, or pecans)
- 1 cup unsweetened almond milk
- 1 tbsp chia seeds
- Sweetener of choice (stevia or erythritol, to taste)

Instructions:

1. Combine all ingredients in a blender.

2. Blend until smooth and creamy.

3. Taste and adjust sweetener as needed.

4. Pour into glasses and serve immediately.

Benefits for Diabetics:

The high protein content from Greek yogurt and nuts helps stabilize blood sugar levels, while the fiber from berries and chia seeds aids in digestion and further controls sugar spikes.

Conclusion:

Berry and Nut Greek Yogurt Smoothie is a quick, easy, and nutritious way to start your day. It's packed with flavors and nutrients, ensuring a satisfying and healthful breakfast option.

Per Serving:

Calories: 280 | Fat: 15g | Carbs: 20g | Fiber: 5g | Protein: 17g

Pumpkin Spice Protein Oats

Serves: 2

Prep time: 5 minutes / Cook time: 15 minutes

Ingredients:

- 1 cup rolled oats
- 1 1/2 cups water or almond milk
- 1/2 cup pumpkin puree
- 1 scoop vanilla protein powder
- 1 tsp pumpkin pie spice
- 1 tbsp chopped nuts (pecans or walnuts)
- Sweetener of choice (stevia or erythritol, to taste)

Instructions:

1. In a saucepan, bring water or almond milk to a boil. Add oats and reduce heat to simmer.

2. Stir in pumpkin puree, protein powder, and pumpkin pie spice until well combined and creamy.

3. Serve hot, topped with chopped nuts and sweetener to taste.

Benefits for Diabetics:

This recipe provides a high fiber and protein content from oats and protein powder, helping to manage blood sugar levels. The pumpkin adds a dose of vitamins and antioxidants without excessive carbs.

Per Serving:

Calories: 280 | Fat: 7g | Carbs: 38g | Fiber: 6g | Protein: 17g

Southwestern Tofu Scramble Wrap

Serves: 2

Prep time: 10 minutes / Cook time: 10 minutes

Ingredients:

- 1 block firm tofu, drained and crumbled
- 2 whole wheat tortillas
- 1/2 cup black beans, drained and rinsed
- 1/4 cup corn kernels
- 1/2 bell pepper, diced
- 1/2 tsp cumin
- 1/2 tsp chili powder
- Salt and pepper to taste
- 1 tbsp olive oil
- Fresh cilantro and avocado slices for garnish

Instructions:

1. Heat olive oil in a skillet over medium heat. Add bell pepper and sauté until soft.

2. Stir in black beans, corn, and crumbled tofu. Season with cumin, chili powder, salt, and pepper.

3. Cook for 5-7 minutes, stirring occasionally, until everything is heated through and flavors are blended.

4. Warm the tortillas, then divide the tofu scramble between them.

5. Top with fresh cilantro and avocado slices, roll up, and serve.

Benefits for Diabetics:

Tofu and black beans provide a solid protein base, aiding in blood sugar control. The spices add flavor without sugar, and the whole wheat tortillas are a good source of fiber.

Per Serving:

Calories: 350 | Fat: 16g | Carbs: 36g | Fiber: 6g | Protein: 20g

Mediterranean Frittata

Serves: 4

Prep time: 10 minutes / Cook time: 20 minutes

Ingredients:

- 8 large eggs
- 1/2 cup diced tomatoes
- 1/2 cup chopped spinach
- 1/4 cup crumbled feta cheese
- 1/4 cup sliced black olives
- 1 tbsp chopped fresh basil
- Salt and pepper to taste
- 1 tbsp olive oil

Instructions:

1. Preheat the oven to 375°F (190°C).

2. Whisk together eggs, salt, and pepper in a bowl.

3. Heat olive oil in an oven-safe skillet over medium heat. Add tomatoes and spinach, sautéing until spinach is wilted.

4. Pour the egg mixture over the vegetables. Sprinkle with feta cheese, olives, and basil.

5. Cook for a few minutes until the edges start to set, then transfer to the oven.

6. Bake for 15-20 minutes until the frittata is set and lightly golden.

7. Serve warm, cut into wedges.

Benefits for Diabetics:

Eggs are a great source of protein and fats that help regulate blood sugar levels. The vegetables add fiber and nutrients, while feta provides flavor without excessive calories or carbs.

Per Serving:

Calories: 220 | Fat: 16g | Carbs: 4g | Fiber: 1g | Protein: 14g

Zucchini and Carrot Pancakes

Serves: 2

Prep time: 15 minutes / Cook time: 10 minutes

Ingredients:

- 1 medium zucchini, grated
- 1 medium carrot, grated
- 2 large eggs
- 1/4 cup almond flour

- Salt and pepper to taste
- 1 tbsp olive oil

Instructions:

1. Squeeze the grated zucchini and carrot to remove excess moisture.
2. In a bowl, mix together grated vegetables, eggs, almond flour, salt, and pepper.
3. Heat olive oil in a skillet over medium heat.
4. Spoon batter into the skillet, forming small pancakes. Cook until golden brown on each side.
5. Serve hot with a side of sour cream or yogurt if desired.

Benefits for Diabetics:

These pancakes are low in carbs and high in nutrients, with a good balance of protein and fiber. The vegetables provide vitamins and minerals, while the almond flour adds a nutty flavor and more protein.

Per Serving:

Calories: 250 | Fat: 18g | Carbs: 12g | Fiber: 3g | Protein: 12g

Pear and Walnut Baked Oatmeal

Serves: 4

Prep time: 10 minutes / Cook time: 40 minutes

Ingredients:

- 2 cups rolled oats
- 1 tsp baking powder
- 1/2 tsp cinnamon
- 1/4 tsp salt
- 2 cups unsweetened almond milk
- 1 large egg
- 1 tsp vanilla extract
- 2 pears, diced
- 1/2 cup walnuts, chopped
- Sweetener of choice (stevia or erythritol, to taste)

Instructions:

1. Preheat oven to 375°F (190°C) and grease a baking dish.
2. In a bowl, mix oats, baking powder, cinnamon, and salt.
3. In another bowl, whisk together almond milk, egg, and vanilla extract.
4. Combine wet and dry ingredients, then fold in diced pears and walnuts.
5. Pour mixture into the prepared baking dish and bake for 35-40 minutes until set and golden.
6. Serve warm, optionally topped with additional milk or yogurt.

Benefits for Diabetics:

Oatmeal is a great source of soluble fiber, aiding in blood sugar control and digestion. Pears add natural sweetness and additional fiber, while walnuts provide healthy fats and a satisfying crunch.

Per Serving:

Calories: 320 | Fat: 12g | Carbs: 44g | Fiber: 6g | Protein: 9g

Savory Breakfast Salad

Serves: 2

Prep time: 10 minutes / Cook time: 5 minutes

Ingredients:

- 4 cups mixed greens (spinach, arugula, kale)
- 1/2 cup cherry tomatoes, halved
- 1/4 cup cucumber, sliced
- 2 hard-boiled eggs, sliced
- 1 avocado, sliced
- 2 tbsp olive oil
- 1 tbsp lemon juice
- Salt and pepper to taste

Instructions:

1. Arrange mixed greens on two plates.
2. Top with cherry tomatoes, cucumber, hard-boiled eggs, and avocado.
3. Drizzle with olive oil and lemon juice, then season with salt and pepper.
4. Serve immediately and enjoy a burst of freshness in every bite.

Benefits for Diabetics:

This breakfast salad is low in carbs and high in fiber, promoting stable blood sugar levels. The combination of vegetables and eggs provides a good balance of nutrients, vitamins, and protein.

Per Serving:

Calories: 300 | Fat: 24g | Carbs: 12g | Fiber: 7g | Protein: 13g

Broccoli and Cheese Breakfast Muffins

Serves: 6

Prep time: 15 minutes / Cook time: 20 minutes

Ingredients:

- 1 cup whole wheat flour
- 1 cup finely chopped broccoli
- 1/2 cup shredded cheddar cheese
- 2 large eggs
- 1/2 cup milk (or unsweetened almond milk)
- 1/4 cup olive oil
- 1 tsp baking powder
- Salt and pepper to taste

Instructions:

1. Preheat the oven to 375°F (190°C) and grease a muffin tin.
2. In a bowl, mix together flour, baking powder, salt, and pepper.
3. In another bowl, whisk together eggs, milk, and olive oil.
4. Combine wet and dry ingredients, then fold in broccoli and cheddar cheese.
5. Spoon the batter into the muffin tin and bake for 20-25 minutes until golden and firm.
6. Allow to cool slightly before serving.

Benefits for Diabetics:

These muffins are a good source of fiber and protein, helping to manage blood sugar levels. Broccoli provides essential nutrients and antioxidants, while whole wheat flour offers a healthier, more fiber-rich alternative to white flour.

Per Serving:

Calories: 220 | Fat: 14g | Carbs: 16g | Fiber: 2g | Protein: 9g

Smoked Salmon and Avocado Toast

Serves: 2

Prep time: 5 minutes / Cook time: 5 minutes

Ingredients:
- 2 slices of whole grain bread
- 4 oz smoked salmon
- 1 ripe avocado
- 1 tbsp lemon juice
- Fresh dill for garnish
- Salt and pepper to taste

Instructions:
1. Toast the whole grain bread until golden and crispy.
2. Mash the avocado with lemon juice, salt, and pepper.
3. Spread the mashed avocado evenly on the toasted bread.
4. Top with smoked salmon and garnish with fresh dill.
5. Serve immediately and enjoy.

Benefits for Diabetics:
This breakfast is high in healthy fats and protein from both salmon and avocado, which can help control blood sugar levels. Whole grain bread provides a good source of fiber, aiding in digestion and further supporting blood sugar management.

Per Serving:
Calories: 320 | Fat: 20g | Carbs: 20g | Fiber: 5g | Protein: 15g

Cottage Cheese and Pineapple Bowl

Serves: 2

Prep time: 5 minutes / Cook time: 0 minutes

Ingredients:
- 1 cup cottage cheese (low-fat or full-fat)
- 1 cup chopped fresh pineapple
- 2 tbsp chopped nuts (almonds or walnuts)
- A sprinkle of cinnamon (optional)

Instructions:
1. Divide the cottage cheese between two bowls.
2. Top with chopped fresh pineapple and nuts.
3. Sprinkle with cinnamon for extra flavor if desired.
4. Serve immediately and enjoy.

Benefits for Diabetics:
Cottage cheese is a great source of protein and calcium, helping to keep you full and satisfied. Pineapple provides vitamin C and sweetness without the need for added sugars. The nuts add healthy fats and a crunchy texture.

Per Serving:
Calories: 200 | Fat: 8g | Carbs: 15g | Fiber: 2g | Protein: 16g

Sweet Potato and Black Bean Breakfast Burrito

Serves: 4

Prep time: 20 minutes / Cook time: 20 minutes

Ingredients:
- 2 medium sweet potatoes, diced
- 1 cup black beans, drained and rinsed
- 4 whole wheat tortillas
- 4 eggs
- 1/2 cup shredded cheese (optional or use a low-fat variety)
- 1/2 tsp cumin
- 1/2 tsp paprika
- 1 tbsp olive oil
- Salt and pepper to taste
- Salsa and avocado for garnish

Instructions:
1. Heat olive oil in a skillet over medium heat. Add sweet potatoes and cook until tender.
2. Add black beans, cumin, paprika, salt, and pepper, cooking for a few more minutes.
3. In another pan, scramble the eggs to your liking.
4. Warm the tortillas, then assemble the burritos by placing sweet potato mixture, scrambled eggs, and cheese on each tortilla.
5. Roll up the tortillas, tucking in the ends.
6. Serve with a side of salsa and avocado slices.

Benefits for Diabetics:
Sweet potatoes are a good source of fiber and vitamins, while black beans provide protein and more fiber, helping to maintain steady blood sugar levels. The whole wheat tortillas are a healthier option, offering additional fiber and nutrients.

Per Serving:
Calories: 350 | Fat: 12g | Carbs: 45g | Fiber: 8g | Protein: 15g

Nutty Banana Quinoa Porridge

Serves: 2

Prep time: 5 minutes / Cook time: 15 minutes

Ingredients:
- 1 cup quinoa, rinsed
- 2 cups unsweetened almond milk
- 1 ripe banana, mashed
- 1/2 tsp cinnamon
- 2 tbsp mixed nuts (almonds, walnuts, pecans), chopped
- Sweetener of choice (stevia or erythritol, to taste)

Instructions:
1. In a saucepan, combine quinoa and almond milk. Bring to a boil, then reduce heat and simmer, covered, until quinoa is cooked and creamy.
2. Stir in mashed banana and cinnamon, cooking for an additional 2 minutes.
3. Divide the porridge between two bowls, top with chopped nuts and sweetener to taste.
4. Serve warm and enjoy.

Benefits for Diabetics:
Quinoa is a complete protein and rich in fiber, aiding in blood sugar management. Bananas provide natural sweetness and potassium, while the nuts add healthy fats and a satisfying crunch.

Per Serving:
Calories: 320 | Fat: 10g | Carbs: 45g | Fiber: 6g | Protein: 12g

Lemon Ricotta Pancakes

Serves: 4

Prep time: 15 minutes / Cook time: 10 minutes

Ingredients:
- 1 cup all-purpose flour (or almond flour for a lower-carb option)
- 1/2 cup ricotta cheese

- 2 large eggs
- 1/2 cup milk (or unsweetened almond milk)
- 2 tbsp lemon juice
- 1 tbsp lemon zest
- 1 tsp baking powder
- 2 tbsp sweetener of choice (stevia or erythritol, to taste)
- Butter or non-stick spray for cooking

Instructions:
1. In a bowl, mix together flour, baking powder, and sweetener.
2. In another bowl, whisk together ricotta cheese, eggs, milk, lemon juice, and lemon zest.
3. Combine the wet and dry ingredients, stirring until just mixed.
4. Heat a non-stick skillet over medium heat and coat with butter or spray.
5. Pour batter to form pancakes, cooking until bubbles appear, then flip and cook until golden brown.
6. Serve warm with a dollop of yogurt or sugar-free syrup.

Benefits for Diabetics:
Using almond flour and a sugar substitute can make these pancakes lower in carbs and suitable for diabetics. Ricotta cheese adds protein and calcium, while lemon provides a dose of vitamin C and a refreshing flavor.

Per Serving:
Calories: 250 | Fat: 12g | Carbs: 20g | Fiber: 2g | Protein: 10g

Savory Spinach and Cheese Breakfast Bread

Serves: 2
Prep time: 20 minutes / Cook time: 35 minutes

Ingredients:
- 1 cup whole wheat flour
- 1/2 tsp baking powder
- 1/4 tsp baking soda
- 1/2 tsp salt
- 2 eggs
- 1/4 cup olive oil
- 1/2 cup Greek yogurt
- 1 cup fresh spinach, chopped
- 1/2 cup shredded cheddar cheese
- 1/4 cup green onions, chopped

Instructions:
1. Preheat oven to 375°F (190°C) and grease a loaf pan.
2. In a large bowl, mix together the whole wheat flour, baking powder, baking soda, and salt.
3. In another bowl, whisk together eggs, olive oil, and Greek yogurt.
4. Stir the wet ingredients into the dry ingredients until just combined.
5. Fold in the spinach, cheddar cheese, and green onions.
6. Pour the batter into the prepared loaf pan and smooth the top.
7. Bake for 35 minutes or until a toothpick inserted into the center comes out clean.
8. Let it cool before slicing and serving.

Benefits for Diabetics:
This bread is high in fiber and protein while being low in sugar, offering a sustained energy release and helping

in managing blood sugar levels. Spinach adds nutrients without adding excess carbohydrates.

Per Serving:
Calories: 300 | Fat: 15g | Carbs: 25g | Fiber: 5g | Protein: 15g

Tomato and Basil Breakfast Tart

Serves: 2
Prep time: 15 minutes / Cook time: 20 minutes

Ingredients:
- 1 cup almond flour
- 2 tablespoons cold butter, diced
- 1 egg, for the crust
- Salt and pepper to taste
- 2 tomatoes, sliced
- Fresh basil leaves
- 1/4 cup mozzarella cheese, shredded

Instructions:
1. Preheat oven to 350°F (175°C) and grease a tart pan.
2. In a bowl, combine almond flour, cold butter, one egg, and a pinch of salt and pepper. Mix until a dough forms.
3. Press the dough into the tart pan evenly. Prick the bottom with a fork.
4. Bake the crust for 10 minutes, then remove from the oven.
5. Arrange the tomato slices and basil leaves over the crust. Sprinkle with mozzarella cheese.
6. Return to oven and bake for an additional 10 minutes or until cheese is melted and slightly golden.
7. Serve warm, garnished with more fresh basil.

Benefits for Diabetics:
The almond flour crust provides a lower carbohydrate base compared to traditional flours, and the tomatoes and basil add flavor without added sugars. It's a balance of protein, healthy fats, and fiber.

Per Serving:
Calories: 320 | Fat: 26g | Carbs: 12g | Fiber: 6g | Protein: 14g

Zucchini and Walnut Breakfast Cookies

Serves: 2
Prep time: 15 minutes / Cook time: 20 minutes

Ingredients:
- 1 cup rolled oats
- 1/2 cup whole wheat flour
- 1/2 tsp baking soda
- 1/4 tsp salt
- 1 tsp cinnamon
- 1 egg
- 1/4 cup honey or a diabetic-friendly sweetener
- 1/2 cup grated zucchini, excess water squeezed out
- 1/2 cup chopped walnuts
- 1/4 cup unsweetened applesauce

Instructions:
1. Preheat oven to 350°F (175°C) and line a baking sheet with parchment paper.
2. In a large bowl, mix together oats, whole wheat flour, baking soda, salt, and cinnamon.
3. In another bowl, whisk together the egg, honey, grated zucchini, and applesauce.
4. Combine the wet and dry ingredients, then fold in the

chopped walnuts.

5. Drop spoonfuls of the dough onto the prepared baking sheet.
6. Bake for 18-20 minutes or until golden brown.
7. Let cool before serving.

Benefits for Diabetics:
These cookies are a fiber-rich treat with the inclusion of whole grains and zucchini. Walnuts provide healthy fats, while the overall low sugar content makes them a suitable choice for blood sugar management.

Per Serving:
Calories: 270 | Fat: 15g | Carbs: 30g | Fiber: 4g | Protein: 6g

Cottage Cheese and Herb Breakfast Muffins

Serves: 2
Prep time: 10 minutes / Cook time: 20 minutes

Ingredients:
- 3/4 cup whole wheat flour
- 1/2 tsp baking powder
- 1/4 cup cottage cheese
- 2 eggs
- 1/4 cup milk
- 1/4 cup chopped fresh herbs (parsley, chives, or dill)
- Salt and pepper to taste

Instructions:
1. Preheat oven to 375°F (190°C) and grease a muffin tin.
2. In a large bowl, whisk together the whole wheat flour and baking powder.
3. In another bowl, mix the cottage cheese, eggs, milk, and chopped herbs. Season with salt and pepper.
4. Add the wet ingredients to the dry ingredients and stir until just combined.
5. Divide the batter evenly among the muffin cups.
6. Bake for 20 minutes or until the muffins are set and lightly golden on top.
7. Allow to cool slightly before serving.

Benefits for Diabetics:
Cottage cheese is high in protein and low in carbs, making it an excellent food for maintaining stable blood sugar levels. The whole wheat flour provides fiber, and the herbs add flavor without extra salt or sugar.

Per Serving:
Calories: 200 | Fat: 8g | Carbs: 18g | Fiber: 3g | Protein: 14g

Cinnamon Almond Breakfast Biscotti

Serves: 2
Prep time: 15 minutes / Cook time: 40 minutes

Ingredients:
- 1 1/2 cups almond flour
- 1/2 tsp baking powder
- 1/4 tsp salt
- 1 tsp cinnamon
- 1/3 cup chopped almonds
- 2 eggs
- 1/4 cup diabetic-friendly sweetener (like stevia or erythritol)
- 1/2 tsp vanilla extract

Instructions:
1. Preheat oven to 350°F (175°C) and line a baking sheet with parchment paper.
2. In a large bowl, mix together almond flour, baking powder, salt, and cinnamon.
3. Stir in the chopped almonds.
4. In another bowl, whisk together eggs, sweetener, and vanilla extract.
5. Add the wet ingredients to the dry ingredients, mixing until a dough forms.
6. Shape the dough into a flat log on the baking sheet.
7. Bake for 20 minutes, then remove from oven and let cool for 10 minutes.
8. Slice the log diagonally into biscotti pieces.
9. Return the slices to the oven and bake for an additional 20 minutes, flipping halfway through, until crisp and golden.
10. Let cool before serving.

Benefits for Diabetics:
These biscotti are low in carbs and high in healthy fats from almonds, making them a great choice for blood sugar control. Cinnamon is also known for its potential benefits in managing blood glucose levels.

Per Serving:
Calories: 280 | Fat: 22g | Carbs: 10g | Fiber: 6g | Protein: 12g

Lemon Poppy Seed Breakfast Loaf

Serves: 2
Prep time: 15 minutes / Cook time: 45 minutes

Ingredients:
- 2 cups almond flour
- 1/2 tsp baking soda
- Pinch of salt
- 3 eggs
- 1/4 cup melted coconut oil
- 1/2 cup diabetic-friendly sweetener
- 2 tbsp lemon juice
- Zest of 1 lemon
- 1 tbsp poppy seeds

Instructions:
1. Preheat the oven to 350°F (175°C) and grease a loaf pan.
2. In a large bowl, combine almond flour, baking soda, and salt.
3. In another bowl, whisk together eggs, melted coconut oil, sweetener, lemon juice, and lemon zest.
4. Mix the wet ingredients into the dry ingredients until well combined. Stir in the poppy seeds.
5. Pour the batter into the prepared loaf pan and smooth the top.
6. Bake for 45 minutes, or until a toothpick inserted into the center comes out clean.
7. Let the loaf cool before slicing and serving.

Benefits for Diabetics:
This loaf is low in carbohydrates and high in fiber, making it suitable for a diabetic diet. The lemon not only adds a refreshing flavor but also provides vitamin C, while the poppy seeds offer a good source of fiber and minerals.

Per Serving:
Calories: 320 | Fat: 28g | Carbs: 12g | Fiber: 6g | Protein: 14g

Chapter 2: Main Recipes

Welcome to Chapter 2, where we embark on a culinary journey through an array of main dishes tailored for a diabetic-friendly diet.

Understanding the importance of managing blood sugar levels without compromising on taste, this chapter is dedicated to offering you a diverse selection of meals from around the world.

From the aromatic spices of Indian cuisine to the robust flavors of Italian pastas and the comforting warmth of American classics, each recipe is crafted with care to ensure nutritional balance, flavor, and satisfaction.

As we delve into these recipes, you'll find dishes rich in lean proteins, complex carbohydrates, and healthy fats, all designed to provide steady energy and maintain blood sugar levels.

We've also focused on incorporating a variety of vegetables and herbs to enhance flavors naturally while boosting the nutritional content. Whether you're craving something exotic, or looking for a new twist on familiar favorites, this chapter is your gateway to delicious, diabetes-friendly meals that promise to delight your palate and support your health.

So, let's turn the page and start cooking some wholesome and delectable main dishes!

Mediterranean Chicken and Vegetable Casserole

Serves: 2

Prep time: 20 minutes / Cook time: 45 minutes

Ingredients:
- 2 boneless, skinless chicken breasts
- 1 zucchini, sliced
- 1 bell pepper, diced
- 1 small onion, diced
- 2 garlic cloves, minced
- 1 can (14.5 oz) diced tomatoes, no salt added
- 1 tsp dried oregano
- 1 tsp dried basil
- 1 tbsp olive oil
- Salt and pepper, to taste
- Fresh basil, for garnish

Instructions:
1. Preheat the oven to 375°F (190°C).
2. In a large baking dish, arrange the chicken breasts, zucchini, bell pepper, and onion.
3. In a bowl, mix the diced tomatoes, garlic, oregano, basil, olive oil, salt, and pepper. Pour this mixture over the chicken and vegetables.
4. Cover with foil and bake for 45 minutes, or until the chicken is cooked through and the vegetables are tender.
5. Garnish with fresh basil before serving.

Benefits for Diabetics:
This casserole is packed with lean protein, fiber, and various vitamins and minerals, all crucial for a balanced diabetic diet. The low glycemic vegetables and herbs provide flavor and nutrients without spiking blood sugar levels.

Per Serving:
Calories: 320 | Fat: 12g | Carbs: 15g | Fiber: 4g | Protein: 38g

Slow-Cooked Beef and Broccoli

Serves: 2

Prep time: 15 minutes / Cook time: 4 hours on high or 7 hours on low

Ingredients:
- 1/2 lb lean beef, sliced into strips
- 2 cups broccoli florets
- 1/2 onion, sliced
- 2 cloves garlic, minced
- 1/4 cup soy sauce, reduced sodium
- 1/4 cup beef broth, low sodium
- 1 tsp sesame oil
- 1 tbsp ginger, grated
- 1 tbsp cornstarch
- Salt and pepper, to taste

Instructions:
1. Place the beef, broccoli, onion, and garlic into the crockpot.
2. In a small bowl, whisk together soy sauce, beef broth, sesame oil, and ginger. Pour over the beef and vegetables.
3. Cook on high for 4 hours or on low for 7 hours.
4. Near the end of cooking, mix cornstarch with a little water and stir into the crockpot to thicken the sauce.
5. Serve hot, seasoned with salt and pepper to taste.

Benefits for Diabetics:
This dish is high in protein and low in carbohydrates, which is ideal for blood sugar management. Broccoli is a non-starchy vegetable, full of nutrients and fiber, helping to maintain a healthy blood sugar level.

Per Serving:
Calories: 250 | Fat: 8g | Carbs: 10g | Fiber: 3g | Protein: 34g

Turkey and Sweet Potato Skillet Casserole

Serves: 2

Prep time: 15 minutes / Cook time: 30 minutes

Ingredients:
- 1/2 lb ground turkey
- 1 large sweet potato, peeled and cubed
- 1 small onion, diced
- 2 cloves garlic, minced
- 1 tsp smoked paprika
- 1/2 tsp ground cumin
- 2 cups spinach leaves
- 1 tbsp olive oil
- Salt and pepper, to taste

Instructions:
1. Heat olive oil in a large skillet over medium heat. Add

onion and garlic, sauté until translucent.

2. Add ground turkey, cook until browned.
3. Stir in sweet potatoes, paprika, and cumin. Cover and cook until sweet potatoes are tender.
4. Add spinach and cook until wilted. Season with salt and pepper to taste.
5. Serve warm directly from the skillet.

Benefits for Diabetics:
Rich in fiber and nutrients, sweet potatoes have a lower glycemic index than regular potatoes, making them a suitable carb choice. Turkey provides high-quality protein, aiding in blood sugar regulation.

Per Serving:
Calories: 300 | Fat: 10g | Carbs: 25g | Fiber: 5g | Protein: 28g

Lemon-Thyme Chicken & Quinoa

Serves: 2

Prep time: 20 minutes / Cook time: 25 minutes

Ingredients:
- 2 boneless, skinless chicken breasts
- 1 cup quinoa
- 2 cups low-sodium chicken broth
- 1 lemon, juice and zest
- 1 tbsp fresh thyme leaves
- 1 tbsp olive oil
- Salt and pepper to taste
- Mixed vegetables (e.g., bell peppers, zucchini) for roasting

Instructions:
1. Rinse quinoa under cold water and drain. In a saucepan, bring chicken broth to a boil, add quinoa, cover, and simmer for 15 minutes or until all liquid is absorbed.
2. Preheat the oven to 375°F (190°C). Place chicken breasts in a baking dish, drizzle with olive oil, and sprinkle with lemon zest, thyme, salt, and pepper.
3. Bake chicken for 20-25 minutes or until fully cooked. Meanwhile, chop vegetables and toss with olive oil, salt, and pepper. Roast in the oven for 20 minutes.
4. Once the chicken is done, let it rest for a few minutes before slicing. Fluff the quinoa with a fork, and stir in lemon juice.
5. Serve the chicken sliced over a bed of quinoa and roasted vegetables on the side.

Benefits for Diabetics:
Chicken provides high-quality protein that helps regulate blood sugar levels, while quinoa is a good source of fiber and protein, contributing to slower digestion and extended energy release. The addition of fresh vegetables enhances the meal's vitamin, mineral, and fiber content, aiding in overall blood sugar management.

Per Serving:
Calories: 400 | Fat: 10g | Carbs: 40g | Fiber: 5g | Protein: 35g

Nordic Salmon with Dill Mustard Sauce

Serves: 2

Prep time: 15 minutes / Cook time: 15 minutes

Ingredients:
- 2 salmon fillets (about 6 oz each)
- 1 tbsp olive oil
- Salt and pepper to taste
- 2 tbsp mustard
- 1 tbsp honey (or a sugar substitute for lower carbs)
- 1 tbsp chopped fresh dill
- 1 tbsp cider vinegar
- Lemon wedges for serving

Instructions:
1. Preheat the oven to 400°F (200°C). Season salmon with salt, pepper, and olive oil. Place on a baking sheet and bake for 12-15 minutes until flaky and cooked.
2. Meanwhile, in a bowl, mix mustard, honey, dill, and cider vinegar to make the sauce.
3. Once the salmon is done, let it rest for a couple of minutes. Serve with the dill mustard sauce and lemon wedges on the side.

Benefits for Diabetics:
Salmon is an excellent source of protein and omega-3 fatty acids, which are beneficial for heart health. The dill mustard sauce provides a burst of flavor without added sugars or unhealthy fats, making it an excellent choice for a diabetic-friendly diet.

Per Serving:
Calories: 300 | Fat: 18g | Carbs: 3g | Fiber: 0g | Protein: 30g

Swedish Turkey Meatballs with Lingonberry

Serves: 2

Prep time: 20 minutes / Cook time: 20 minutes

Ingredients:
- 1/2 lb ground turkey
- 1/4 cup almond flour
- 1 egg
- 1/2 onion, finely chopped
- 1/2 tsp allspice
- Salt and pepper to taste
- 1 cup low-sodium beef broth
- 1 tbsp olive oil
- Lingonberry sauce (or sugar-free cranberry sauce as substitute)

Instructions:
1. Combine ground turkey, almond flour, egg, onion, allspice, salt, and pepper in a bowl. Form into small meatballs.
2. Heat olive oil in a pan over medium heat. Add meatballs and cook until browned on all sides and cooked through, about 10 minutes.
3. Remove meatballs and to the same pan, add beef broth to deglaze. Simmer until the sauce thickens slightly.
4. Serve meatballs with the sauce and a side of lingonberry sauce.

Benefits for Diabetics:
Turkey is lower in fat than beef, making it a healthier choice for maintaining cholesterol levels. Almond flour provides a low-carb alternative to breadcrumbs, and lingonberries are

low in sugar, high in antioxidants, making them a diabetic-friendly fruit.

Per Serving:
Calories: 350 | Fat: 20g | Carbs: 8g | Fiber: 2g | Protein: 35g

Finnish Mushroom Soup

Serves: 2
Prep time: 10 minutes / Cook time: 20 minutes

Ingredients:
- 2 cups mixed wild mushrooms, sliced
- 1 small onion, diced
- 2 cups vegetable broth
- 1 cup unsweetened almond milk
- 1 tbsp olive oil
- 1 tbsp fresh thyme
- Salt and pepper to taste

Instructions:
1. In a pot, heat olive oil over medium heat. Add onions and sauté until translucent. Add mushrooms and thyme, cook until mushrooms are soft.
2. Pour in vegetable broth and bring to a simmer. Let cook for about 10 minutes.
3. Stir in almond milk, and continue to cook for another 5 minutes. Season with salt and pepper.
4. Serve hot, garnished with a sprig of thyme or chopped parsley.

Benefits for Diabetics:
Mushrooms are low in carbohydrates and calories, making them an ideal component of a diabetic-friendly meal. Almond milk provides a creamy texture without the added sugars found in traditional cream, making it a healthier choice.

Per Serving:
Calories: 150 | Fat: 10g | Carbs: 10g | Fiber: 2g | Protein: 4g

Danish Rye Bread Open Sandwich (Smørrebrød)

Serves: 2
Prep time: 10 minutes / Cook time: 0 minutes

Ingredients:
- 2 slices dark rye bread
- 4 oz smoked salmon
- 1/4 cucumber, thinly sliced
- 1 hard-boiled egg, sliced
- Fresh dill for garnish
- Mustard or light cream cheese for spread

Instructions:
1. Spread a thin layer of mustard or light cream cheese on each slice of rye bread.
2. Layer smoked salmon, cucumber slices, and egg slices on the bread.
3. Garnish with fresh dill and serve immediately.

Benefits for Diabetics:
Rye bread is an excellent source of fiber, which helps in slow digestion and steady blood sugar levels. Smoked salmon provides omega-3 fatty acids, and the addition of vegetables adds vitamins and minerals without extra carbs

or calories.
Per Serving:
Calories: 250 | Fat: 10g | Carbs: 20g | Fiber: 5g | Protein: 20g

Norwegian Cod with Root Vegetables

Serves: 2
Prep time: 15 minutes / Cook time: 25 minutes

Ingredients:
- 2 cod fillets (about 6 oz each)
- 1 cup chopped carrots
- 1 cup chopped parsnips
- 1 cup chopped turnips
- 2 tbsp olive oil
- Salt and pepper to taste
- Fresh parsley for garnish

Instructions:
1. Preheat the oven to 400°F (200°C).
2. Toss chopped root vegetables with olive oil, salt, and pepper. Spread them on a baking sheet and roast for 20 minutes or until tender.
3. Season cod fillets with salt and pepper, and place them on top of the vegetables in the last 10 minutes of cooking.
4. Bake until the fish is flaky and vegetables are tender.
5. Serve hot, garnished with fresh parsley.

Benefits for Diabetics:
Cod is an excellent source of lean protein, and root vegetables are rich in fiber, aiding in blood sugar control and satiety. This dish is low in unhealthy fats and carbs, focusing on nutrient density and flavor.

Per Serving:
Calories: 300 | Fat: 10g | Carbs: 20g | Fiber: 6g | Protein: 35g

Icelandic Barley and Lamb Stew

Serves: 2
Prep time: 20 minutes / Cook time: 2 hours

Ingredients:
- 1/2 lb lamb shoulder, cut into cubes
- 1/2 cup pearl barley
- 2 cups low-sodium beef broth
- 1 cup chopped carrots
- 1 cup chopped onions
- 2 garlic cloves, minced
- 1 tbsp olive oil
- Salt and pepper to taste
- Fresh thyme for flavor

Instructions:
1. Heat olive oil in a large pot. Add lamb cubes and brown on all sides. Remove lamb and set aside.
2. In the same pot, add onions, garlic, carrots, and cook until softened.
3. Return lamb to the pot, add pearl barley, beef broth, thyme, salt, and pepper. Bring to a boil.
4. Reduce heat, cover, and simmer for about 2 hours or until the lamb is tender and barley is cooked.
5. Adjust seasoning and serve hot, garnished with fresh

herbs if desired.

Benefits for Diabetics:
Lamb is a good source of protein and iron, while barley is a whole grain that provides a slow release of energy. The fiber in the vegetables and barley aids in digestion and blood sugar control, making this a hearty and healthy option.

Per Serving:
Calories: 350 | Fat: 12g | Carbs: 30g | Fiber: 6g | Protein: 30g

Maple Glazed Salmon

Serves: 2
Prep time: 10 minutes / Cook time: 15 minutes

Ingredients:
- 2 salmon fillets (about 6 oz each)
- 2 tbsp sugar-free maple syrup
- 1 tbsp soy sauce (low sodium)
- 1 garlic clove, minced
- 1 tsp fresh grated ginger
- Salt and pepper to taste

Instructions:
1. Preheat the oven to 400°F (200°C).
2. In a small bowl, mix together the sugar-free maple syrup, soy sauce, garlic, and ginger.
3. Place the salmon fillets on a baking sheet lined with parchment paper. Season with salt and pepper.
4. Brush the maple mixture over the salmon fillets.
5. Bake for 12-15 minutes until the salmon is cooked through and flakes easily with a fork.

Benefits for Diabetics:
Salmon is rich in omega-3 fatty acids and protein, making it excellent for heart health and blood sugar stabilization. The sugar-free maple syrup provides the sweetness without the added sugars, making it a diabetic-friendly indulgence.

Per Serving:
Calories: 300 | Fat: 14g | Carbs: 3g | Fiber: 0g | Protein: 38g

Poutine with Oven-Baked Fries

Serves: 2
Prep time: 15 minutes / Cook time: 30 minutes

Ingredients:
- 2 large russet potatoes, cut into fries
- 1 tbsp olive oil
- 1 cup low-fat cheese curds or shredded cheese
- 1 cup low-sodium beef or chicken gravy

Instructions:
1. Preheat the oven to 425°F (220°C). Toss the cut potatoes with olive oil and spread them on a baking sheet.
2. Bake for 25-30 minutes, turning once until golden and crisp.
3. Heat the gravy in a saucepan over medium heat.
4. Once the fries are done, divide them between two plates. Sprinkle cheese curds over the hot fries and pour the warm gravy on top.

Benefits for Diabetics:
Oven-baked fries provide a lower-fat alternative to

traditional deep-fried potatoes, and using low-fat cheese and low-sodium gravy reduces the overall calorie and salt content. This version is more blood sugar friendly while still satisfying cravings for comfort food.

Per Serving:
Calories: 350 | Fat: 12g | Carbs: 45g | Fiber: 5g | Protein: 15g

Wild Rice and Chicken Casserole

Serves: 2
Prep time: 20 minutes / Cook time: 45 minutes

Ingredients:
- 1 cup wild rice
- 2 cups low-sodium chicken broth
- 1/2 lb chicken breast, cubed
- 1 cup mixed vegetables (carrots, peas, corn)
- 1 onion, diced
- 1 garlic clove, minced
- 1 tsp olive oil
- Salt and pepper to taste
- 1 tsp thyme

Instructions:
1. Preheat oven to 375°F (190°C).
2. Cook wild rice in chicken broth according to package instructions until tender.
3. In a skillet, heat olive oil over medium heat. Add onion and garlic, sauté until translucent.
4. Add cubed chicken to the skillet and cook until no longer pink. Season with salt, pepper, and thyme.
5. In a casserole dish, combine cooked wild rice, chicken, and vegetables. Stir to mix well.
6. Cover with foil and bake for 30 minutes until everything is heated through and flavors have melded.

Benefits for Diabetics:
Wild rice is a good source of fiber and nutrients, which helps in blood sugar management. Chicken provides lean protein, and the vegetables add vitamins and minerals without a significant amount of carbs.

Per Serving:
Calories: 400 | Fat: 9g | Carbs: 45g | Fiber: 6g | Protein: 35g

Roasted Beet and Goat Cheese Salad

Serves: 2
Prep time: 15 minutes / Cook time: 30 minutes

Ingredients:
- 4 medium beets, peeled and cubed
- 2 cups mixed greens
- 1/4 cup crumbled goat cheese
- 1/4 cup walnuts, chopped
- 2 tbsp balsamic vinegar
- 1 tbsp olive oil
- Salt and pepper to taste

Instructions:
1. Preheat the oven to 400°F (200°C). Toss cubed beets with 1/2 tbsp olive oil, salt, and pepper. Spread on a baking sheet and roast for 30 minutes or until tender.
2. In a large bowl, combine mixed greens, roasted beets, goat cheese, and walnuts.

3. Drizzle with balsamic vinegar and the remaining olive oil. Toss to coat and season with salt and pepper to taste.

Benefits for Diabetics:
Beets are low in calories and high in fiber, helping to manage blood sugar levels. Goat cheese is a good source of protein and healthy fats, and walnuts add omega-3 fatty acids, beneficial for heart health.

Per Serving:
Calories: 250 | Fat: 18g | Carbs: 15g | Fiber: 5g | Protein: 10g

Lentil Shepherd's Pie

Serves: 2
Prep time: 30 minutes / Cook time: 20 minutes

Ingredients:
- 1 cup lentils, cooked
- 2 cups cauliflower florets
- 1 cup mixed vegetables (carrots, peas, corn)
- 1 onion, diced
- 1 garlic clove, minced
- 1 cup low-sodium vegetable broth
- 1 tbsp olive oil
- Salt and pepper to taste
- 1 tsp paprika

Instructions:
1. Preheat oven to 375°F (190°C).
2. In a pan, heat olive oil over medium heat. Add onion and garlic, sauté until translucent. Add mixed vegetables, cooked lentils, vegetable broth, paprika, salt, and pepper. Simmer until thickened.
3. Meanwhile, steam cauliflower until tender. Mash with a fork or blender, seasoning with salt and pepper.
4. In a baking dish, layer the lentil mixture. Top with mashed cauliflower, smoothing the surface.
5. Bake for 20 minutes or until the top is slightly golden.

Benefits for Diabetics:
Lentils are an excellent source of fiber and plant-based protein, aiding in blood sugar control. Cauliflower provides a low-carb alternative to mashed potatoes, making the dish lighter and more suitable for a diabetic diet.

Per Serving:
Calories: 350 | Fat: 8g | Carbs: 50g | Fiber: 15g | Protein: 20g

Baked Cod with Maple Balsamic Brussels Sprouts

Serves: 2
Prep time: 15 minutes / Cook time: 20 minutes

Ingredients:
- 2 cod fillets (about 6 oz each)
- 2 cups Brussels sprouts, halved
- 2 tbsp balsamic vinegar
- 1 tbsp sugar-free maple syrup
- 1 tbsp olive oil
- Salt and pepper to taste

Instructions:
1. Preheat the oven to 400°F (200°C).

2. Toss Brussels sprouts with olive oil, salt, and pepper. Spread on a baking sheet and roast for 15 minutes until tender and caramelized.
3. In the last 10 minutes of cooking the Brussels sprouts, add the cod fillets to the baking sheet. Season with salt and pepper.
4. Bake until the cod is flaky and cooked through.
5. Mix balsamic vinegar and sugar-free maple syrup in a small bowl. Drizzle over the cooked cod and Brussels sprouts before serving.

Benefits for Diabetics:
Cod is an excellent source of lean protein, and Brussels sprouts are high in fiber and nutrients. The sugar-free maple and balsamic glaze adds a touch of sweetness and acidity without the added sugars, making it a balanced and flavorful meal.

Per Serving:
Calories: 300 | Fat: 10g | Carbs: 20g | Fiber: 5g | Protein: 35g

Crockpot Turkey Chili

Serves: 2
Prep time: 15 minutes / Cook time: 6 hours on low

Ingredients:
- 1/2 lb ground turkey
- 1 can (15 oz) low-sodium black beans, drained and rinsed
- 1 can (15 oz) low-sodium diced tomatoes
- 1 bell pepper, chopped
- 1 onion, chopped
- 2 cloves garlic, minced
- 1 tbsp chili powder
- 1 tsp cumin
- Salt and pepper to taste

Instructions:
1. Brown the ground turkey in a skillet, then transfer to the crockpot.
2. Add the black beans, diced tomatoes, bell pepper, onion, garlic, chili powder, and cumin to the crockpot.
3. Stir well to combine, then cover and cook on low for 6 hours.
4. Season with salt and pepper to taste before serving.

Benefits for Diabetics:
Turkey is a great source of lean protein, and black beans provide fiber, which helps regulate blood sugar levels. The slow cooking process allows the flavors to meld beautifully while keeping the nutritional integrity of the ingredients.

Per Serving:
Calories: 350 | Fat: 5g | Carbs: 45g | Fiber: 12g | Protein: 35g

Beef Stew with Root Vegetables

Serves: 2
Prep time: 20 minutes / Cook time: 8 hours on low

Ingredients:
- 1/2 lb beef stew meat, trimmed
- 1 cup low-sodium beef broth
- 2 carrots, chopped

- 2 parsnips, chopped
- 1 small sweet potato, cubed
- 1 onion, diced
- 2 cloves garlic, minced
- Salt and pepper to taste
- 1 tsp dried thyme

Instructions:
1. Place the beef, carrots, parsnips, sweet potato, onion, and garlic in the crockpot.
2. Pour the beef broth over the ingredients. Add thyme, salt, and pepper.
3. Cover and cook on low for 8 hours until the meat is tender and the vegetables are cooked.
4. Adjust the seasoning if necessary and serve hot.

Benefits for Diabetics:
Lean beef provides protein, and the variety of root vegetables offers fiber and essential nutrients. This slow-cooked stew maximizes flavor without adding unnecessary fats or sugars.

Per Serving:
Calories: 400 | Fat: 12g | Carbs: 40g | Fiber: 6g | Protein: 35g

Slow-Cooked Pulled Pork

Serves: 2

Prep time: 10 minutes / Cook time: 8 hours on low

Ingredients:
- 1 lb pork tenderloin
- 1 cup sugar-free barbecue sauce
- 1 onion, sliced
- 2 cloves garlic, minced
- Salt and pepper to taste

Instructions:
1. Season the pork tenderloin with salt and pepper and place it in the crockpot.
2. Add the sliced onion and minced garlic around the pork.
3. Pour the sugar-free barbecue sauce over the pork.
4. Cover and cook on low for 8 hours until the pork is very tender.
5. Shred the pork with two forks and mix with the sauce in the crockpot.
6. Serve with a side of steamed vegetables or a small portion of whole grain bread.

Benefits for Diabetics:
Pulled pork provides a high-protein meal, and using a sugar-free barbecue sauce keeps the sugar content low. The long, slow cooking process keeps the meat tender and flavorful without needing added fats.

Per Serving:
Calories: 300 | Fat: 8g | Carbs: 10g | Fiber: 0g | Protein: 45g

Crockpot Chicken Cacciatore

Serves: 2

Prep time: 15 minutes / Cook time: 6 hours on low

Ingredients:
- 2 boneless, skinless chicken breasts
- 1 can (15 oz) low-sodium diced tomatoes
- 1 bell pepper, sliced

- 1 onion, sliced
- 2 cloves garlic, minced
- 1 tsp dried oregano
- 1 tsp dried basil
- Salt and pepper to taste

Instructions:
1. Place the chicken breasts in the bottom of the crockpot.
2. Top with the diced tomatoes, bell pepper, onion, and garlic.
3. Sprinkle with oregano, basil, salt, and pepper.
4. Cover and cook on low for 6 hours until the chicken is tender and cooked through.
5. Serve hot, garnished with additional fresh herbs if desired.

Benefits for Diabetics:
Chicken is a lean protein source, and the vegetables add fiber and nutrients with minimal impact on blood sugar. This dish is filling, nutritious, and aligns with the dietary needs of diabetics.

Per Serving:
Calories: 300 | Fat: 6g | Carbs: 20g | Fiber: 5g | Protein: 40g

Slow-Cooker Salsa Verde Chicken

Serves: 2

Prep time: 10 minutes / Cook time: 4 hours on high

Ingredients:
- 2 boneless, skinless chicken breasts
- 1 cup salsa verde (low-sodium, sugar-free)
- 1 onion, chopped
- 1 tsp cumin
- Salt and pepper to taste

Instructions:
1. Place the chicken breasts in the crockpot.
2. Top with salsa verde, onion, cumin, salt, and pepper.
3. Cover and cook on high for 4 hours until the chicken is tender and easy to shred.
4. Shred the chicken in the crockpot with two forks and stir to mix with the salsa.
5. Serve over a small portion of brown rice or wrapped in a low-carb tortilla with additional vegetables if desired.

Benefits for Diabetics:
This dish is high in protein from the chicken and low in sugar with the use of sugar-free salsa verde. It's a satisfying meal that's easy to digest and gentle on blood sugar levels.

Per Serving:
Calories: 250 | Fat: 3g | Carbs: 10g | Fiber: 2g | Protein: 45g

Crockpot Beef and Broccoli

Serves: 2

Prep time: 15 minutes / Cook time: 6 hours on low

Ingredients:
- 1/2 lb beef chuck, sliced thinly
- 2 cups broccoli florets
- 1/4 cup low-sodium soy sauce
- 1/4 cup beef broth
- 2 cloves garlic, minced
- 1 tbsp ginger, minced
- 2 tsp sugar substitute

- 1 tbsp cornstarch (optional, for thickening)
- Salt and pepper to taste

Instructions:
1. Place the sliced beef in the crockpot.
2. In a bowl, mix the soy sauce, beef broth, garlic, ginger, and sugar substitute. Pour over the beef.
3. Cook on low for 5 hours. Then add the broccoli and cook for an additional hour until the broccoli is tender and the beef is cooked through.
4. If a thicker sauce is desired, mix cornstarch with a little water and stir into the crockpot. Allow to cook and thicken for the last 30 minutes.
5. Adjust seasoning with salt and pepper, and serve hot.

Benefits for Diabetics:
Beef provides protein and iron, while broccoli offers fiber and essential nutrients. The dish is low in carbohydrates and sugars, making it a balanced option for managing blood sugar levels.

Per Serving:
Calories: 300 | Fat: 10g | Carbs: 15g | Fiber: 3g | Protein: 35g

Whole Wheat Spaghetti with Grilled Vegetables

Serves: 2
Prep time: 15 minutes / Cook time: 20 minutes

Ingredients:
- 6 oz whole wheat spaghetti
- 2 cups mixed vegetables (zucchini, bell peppers, cherry tomatoes)
- 2 cloves garlic, minced
- 1 tbsp olive oil
- Salt and pepper to taste
- Fresh basil for garnish
- Parmesan cheese, grated (optional)

Instructions:
1. Cook whole wheat spaghetti according to package instructions until al dente. Drain and set aside.
2. Preheat a grill or grill pan over medium heat. Toss the vegetables with olive oil, salt, and pepper. Grill until charred and tender.
3. In a large pan, sauté garlic in a bit of olive oil until fragrant. Add the grilled vegetables and cooked spaghetti. Toss to combine.
4. Serve hot, garnished with fresh basil and a sprinkle of Parmesan cheese if desired.

Benefits for Diabetics:
Whole wheat pasta has a lower glycemic index than regular pasta, helping to maintain stable blood sugar levels. The grilled vegetables add fiber and antioxidants without extra carbs.

Per Serving:
Calories: 350 | Fat: 8g | Carbs: 60g | Fiber: 10g | Protein: 12g

Chicken and Mushroom Risotto

Serves: 2
Prep time: 15 minutes / Cook time: 30 minutes

Ingredients:
- 1/2 cup arborio rice
- 1/2 lb chicken breast, cubed
- 2 cups sliced mushrooms
- 1 small onion, diced
- 2 cloves garlic, minced
- 3 cups low-sodium chicken broth
- 1 tbsp olive oil
- Salt and pepper to taste
- Fresh parsley for garnish

Instructions:
1. In a large pan, heat olive oil over medium heat. Add onion and garlic, sauté until translucent.
2. Add the chicken and cook until browned and cooked through. Remove the chicken and set aside.
3. In the same pan, add a bit more oil if needed and sauté the mushrooms until they're soft.
4. Add the arborio rice to the mushrooms and stir for a minute to toast the rice. Begin adding chicken broth one cup at a time, stirring frequently, allowing the rice to absorb the liquid before adding more.
5. Once the rice is tender and creamy, add back the cooked chicken. Season with salt and pepper.
6. Serve hot, garnished with fresh parsley.

Benefits for Diabetics:
This dish offers a good balance of protein from the chicken, complex carbohydrates from the arborio rice, and nutrients from the mushrooms. The controlled portion of rice and the slow release of carbohydrates help manage blood sugar levels.

Per Serving:
Calories: 400 | Fat: 10g | Carbs: 50g | Fiber: 3g | Protein: 30g

Shrimp and Zucchini Noodles

Serves: 2
Prep time: 10 minutes / Cook time: 10 minutes

Ingredients:
- 2 medium zucchinis, spiralized
- 1/2 lb shrimp, peeled and deveined
- 2 cloves garlic, minced
- 1 lemon, juice, and zest
- 1 tbsp olive oil
- Salt and pepper to taste
- Red pepper flakes (optional)

Instructions:
1. Heat olive oil in a large pan over medium heat. Add garlic and cook until fragrant.
2. Add shrimp, season with salt, pepper, and red pepper flakes if using. Cook until shrimp are pink and opaque.
3. Add the zucchini noodles and lemon zest to the pan. Cook for 2-3 minutes until the zoodles are tender.
4. Stir in lemon juice and adjust seasoning as needed.
5. Serve immediately, garnished with additional lemon zest or parsley if desired.

Benefits for Diabetics:
Zucchini noodles are a low-carb alternative to pasta, significantly reducing the dish's glycemic load. Shrimp

provides a high-quality protein source, and the whole dish is light on calories yet rich in flavor.

Per Serving:
Calories: 250 | Fat: 8g | Carbs: 10g | Fiber: 2g | Protein: 35g

Eggplant Parmesan with Almond Flour

Serves: 2
Prep time: 20 minutes / Cook time: 30 minutes

Ingredients:
- 1 large eggplant, sliced into 1/2 inch rounds
- 1 cup almond flour
- 2 eggs, beaten
- 1 cup sugar-free marinara sauce
- 1/2 cup shredded mozzarella cheese (low-fat)
- 1/4 cup grated Parmesan cheese
- 1 tbsp olive oil
- Salt and pepper to taste
- Fresh basil for garnish

Instructions:
1. Preheat the oven to 375°F (190°C). Line a baking sheet with parchment paper.
2. Season the eggplant slices with salt and let them sit for 10 minutes. Wipe away the moisture with a paper towel.
3. Dip eggplant slices first in the beaten eggs, then coat with almond flour.
4. Arrange the eggplant on the baking sheet and drizzle with olive oil. Bake for 20 minutes until golden brown.
5. In a baking dish, layer the baked eggplant with marinara sauce, mozzarella, and Parmesan cheese. Repeat the layers.
6. Bake for an additional 10 minutes until the cheese is melted and bubbly.
7. Serve hot, garnished with fresh basil.

Benefits for Diabetics:
Eggplant is a low-carbohydrate vegetable, and almond flour offers a lower-carb alternative to traditional breadcrumbs. The cheese provides calcium and protein, making this a balanced and nutritious dish.

Per Serving:
Calories: 400 | Fat: 25g | Carbs: 20g | Fiber: 10g | Protein: 25g

Italian Sausage and Peppers over Cauliflower Rice

Serves: 2
Prep time: 15 minutes / Cook time: 20 minutes

Ingredients:
- 2 Italian chicken sausages, sliced
- 1 bell pepper, sliced
- 1 onion, sliced
- 2 cups cauliflower rice
- 1 tbsp olive oil
- Salt and pepper to taste
- 1 tsp Italian seasoning

Instructions:
1. In a large pan, heat olive oil over medium heat. Add the sausage slices and cook until browned. Remove and set aside.
2. In the same pan, add onions and bell peppers. Cook until softened and slightly caramelized.
3. Stir in the cooked sausage, cauliflower rice, and Italian seasoning. Cook for an additional 5-7 minutes until everything is heated through and flavors are combined.
4. Season with salt and pepper to taste and serve hot.

Benefits for Diabetics:
Cauliflower rice is an excellent low-carb substitute for grains, and chicken sausage is a leaner protein option than traditional pork sausage. The vegetables add fiber and nutrients, making this a well-rounded, diabetes-friendly dish.

Per Serving:
Calories: 300 | Fat: 18g | Carbs: 15g | Fiber: 5g | Protein: 20g

Lean Beef Bolognese over Spaghetti Squash

Serves: 2
Prep time: 15 minutes / Cook time: 45 minutes

Ingredients:
- 1 medium spaghetti squash
- 1/2 lb lean ground beef
- 1 cup sugar-free marinara sauce
- 1 onion, diced
- 2 cloves garlic, minced
- 1 carrot, diced
- 1 celery stalk, diced
- 1 tbsp olive oil
- Salt and pepper to taste
- Fresh basil for garnish

Instructions:
1. Preheat the oven to 400°F (200°C). Halve the spaghetti squash and scoop out the seeds. Place cut side down on a baking sheet and bake for 30-35 minutes until tender.
2. In a large pan, heat olive oil over medium heat. Add onions, garlic, carrot, and celery. Cook until softened.
3. Add the ground beef and cook until browned. Drain any excess fat.
4. Stir in the marinara sauce and simmer for 10 minutes until the flavors meld.
5. Once the spaghetti squash is cooked, use a fork to scrape out the strands.
6. Serve the Bolognese sauce over the spaghetti squash, garnished with fresh basil.

Benefits for Diabetics:
Spaghetti squash is a fantastic low-carb alternative to pasta, high in fiber and nutrients. Lean beef provides protein without excess fat, and the homemade, sugar-free marinara keeps the sugar content minimal.

Per Serving:
Calories: 350 | Fat: 15g | Carbs: 30g | Fiber: 7g | Protein: 25g

Grilled Chicken Caprese

Serves: 2
Prep time: 15 minutes / Cook time: 20 minutes

Ingredients:
- 2 boneless, skinless chicken breasts
- 1 large tomato, sliced
- 4 oz fresh mozzarella cheese, sliced
- Fresh basil leaves
- 1 tbsp balsamic glaze
- 1 tbsp olive oil
- Salt and pepper to taste

Instructions:
1. Preheat the grill to medium-high heat. Brush the chicken breasts with olive oil and season with salt and pepper.
2. Grill the chicken for 6-7 minutes on each side or until fully cooked and internal temperature reaches 165°F (75°C).
3. Once cooked, top each chicken breast with tomato slices, mozzarella, and basil leaves.
4. Cover the grill for 2-3 minutes, allowing the cheese to melt slightly.
5. Drizzle with balsamic glaze before serving.

Benefits for Diabetics:
This dish is high in protein and low in carbs, making it ideal for blood sugar control. The fresh ingredients provide vitamins and minerals, and the balsamic glaze offers a hint of sweetness without a significant sugar spike.

Per Serving:
Calories: 350 | Fat: 18g | Carbs: 8g | Fiber: 1g | Protein: 38g

Tuscan Bean Soup

Serves: 2
Prep time: 15 minutes / Cook time: 30 minutes

Ingredients:
- 1 can (15 oz) cannellini beans, drained and rinsed
- 2 cups kale, chopped
- 1 carrot, diced
- 1 celery stalk, diced
- 1 small onion, diced
- 2 cloves garlic, minced
- 1 can (15 oz) low-sodium diced tomatoes
- 3 cups low-sodium vegetable broth
- 1 tsp dried Italian herbs
- 1 tbsp olive oil
- Salt and pepper to taste

Instructions:
1. In a large pot, heat olive oil over medium heat. Add onion, carrot, and celery. Cook until softened.
2. Add garlic and cook for an additional minute until fragrant.
3. Stir in the diced tomatoes, vegetable broth, cannellini beans, and Italian herbs. Bring to a boil.
4. Reduce heat and simmer for 20 minutes.
5. Add the kale and cook until wilted and tender.
6. Season with salt and pepper to taste and serve warm.

Benefits for Diabetics:
Beans are a great source of fiber and protein, helping to regulate blood sugar levels. Kale and other vegetables add a wealth of nutrients and antioxidants, while the low-sodium ingredients keep the dish heart-healthy.

Per Serving:
Calories: 300 | Fat: 7g | Carbs: 45g | Fiber: 12g | Protein: 15g

Baked Cod with Olive Tapenade

Serves: 2
Prep time: 10 minutes / Cook time: 15 minutes

Ingredients:
- 2 cod fillets (about 6 oz each)
- 1/2 cup black olives, pitted and chopped
- 1 tbsp capers, rinsed and chopped
- 1 clove garlic, minced
- 1 tbsp lemon juice
- 2 tsp olive oil
- Fresh parsley, chopped
- Salt and pepper to taste

Instructions:
1. Preheat the oven to 400°F (200°C).
2. In a small bowl, mix together the olives, capers, garlic, lemon juice, and olive oil to create the tapenade.
3. Place the cod fillets on a baking sheet lined with parchment paper. Season with salt and pepper.
4. Spread the olive tapenade over the cod fillets.
5. Bake for 12-15 minutes or until the cod is flaky and cooked through.
6. Garnish with fresh parsley before serving.

Benefits for Diabetics:
Cod is an excellent source of lean protein, essential for blood sugar regulation. The olive tapenade provides healthy fats and adds a burst of flavor without the need for heavy sauces or additional salt.

Per Serving:
Calories: 250 | Fat: 10g | Carbs: 5g | Fiber: 1g | Protein: 35g

Italian-Style Stuffed Peppers

Serves: 2
Prep time: 20 minutes / Cook time: 30 minutes

Ingredients:
- 2 bell peppers, halved and seeded
- 1/2 lb lean ground turkey
- 1/2 cup cooked quinoa
- 1 small onion, diced
- 1 clove garlic, minced
- 1 cup spinach, chopped
- 1/4 cup grated Parmesan cheese
- 1 cup low-sodium tomato sauce
- 1 tsp olive oil
- Salt and pepper to taste
- Fresh basil for garnish

Instructions:
1. Preheat the oven to 375°F (190°C).
2. In a skillet, heat olive oil over medium heat. Add the ground turkey, onion, and garlic. Cook until the turkey is browned.
3. Stir in the cooked quinoa, spinach, half of the tomato sauce, and Parmesan cheese. Cook until the spinach is wilted.
4. Season the mixture with salt and pepper.
5. Stuff the bell pepper halves with the turkey and quinoa mixture.
6. Place the stuffed peppers in a baking dish and pour the

remaining tomato sauce over the top.

7. Cover with foil and bake for 25-30 minutes until the peppers are tender.
8. Uncover and bake for an additional 5 minutes.
9. Garnish with fresh basil and serve hot.

Benefits for Diabetics:
Stuffed peppers are a balanced meal with a good mix of protein, fiber, and healthy carbs. The lean ground turkey and quinoa provide a satisfying base, while the bell peppers add sweetness and vitamins without excess calories or carbs.

Per Serving:
Calories: 350 | Fat: 12g | Carbs: 30g | Fiber: 6g | Protein: 28g

Mediterranean Stuffed Baked Potato

Serves: 2
Prep time: 10 minutes / Cook time: 1 hour

Ingredients:
- 2 large russet potatoes
- 1/2 cup chopped spinach
- 1/4 cup sun-dried tomatoes, chopped
- 1/4 cup feta cheese, crumbled
- 1/4 cup kalamata olives, sliced
- 1 tbsp olive oil
- Salt and pepper to taste
- 1 tsp dried oregano

Instructions:
1. Preheat the oven to 425°F (220°C). Wash the potatoes and prick them with a fork. Bake directly on the oven rack for about 1 hour or until tender.
2. Once done, let the potatoes cool slightly, then cut them open and scoop out some of the insides to make room for the filling, leaving some potato along the skin for structure.
3. In a bowl, mix the scooped-out potato with spinach, sun-dried tomatoes, feta cheese, kalamata olives, olive oil, salt, pepper, and oregano.
4. Stuff the mixture back into the potato skins and return them to the oven for an additional 10 minutes until everything is heated through and the top is slightly crispy.
5. Serve warm, garnished with extra feta or herbs if desired.

Benefits for Diabetics:
This dish is packed with fiber from the potato skin and spinach, healthy fats from the olives and olive oil, and protein from the feta cheese. The variety of flavors and nutrients makes it a satisfying meal without a high glycemic load.

Per Serving:
Calories: 300 | Fat: 12g | Carbs: 40g | Fiber: 5g | Protein: 8g

BBQ Chicken Stuffed Baked Potato

Serves: 2
Prep time: 15 minutes / Cook time: 1 hour

Ingredients:
- 2 large russet potatoes
- 1/2 lb cooked chicken breast, shredded
- 1/2 cup sugar-free BBQ sauce
- 1/4 cup cheddar cheese, shredded
- 2 green onions, sliced
- 1 tbsp olive oil
- Salt and pepper to taste

Instructions:
1. Preheat the oven to 425°F (220°C). Wash the potatoes and prick them with a fork. Bake directly on the oven rack for about 1 hour or until tender.
2. In a bowl, mix the shredded chicken with the sugar-free BBQ sauce.
3. Once the potatoes are cooked, slice them open and fluff the inside with a fork.
4. Stuff the BBQ chicken mixture into the potato and top with shredded cheddar cheese.
5. Return the potatoes to the oven and bake for an additional 10 minutes until the cheese is melted and bubbly.
6. Garnish with sliced green onions and serve hot.

Benefits for Diabetics:
The chicken provides a high-quality protein source, essential for blood sugar management. Using a sugar-free BBQ sauce reduces the overall sugar content, and the potato, when eaten with its skin, offers fiber to help slow glucose absorption.

Per Serving:
Calories: 400 | Fat: 10g | Carbs: 45g | Fiber: 5g | Protein: 30g

Broccoli and Cheddar Twice-Baked Potato

Serves: 2
Prep time: 15 minutes / Cook time: 1 hour 20 minutes

Ingredients:
- 2 large russet potatoes
- 1 cup broccoli florets, steamed and chopped
- 1/2 cup low-fat cheddar cheese, shredded
- 1/4 cup Greek yogurt or low-fat sour cream
- 1 tbsp olive oil
- Salt and pepper to taste
- Paprika for garnish

Instructions:
1. Preheat the oven to 425°F (220°C). Wash the potatoes and prick them with a fork. Bake directly on the oven rack for about 1 hour or until tender.
2. Once the potatoes are cool enough to handle, cut them in half and scoop out the insides, leaving a thin layer of potato on the skin.
3. In a bowl, mash the scooped-out potato with Greek yogurt or sour cream, salt, and pepper.
4. Mix in the steamed broccoli and half of the cheddar cheese.
5. Spoon the mixture back into the potato skins. Top with the remaining cheddar cheese and sprinkle with paprika.
6. Bake for an additional 20 minutes or until the tops are golden and cheese is melted.
7. Serve warm, with extra Greek yogurt or sour cream on

the side if desired.
Benefits for Diabetics:
Broccoli is high in fiber and nutrients while being low in calories, making it great for blood sugar management. Greek yogurt adds creaminess and protein without the fat of traditional ingredients, and the whole dish is balanced with complex carbohydrates and protein.
Per Serving:
Calories: 350 | Fat: 12g | Carbs: 45g | Fiber: 6g | Protein: 15g

Coq Au Vin (Light Version)

Serves: 2
Prep time: 30 minutes / Cook time: 1 hour

Ingredients:
- 2 skinless chicken breasts or thighs
- 1 cup red wine (or low-sodium chicken broth for a non-alcoholic version)
- 1 cup mushrooms, sliced
- 1 small onion, diced
- 1 carrot, sliced
- 2 cloves garlic, minced
- 2 slices turkey bacon, chopped
- 1 tbsp olive oil
- 1 tsp dried thyme
- Salt and pepper to taste
- Fresh parsley for garnish

Instructions:
1. In a large pan, heat olive oil over medium heat. Add turkey bacon and cook until crispy. Remove and set aside.
2. In the same pan, add chicken pieces and brown on all sides. Remove and set aside.
3. Add onions, garlic, carrots, and mushrooms to the pan. Sauté until vegetables are softened.
4. Return the chicken and bacon to the pan. Add red wine (or chicken broth), thyme, salt, and pepper.
5. Cover and simmer for about 45 minutes to 1 hour, until the chicken is tender and the sauce has thickened.
6. Adjust seasoning and serve hot, garnished with fresh parsley.

Benefits for Diabetics:
This dish offers a high protein content from the chicken, essential for maintaining muscle health and satiety. The vegetables add fiber and nutrients, and by using skinless chicken and turkey bacon, the overall fat content is reduced.
Per Serving:
Calories: 350 | Fat: 10g | Carbs: 10g | Fiber: 2g | Protein: 40g

French-Style Baked Fish with Herbs and Lemon

Serves: 2
Prep time: 10 minutes / Cook time: 20 minutes

Ingredients:
- 2 white fish fillets (cod, halibut, or similar)
- 1 lemon, sliced
- 1 tbsp olive oil
- 1 tbsp fresh parsley, chopped
- 1 tsp dried tarragon or thyme
- Salt and pepper to taste

Instructions:
1. Preheat the oven to 375°F (190°C). Line a baking dish with parchment paper.
2. Place the fish fillets in the dish and season with salt, pepper, and dried herbs.
3. Drizzle with olive oil and top with lemon slices and parsley.
4. Bake for 15-20 minutes, depending on the thickness of the fillets, until fish flakes easily with a fork.
5. Serve hot, garnished with additional fresh herbs and lemon wedges if desired.

Benefits for Diabetics:
White fish is a great source of high-quality protein and omega-3 fatty acids, with minimal saturated fat. The herbs and lemon add flavor without additional salt or sugar, making this a heart-healthy and diabetic-friendly option.
Per Serving:
Calories: 200 | Fat: 7g | Carbs: 2g | Fiber: 0.5g | Protein: 30g

French Lentil Salad with Dijon Vinaigrette

Serves: 2
Prep time: 15 minutes / Cook time: 25 minutes

Ingredients:
- 1 cup French green lentils (Puy lentils)
- 2 cups water or vegetable broth
- 1/2 red onion, diced
- 1 carrot, diced
- 1 celery stalk, diced
- 2 tbsp fresh parsley, chopped
- For the Dijon Vinaigrette:
- 2 tbsp olive oil
- 1 tbsp Dijon mustard
- 1 tbsp red wine vinegar
- Salt and pepper to taste

Instructions:
1. Rinse the lentils and cook in water or vegetable broth according to package instructions until tender but firm.
2. Drain the lentils and let them cool slightly.
3. In a large bowl, combine cooked lentils, red onion, carrot, celery, and parsley.
4. In a small bowl, whisk together the olive oil, Dijon mustard, red wine vinegar, salt, and pepper to make the vinaigrette.
5. Pour the vinaigrette over the lentil mixture and toss to combine.
6. Serve at room temperature or chilled, garnished with extra parsley if desired.

Benefits for Diabetics:
Lentils are a great source of plant-based protein and fiber, which are beneficial for blood sugar control and heart health. The vegetables add vitamins and minerals, and the vinaigrette provides healthy fats and flavor without added sugars.
Per Serving:
Calories: 350 | Fat: 14g | Carbs: 40g | Fiber: 16g | Protein: 18g

Baked Ratatouille Gratin

Serves: 2
Prep time: 30 minutes / Cook time: 45 minutes

Ingredients:
- 1 small eggplant, thinly sliced
- 1 zucchini, thinly sliced
- 1 yellow squash, thinly sliced
- 1 bell pepper, thinly sliced
- 2 tomatoes, thinly sliced
- 1/2 cup low-sodium tomato sauce
- 1/4 cup grated low-fat cheese (optional)
- 1 tbsp olive oil
- 1 tsp dried basil
- 1 tsp dried thyme
- Salt and pepper to taste

Instructions:
1. Preheat the oven to 375°F (190°C). Spread tomato sauce at the bottom of a baking dish.
2. Arrange slices of eggplant, zucchini, yellow squash, bell pepper, and tomatoes in a spiral or layered pattern over the sauce.
3. Drizzle with olive oil and sprinkle with basil, thyme, salt, and pepper.
4. Cover with foil and bake for 35 minutes.
5. Remove foil, sprinkle with cheese, and bake for another 10 minutes or until the cheese is melted and golden.
6. Serve hot, garnished with fresh herbs if desired.

Benefits for Diabetics:
This gratin is loaded with vegetables, providing an array of nutrients and fiber. The use of low-fat cheese adds calcium and protein without too much fat, making it a balanced and nutritious dish suitable for diabetics.

Per Serving:
Calories: 250 | Fat: 12g | Carbs: 30g | Fiber: 9g | Protein: 10g

Spiced Pork Chops with Vegetable Stir Fry

Serves: 2
Prep time: 15 minutes / Cook time: 20 minutes

Ingredients:
- 2 boneless pork chops
- 1 tbsp olive oil
- 1 tsp smoked paprika
- 1/2 tsp garlic powder
- Salt and pepper to taste
- 2 cups mixed vegetables (bell peppers, broccoli, carrots)
- 1 tbsp low-sodium soy sauce
- 1 tsp sesame oil

Instructions:
1. Season pork chops with smoked paprika, garlic powder, salt, and pepper.
2. Heat olive oil in a pan over medium heat and cook pork chops for about 4-5 minutes on each side or until fully cooked.
3. Remove pork chops and set aside. In the same pan, add the mixed vegetables, soy sauce, and sesame oil, and stir-fry until vegetables are tender-crisp.
4. Serve the pork chops with the vegetable stir-fry on the side.

Benefits for Diabetics:
This meal is low in carbs and high in fiber, aiding in blood sugar control. The lean protein from pork along with the nutrients from the vegetables make it a balanced meal that won't spike blood sugar levels.

Per Serving:
Calories: 260 | Fat: 15g | Carbs: 8g | Fiber: 3g | Protein: 25g

Spiced Pork Chops with Vegetable Stir Fry

Serves: 2
Prep time: 15 minutes / Cook time: 20 minutes

Ingredients:
- 2 boneless pork chops
- 1 tbsp olive oil
- 1 tsp smoked paprika
- 1/2 tsp garlic powder
- Salt and pepper to taste
- 2 cups mixed vegetables (bell peppers, broccoli, carrots)
- 1 tbsp low-sodium soy sauce
- 1 tsp sesame oil

Instructions:
1. Season pork chops with smoked paprika, garlic powder, salt, and pepper.
2. Heat olive oil in a pan over medium heat and cook pork chops for about 4-5 minutes on each side or until fully cooked.
3. Remove pork chops and set aside. In the same pan, add the mixed vegetables, soy sauce, and sesame oil, and stir-fry until vegetables are tender-crisp.
4. Serve the pork chops with the vegetable stir-fry on the side.

Benefits for Diabetics:
This meal is low in carbs and high in fiber, aiding in blood sugar control. The lean protein from pork along with the nutrients from the vegetables make it a balanced meal that won't spike blood sugar levels.

Per Serving:
Calories: 260 | Fat: 15g | Carbs: 8g | Fiber: 3g | Protein: 25g

Lemon-Herb Grilled Pork and Zucchini

Serves: 2
Prep time: 10 minutes / Cook time: 15 minutes

Ingredients:
- 2 pork loin steaks
- 2 medium zucchinis, sliced lengthwise
- 2 tbsp olive oil
- 1 lemon, juice and zest
- 1 tbsp mixed herbs (such as thyme, oregano, and parsley)
- Salt and pepper to taste

Instructions:
1. Preheat grill to medium-high heat.
2. Season pork loin steaks and zucchini slices with salt and pepper.

3. In a small bowl, combine olive oil, lemon juice, lemon zest, and mixed herbs.
4. Brush the pork and zucchini with the lemon-herb mixture.
5. Grill pork for about 6-7 minutes per side or until fully cooked. Grill zucchini for about 3-4 minutes per side or until tender.
6. Serve the grilled pork and zucchini with extra lemon wedges on the side.

Benefits for Diabetics:
Grilled pork and zucchini offer a meal high in protein and low in carbohydrates, ideal for blood sugar management. The added lemon and herbs provide a burst of flavor without added sugar or fat.

Per Serving:
Calories: 280 | Fat: 16g | Carbs: 6g | Fiber: 2g | Protein: 30g

Maple-Dijon Pork Tenderloin with Cauliflower Mash

Serves: 2
Prep time: 15 minutes / Cook time: 25 minutes

Ingredients:
- 1 pork tenderloin (about 1 lb)
- 2 tbsp Dijon mustard
- 1 tbsp maple syrup (sugar-free)
- 1 head cauliflower, cut into florets
- 2 tbsp olive oil
- Salt and pepper to taste

Instructions:
1. Preheat oven to 375°F (190°C).
2. Season the pork tenderloin with salt and pepper. In a small bowl, mix together Dijon mustard and maple syrup. Brush the mixture over the pork.
3. Roast the pork in the oven for 20-25 minutes or until cooked to desired doneness.
4. While the pork is roasting, steam the cauliflower florets until tender. Mash the cauliflower with olive oil, salt, and pepper until smooth.
5. Slice the pork tenderloin and serve with a side of cauliflower mash.

Benefits for Diabetics:
This meal offers a low-glycemic load, crucial for blood sugar control. The cauliflower mash is a nutritious substitute for high-carb sides, and the pork tenderloin is an excellent source of lean protein.

Per Serving:
Calories: 330 | Fat: 15g | Carbs: 10g | Fiber: 4g | Protein: 40g

Smoky BBQ Pork Skewers with Avocado Salad

Serves: 2
Prep time: 20 minutes (plus marinating) / Cook time: 10 minutes

Ingredients:
- 1 lb pork shoulder, cut into 1-inch cubes
- 2 tbsp sugar-free BBQ sauce
- 1 tbsp olive oil
- 1 tsp smoked paprika
- Salt and pepper to taste
- 1 avocado, diced
- 1 cup cherry tomatoes, halved
- 1/4 red onion, thinly sliced
- 1 lime, juice and zest
- Fresh cilantro for garnish

Instructions:
1. In a bowl, mix pork cubes with BBQ sauce, olive oil, smoked paprika, salt, and pepper. Marinate for at least 30 minutes.
2. Thread the marinated pork onto skewers.
3. Preheat grill to medium-high and grill skewers for 4-5 minutes on each side or until fully cooked.
4. For the salad, combine diced avocado, cherry tomatoes, red onion, lime juice, and zest. Toss gently.
5. Serve BBQ pork skewers with a side of avocado salad and garnish with fresh cilantro.

Benefits for Diabetics:
Pork provides a high-quality protein source, while the avocado salad offers healthy fats and fiber, promoting satiety and supporting blood sugar control. The use of sugar-free BBQ sauce ensures a lower carbohydrate content.

Per Serving:
Calories: 350 | Fat: 22g | Carbs: 12g | Fiber: 6g | Protein: 28g

Garlic and Rosemary Pork Medallions with Green Beans

Serves: 2
Prep time: 10 minutes / Cook time: 15 minutes

Ingredients:
- 1 lb pork tenderloin, sliced into medallions
- 2 tbsp olive oil
- 2 garlic cloves, minced
- 1 tbsp fresh rosemary, chopped
- 2 cups green beans, trimmed
- Salt and pepper to taste

Instructions:
1. Season pork medallions with salt and pepper.
2. In a large skillet, heat olive oil over medium heat. Add garlic and rosemary, and sauté for 1 minute.
3. Add pork medallions to the skillet and cook for 3-4 minutes on each side or until golden and cooked through.
4. In another pan, blanch the green beans in boiling water for 2-3 minutes, then drain.
5. Serve the pork medallions with a side of green beans.

Benefits for Diabetics:
This meal is a great source of lean protein from the pork, while the green beans provide a good amount of fiber, important for blood sugar regulation. The garlic and rosemary not only add flavor but also offer potential health benefits.

Per Serving:
Calories: 310 | Fat: 16g | Carbs: 8g | Fiber: 3g | Protein: 35g

Chapter 3: Healthy Vegetables Recipes

Welcome to the Diabetic Vegetarian Chapter, a collection meticulously crafted for those seeking to enjoy vegetarian cuisine while managing diabetes.

This chapter understands the unique balance required in a diet that is both blood sugar-friendly and devoid of meat, offering a variety of meals packed with nutrients, fiber, and flavors that cater to these needs.

Our recipes emphasize low-glycemic vegetables, wholesome grains, and quality proteins from plant-based sources, ensuring each dish supports your health goals without sacrificing taste.

From hearty soups and stews to light salads, from comforting casseroles to vibrant stir-fries, each recipe is designed to delight the palate while contributing to a stable and healthy blood sugar level.

We believe that a diabetic diet can be diverse, satisfying, and full of culinary discoveries. With each recipe, you'll find detailed nutritional information, making it easier for you to make informed choices about your meals. So, embark on this journey of health and flavor with our Diabetic Vegetarian Chapter, where managing your diabetes does not mean compromising on the joy of eating.

Spinach and Mushroom Stuffed Bell Peppers

Serves: 4

Prep time: 20 minutes / Cook time: 25 minutes

Ingredients:
- 4 large bell peppers, tops cut off and seeded
- 1 cup cooked quinoa or brown rice
- 1 cup chopped mushrooms
- 1 cup chopped spinach
- 1/2 cup diced onions
- 2 cloves garlic, minced
- 1 cup shredded cheese (optional or use a low-fat variety)
- 1 tsp olive oil
- Salt and pepper to taste

Instructions:
1. Preheat the oven to 375°F (190°C).
2. Heat olive oil in a skillet over medium heat. Add onions and garlic, sautéing until translucent.
3. Add mushrooms and cook until they release their moisture and begin to brown.
4. Stir in spinach and cook until wilted. Remove from heat and mix in the cooked quinoa or rice.
5. Spoon the vegetable and grain mixture into the hollowed-out bell peppers. Top with cheese if desired.
6. Place stuffed peppers in a baking dish and bake for 25 minutes until peppers are tender and filling is hot.
7. Serve warm, garnished with fresh herbs or additional cheese if desired.

Benefits for Diabetics:
This dish is high in fiber and nutrients, thanks to the combination of vegetables and whole grains. It's a balanced meal that can help manage blood sugar levels while providing a generous serving of vitamins and minerals.

Per Serving:
Calories: 220 | Fat: 8g | Carbs: 30g | Fiber: 6g | Protein: 10g

Creamy Avocado Pasta

Serves: 4

Prep time: 10 minutes / Cook time: 10 minutes

Ingredients:
- 8 oz whole wheat spaghetti or your favorite pasta
- 2 ripe avocados, pitted and peeled
- 1/2 cup fresh basil leaves
- 2 cloves garlic
- 2 tbsp lemon juice
- 1/4 cup olive oil
- Salt and pepper to taste
- Cherry tomatoes and additional basil for garnish

Instructions:
1. Cook pasta according to package instructions until al dente. Drain and set aside, reserving some pasta water.
2. In a food processor, blend avocados, basil, garlic, lemon juice, and olive oil until smooth. Season with salt and pepper.
3. Toss the avocado sauce with the cooked pasta, adding a little pasta water if needed to reach desired consistency.
4. Serve immediately, garnished with cherry tomatoes and additional basil.

Benefits for Diabetics:
Whole wheat pasta offers more fiber and nutrients than white pasta, aiding in blood sugar management. Avocados provide healthy fats and fiber, contributing to a feeling of fullness and further supporting blood sugar control.

Per Serving:
Calories: 350 | Fat: 20g | Carbs: 38g | Fiber: 8g | Protein: 10g

Lentil and Vegetable Curry

Serves: 4

Prep time: 15 minutes / Cook time: 30 minutes

Ingredients:
- 1 cup dry lentils, rinsed and drained
- 1 large carrot, diced
- 1 bell pepper, diced
- 1 small zucchini, diced
- 1 onion, diced
- 2 cloves garlic, minced
- 1 can (14 oz) diced tomatoes
- 2 cups vegetable broth
- 1 tbsp curry powder
- 1 tsp cumin
- 1/2 tsp turmeric
- 1/2 tsp ginger

- Salt and pepper to taste
- 1 tbsp olive oil
- Fresh cilantro for garnish

Instructions:

1. Heat olive oil in a large pot over medium heat. Add onions and garlic, sautéing until translucent.
2. Add carrots, bell pepper, and zucchini, cooking for a few minutes until slightly soft.
3. Stir in lentils, diced tomatoes, vegetable broth, curry powder, cumin, turmeric, ginger, salt, and pepper.
4. Bring to a boil, then reduce heat and simmer for 25-30 minutes until lentils are tender and flavors are well combined.
5. Serve hot, garnished with fresh cilantro.

Benefits for Diabetics:
Lentils are a great source of plant-based protein and fiber, which can help in managing blood sugar levels. The variety of vegetables increases the dish's vitamin and mineral content, making it a nutritious and balanced meal.

Per Serving:
Calories: 280 | Fat: 5g | Carbs: 45g | Fiber: 15g | Protein: 18g

Quinoa Stuffed Acorn Squash

Serves: 4
Prep time: 20 minutes / Cook time: 40 minutes

Ingredients:

- 2 acorn squashes, halved and seeds removed
- 1 cup quinoa, rinsed
- 2 cups vegetable broth
- 1 small onion, diced
- 1/2 cup diced bell pepper
- 1/2 cup diced mushrooms
- 1/4 cup dried cranberries
- 1/4 cup chopped walnuts
- 1 tsp thyme
- Salt and pepper to taste
- 2 tbsp olive oil

Instructions:

1. Preheat oven to 375°F (190°C). Place acorn squash halves on a baking sheet, cut side up. Drizzle with olive oil and season with salt and pepper. Roast for 25-30 minutes until tender.
2. Meanwhile, cook quinoa in vegetable broth according to package instructions.
3. Heat a little olive oil in a skillet over medium heat. Sauté onion, bell pepper, and mushrooms until softened.
4. Mix cooked quinoa, sautéed vegetables, cranberries, walnuts, thyme, salt, and pepper in a bowl.
5. Spoon the quinoa mixture into the roasted acorn squash halves.
6. Return to the oven and bake for an additional 10 minutes.
7. Serve warm, garnished with extra herbs or nuts if desired.

Benefits for Diabetics:
Acorn squash and quinoa both offer a good amount of fiber,

which is beneficial for blood sugar control. The nuts and vegetables add healthy fats, protein, and essential nutrients, making this a well-rounded, diabetic-friendly meal.

Per Serving:
Calories: 300 | Fat: 10g | Carbs: 48g | Fiber: 7g | Protein: 8g

Tofu and Veggie Stir-Fry

Serves: 4
Prep time: 15 minutes / Cook time: 10 minutes

Ingredients:

- 1 block firm tofu, drained and cut into cubes
- 2 cups mixed vegetables (bell peppers, broccoli, carrots, snap peas)
- 1 onion, sliced
- 2 cloves garlic, minced
- 2 tbsp soy sauce
- 1 tbsp sesame oil
- 1 tsp ginger, grated
- Salt and pepper to taste
- 1 tbsp olive oil
- Sesame seeds for garnish

Instructions:

1. Heat olive oil in a large skillet or wok over medium-high heat. Add tofu cubes and cook until golden on all sides. Remove and set aside.
2. In the same skillet, add a little more oil if needed. Sauté onions and garlic until fragrant.
3. Add the mixed vegetables, cooking until they are tender but still crisp.
4. Return the tofu to the skillet. Stir in soy sauce, sesame oil, and ginger. Cook for a few more minutes until everything is heated through and coated in sauce.
5. Season with salt and pepper to taste.
6. Serve hot, sprinkled with sesame seeds.

Benefits for Diabetics:
Tofu is a low-carb, high-protein food that can help stabilize blood sugar levels. The mixed vegetables provide a wealth of nutrients and fiber, aiding in overall digestion and health.

Per Serving:
Calories: 200 | Fat: 12g | Carbs: 10g | Fiber: 3g | Protein: 12g

Chickpea and Spinach Curry

Serves: 4
Prep time: 10 minutes / Cook time: 20 minutes

Ingredients:

- 2 cans (15 oz each) chickpeas, drained and rinsed
- 1 large onion, diced
- 2 cloves garlic, minced
- 1 tbsp ginger, grated
- 1 bag (6 oz) fresh spinach
- 1 can (14 oz) diced tomatoes
- 1 can (14 oz) coconut milk
- 2 tbsp curry powder
- 1 tsp cumin
- 1/2 tsp turmeric
- Salt and pepper to taste
- 2 tbsp olive oil

- Fresh cilantro for garnish

Instructions:
1. Heat olive oil in a large pot over medium heat. Add onions, garlic, and ginger, sautéing until the onions are translucent.
2. Stir in curry powder, cumin, and turmeric, cooking for a minute until fragrant.
3. Add chickpeas, diced tomatoes, and coconut milk. Bring to a boil, then reduce heat and simmer for 15 minutes.
4. Add spinach, stirring until it wilts into the curry.
5. Season with salt and pepper to taste.
6. Serve hot, garnished with fresh cilantro.

Benefits for Diabetics:
Chickpeas are an excellent source of protein and fiber, helping to maintain stable blood sugar levels. Spinach adds a nutrient-rich component, while the spices provide flavor without the need for additional sugar or fat.

Per Serving:
Calories: 350 | Fat: 15g | Carbs: 40g | Fiber: 12g | Protein: 14g

Veggie and Hummus Sandwich

Serves: 2

Prep time: 10 minutes / Cook time: 0 minutes

Ingredients:
- 4 slices whole grain bread
- 1/2 cup hummus (see in sauces chapter)
- 1/4 cucumber, sliced
- 1 small carrot, grated
- 1/4 bell pepper, sliced
- 1 handful of baby spinach leaves
- Salt and pepper to taste

Instructions:
1. Spread hummus evenly on two slices of bread.
2. Layer cucumber, carrot, bell pepper, and spinach on top of the hummus.
3. Season with salt and pepper to taste.
4. Top with the remaining slices of bread, cut in half, and serve.

Benefits for Diabetics:
Hummus provides a good source of protein and fiber, helping to manage blood sugar levels. The whole grain bread and vegetables add extra fiber and nutrients, making this sandwich a balanced, healthy choice for diabetics.

Per Serving:
Calories: 300 | Fat: 12g | Carbs: 40g | Fiber: 8g | Protein: 12g

Eggplant and Chickpea Stew

Serves: 4

Prep time: 15 minutes / Cook time: 30 minutes

Ingredients:
- 1 large eggplant, diced
- 1 can (15 oz) chickpeas, drained and rinsed
- 1 onion, diced
- 2 cloves garlic, minced
- 1 can (14 oz) diced tomatoes

- 2 cups vegetable broth
- 1 tsp paprika
- 1/2 tsp cumin
- Salt and pepper to taste
- 2 tbsp olive oil
- Fresh parsley for garnish

Instructions:
1. Heat olive oil in a large pot over medium heat. Add onions and garlic, cooking until the onions are soft.
2. Add eggplant, cooking for 10 minutes until it begins to soften.
3. Stir in chickpeas, diced tomatoes, vegetable broth, paprika, and cumin. Bring to a boil, then reduce heat and simmer for 20 minutes until the stew thickens and flavors meld.
4. Season with salt and pepper to taste.
5. Serve hot, garnished with fresh parsley.

Benefits for Diabetics:
This stew is rich in fiber from both the eggplant and chickpeas, aiding in blood sugar control. The vegetables provide vitamins and minerals, while the spices add depth of flavor without added sugar or fat.

Per Serving:
Calories: 250 | Fat: 10g | Carbs: 35g | Fiber: 12g | Protein: 9g

Mushroom and Leek Quiche

Serves: 6

Prep time: 20 minutes / Cook time: 35 minutes

Ingredients:
- 1 ready-made pie crust (or homemade if preferred)
- 1 tbsp olive oil
- 1 leek, cleaned and sliced
- 1 cup mushrooms, sliced
- 4 large eggs
- 1 cup milk (or a non-dairy alternative)
- 1/2 cup shredded cheese (optional or use a low-fat variety)
- Salt and pepper to taste

Instructions:
1. Preheat oven to 375°F (190°C). Place the pie crust in a pie dish and set aside.
2. Heat olive oil in a skillet over medium heat. Add leeks and mushrooms, cooking until softened.
3. In a bowl, whisk together eggs and milk. Season with salt and pepper.
4. Spread the cooked leeks and mushrooms evenly over the pie crust. Pour the egg mixture on top. Sprinkle with cheese if using.
5. Bake for 35-40 minutes until the quiche is set and the crust is golden.
6. Let cool slightly before cutting into wedges and serving.

Benefits for Diabetics:
The eggs in this quiche provide a high-quality protein source, helping to keep blood sugar levels stable. Leeks and mushrooms add fiber and nutrients, making this dish both filling and nutritious.

Per Serving:
Calories: 270 | Fat: 16g | Carbs: 22g | Fiber: 2g | Protein: 10g

Roasted Vegetable Buddha Bowl

Serves: 4
Prep time: 20 minutes / Cook time: 30 minutes

Ingredients:
- 2 cups mixed vegetables (broccoli, carrots, bell peppers, zucchini)
- 1 cup quinoa or brown rice, cooked
- 1 avocado, sliced
- 1/4 cup tahini
- 2 tbsp lemon juice
- 1 clove garlic, minced
- Salt and pepper to taste
- 2 tbsp olive oil

Instructions:
1. Preheat oven to 425°F (220°C). Toss the mixed vegetables with olive oil, salt, and pepper. Spread on a baking sheet and roast for 25-30 minutes until tender and slightly charred.
2. In a small bowl, whisk together tahini, lemon juice, garlic, and a little water to reach desired consistency. Season with salt and pepper.
3. Assemble the Buddha bowls by dividing the cooked quinoa or rice among four bowls. Top with roasted vegetables and sliced avocado.
4. Drizzle tahini dressing over each bowl and serve.

Benefits for Diabetics:
The fiber in the vegetables and whole grains helps to slow digestion and prevent rapid blood sugar spikes. Avocado provides healthy fats, aiding in satiety and blood sugar control, while tahini adds a creamy texture and a dose of calcium.

Per Serving:
Calories: 350 | Fat: 18g | Carbs: 40g | Fiber: 10g | Protein: 10g

Spinach and Ricotta Stuffed Shells

Serves: 4
Prep time: 20 minutes / Cook time: 30 minutes

Ingredients:
- 20 jumbo pasta shells
- 1 1/2 cups ricotta cheese
- 1 cup chopped spinach (fresh or frozen and thawed)
- 1/2 cup grated Parmesan cheese
- 1 egg
- 2 cups marinara sauce
- Salt and pepper to taste
- 1 tbsp olive oil
- Fresh basil for garnish

Instructions:
1. Preheat oven to 375°F (190°C). Cook pasta shells according to package instructions until al dente. Drain and set aside.
2. In a bowl, mix together ricotta cheese, spinach, Parmesan cheese, egg, salt, and pepper.

3. Spread a thin layer of marinara sauce on the bottom of a baking dish.
4. Fill each pasta shell with the ricotta mixture and place in the baking dish.
5. Pour the remaining marinara sauce over the stuffed shells.
6. Cover with foil and bake for 25 minutes. Remove foil and bake for an additional 5 minutes until the top is slightly golden.
7. Serve hot, garnished with fresh basil.

Benefits for Diabetics:
The combination of ricotta and spinach provides a good source of protein and iron, along with other essential nutrients. Using a moderate amount of cheese helps maintain a balance of flavor and nutrition.

Per Serving:
Calories: 400 | Fat: 16g | Carbs: 40g | Fiber: 4g | Protein: 22g

Zucchini Noodle Alfredo

Serves: 4
Prep time: 10 minutes / Cook time: 10 minutes

Ingredients:
- 2 large zucchinis, spiralized
- 1/2 cup Greek yogurt (or a non-dairy alternative)
- 1/4 cup grated Parmesan cheese
- 1 clove garlic, minced
- Salt and pepper to taste
- 1 tbsp olive oil
- Fresh parsley for garnish

Instructions:
1. Heat olive oil in a large skillet over medium heat. Add garlic and sauté until fragrant.
2. Add spiralized zucchini noodles and cook for 2-3 minutes until just tender.
3. In a bowl, mix together Greek yogurt and Parmesan cheese. Add to the skillet with zucchini noodles, stirring gently until heated through and evenly coated.
4. Season with salt and pepper to taste.
5. Serve immediately, garnished with fresh parsley.

Benefits for Diabetics:
Zucchini noodles are a low-carb alternative to traditional pasta, helping to reduce the overall glycemic load of the dish. Greek yogurt provides a creamy texture and protein without the excess fat of traditional Alfredo sauce.

Per Serving:
Calories: 200 | Fat: 10g | Carbs: 14g | Fiber: 3g | Protein: 14g

Eggplant Parmesan

Serves: 4
Prep time: 20 minutes / Cook time: 30 minutes

Ingredients:
- 2 large eggplants, sliced into 1/2 inch rounds
- 2 cups marinara sauce
- 2 cups shredded mozzarella cheese (or a low-fat variety)
- 1/2 cup grated Parmesan cheese
- 1 cup whole wheat breadcrumbs

- 2 eggs, beaten
- Salt and pepper to taste
- 1/4 cup olive oil
- Fresh basil leaves for garnish

Instructions:

1. Preheat the oven to 375°F (190°C).
2. Season eggplant slices with salt and let them sit for 10-15 minutes to draw out moisture. Pat dry with paper towels.
3. Dip eggplant slices in beaten eggs, then coat with breadcrumbs.
4. Heat olive oil in a skillet over medium heat. Fry eggplant slices until golden on each side. Drain on paper towels.
5. In a baking dish, layer marinara sauce, eggplant slices, mozzarella, and Parmesan cheese. Repeat layers.
6. Bake for 25-30 minutes until cheese is melted and bubbly.
7. Garnish with fresh basil leaves and serve warm.

Benefits for Diabetics:

Eggplant is a low-carbohydrate vegetable rich in fiber and nutrients, making it a good choice for blood sugar management. The cheese adds protein and calcium, contributing to a balanced meal.

Per Serving:

Calories: 350 | Fat: 20g | Carbs: 28g | Fiber: 9g | Protein: 18g

Vegetarian Shepherd's Pie

Serves: 6

Prep time: 30 minutes / Cook time: 20 minutes

Ingredients:

- 1 cup green lentils, cooked
- 2 large potatoes, peeled and cubed
- 1/4 cup milk (or unsweetened almond milk)
- 2 tbsp butter (or olive oil)
- 1 onion, diced
- 2 carrots, diced
- 1 cup frozen peas
- 2 cloves garlic, minced
- 1 tbsp tomato paste
- 1 tsp thyme
- 2 cups vegetable broth
- Salt and pepper to taste

Instructions:

1. Boil potatoes until tender. Drain and mash with milk and butter, seasoning with salt and pepper.
2. Preheat the oven to 400°F (200°C).
3. Heat oil in a large skillet. Sauté onions, carrots, and garlic until soft.
4. Add cooked lentils, peas, tomato paste, thyme, and vegetable broth. Simmer until thickened.
5. Pour the lentil mixture into a baking dish. Spread mashed potatoes on top.
6. Bake for 20 minutes or until the top is golden.
7. Serve warm.

Benefits for Diabetics:

Lentils are an excellent source of plant-based protein and fiber, helping to manage blood sugar levels. The vegetables add essential nutrients, while the mashed potatoes provide a comforting and satisfying topping.

Per Serving:

Calories: 300 | Fat: 5g | Carbs: 50g | Fiber: 10g | Protein: 15g

Spicy Chickpea and Spinach Stew

Serves: 4

Prep time: 10 minutes / Cook time: 20 minutes

Ingredients:

- 2 cans chickpeas, drained and rinsed
- 4 cups fresh spinach
- 1 onion, diced
- 2 cloves garlic, minced
- 1 can diced tomatoes
- 1 tsp cumin
- 1 tsp paprika
- 1/2 tsp chili powder
- 2 tbsp olive oil
- Salt and pepper to taste
- Fresh cilantro for garnish

Instructions:

1. Heat olive oil in a large pot over medium heat. Add onions and garlic, sautéing until translucent.
2. Add chickpeas, diced tomatoes, cumin, paprika, and chili powder. Cook for 10 minutes.
3. Stir in spinach and cook until wilted.
4. Season with salt and pepper to taste.
5. Serve hot, garnished with fresh cilantro.

Benefits for Diabetics:

Chickpeas are a great source of protein and fiber, which can help stabilize blood sugar levels. Spinach adds a wealth of vitamins and minerals, making this stew both nutritious and filling.

Conclusion:

Spicy Chickpea and Spinach Stew is a simple yet delicious dish that's perfect for a quick and healthy meal. It's a great way to enjoy a variety of flavors and nutrients in one comforting bowl.

Per Serving:

Calories: 280 | Fat: 10g | Carbs: 38g | Fiber: 12g | Protein: 12g

Zucchini Noodles with Pesto

Serves: 4

Prep time: 15 minutes / Cook time: 5 minutes

Ingredients:

- 4 medium zucchinis, spiralized
- 1 cup fresh basil leaves
- 1/4 cup pine nuts
- 2 cloves garlic
- 1/4 cup grated Parmesan cheese (or nutritional yeast for vegan option)
- 1/4 cup olive oil
- Salt and pepper to taste
- Cherry tomatoes for garnish

Instructions:

1. In a food processor, blend basil, pine nuts, garlic,

Parmesan cheese, and olive oil until smooth. Season with salt and pepper.

2. Heat a large skillet over medium heat. Add zucchini noodles, cooking for 2-3 minutes until tender.

3. Remove from heat and toss with pesto sauce until well coated.

4. Serve immediately, garnished with cherry tomatoes and additional Parmesan cheese if desired.

Benefits for Diabetics:
Zucchini noodles are a low-carbohydrate alternative to pasta, helping to reduce blood sugar spikes. The pesto provides healthy fats from olive oil and pine nuts, while basil offers anti-inflammatory properties.

Per Serving:
Calories: 280 | Fat: 24g | Carbs: 10g | Fiber: 3g | Protein: 6g

Butternut Squash and Chickpea Salad

Serves: 4
Prep time: 15 minutes / Cook time: 25 minutes

Ingredients:
- 1 medium butternut squash, peeled and cubed
- 1 can chickpeas, drained and rinsed
- 1/2 red onion, thinly sliced
- 4 cups mixed greens (spinach, arugula, kale)
- 1/4 cup dried cranberries
- 1/4 cup chopped walnuts
- 3 tbsp olive oil
- 2 tbsp balsamic vinegar
- 1 tsp honey (or maple syrup for vegan option)
- 1 tsp cinnamon
- Salt and pepper to taste

Instructions:
1. Preheat the oven to 400°F (200°C). Toss butternut squash cubes with 1 tbsp olive oil, cinnamon, salt, and pepper. Roast for 25 minutes until tender and slightly caramelized.

2. In a large bowl, mix roasted squash, chickpeas, red onion, mixed greens, cranberries, and walnuts.

3. In a small bowl, whisk together remaining olive oil, balsamic vinegar, and honey. Drizzle over the salad and toss to combine.

4. Serve immediately or let sit for flavors to meld.

Benefits for Diabetics:
Butternut squash is a good source of vitamins and fiber, while chickpeas provide protein and more fiber, both important for blood sugar management. The salad is rich in nutrients and antioxidants, offering a balanced meal with a variety of textures and flavors.

Per Serving:
Calories: 280 | Fat: 12g | Carbs: 38g | Fiber: 9g | Protein: 8g

Sweet and Sour Tofu Stir-Fry

Serves: 4
Prep time: 20 minutes / Cook time: 10 minutes

Ingredients:
- 1 block firm tofu, drained and cut into cubes
- 2 cups mixed bell peppers, sliced
- 1 cup pineapple chunks
- 1/2 red onion, sliced
- 2 cloves garlic, minced
- 1/4 cup apple cider vinegar
- 2 tbsp soy sauce
- 2 tbsp honey (or maple syrup for vegan option)
- 1 tbsp cornstarch
- 2 tbsp water
- 3 tbsp olive oil
- Sesame seeds for garnish

Instructions:
1. Press tofu to remove excess water. Heat 2 tbsp olive oil in a large skillet over medium-high heat. Add tofu and fry until golden on all sides. Set aside.

2. In the same skillet, add remaining oil. Sauté bell peppers, pineapple, red onion, and garlic until vegetables are tender but crisp.

3. In a bowl, whisk together vinegar, soy sauce, honey, cornstarch, and water until smooth. Pour over the vegetables in the skillet, stirring until the sauce thickens.

4. Add fried tofu back to the skillet, tossing to coat with the sauce and vegetables.

5. Serve hot, sprinkled with sesame seeds.

Benefits for Diabetics:
Tofu is a low-carb protein source, ideal for managing blood sugar. Vegetables and pineapple provide vitamins, minerals, and fiber, contributing to a balanced meal.

Per Serving:
Calories: 250 | Fat: 14g | Carbs: 22g | Fiber: 2g | Protein: 12g

Roasted Cauliflower and Chickpea Tacos

Serves: 4
Prep time: 15 minutes / Cook time: 25 minutes

Ingredients:
- 1 head cauliflower, cut into florets
- 1 can chickpeas, drained and rinsed
- 2 avocados, sliced
- 8 small whole wheat tortillas
- 1/2 cup Greek yogurt (or dairy-free alternative)
- 2 limes, one juiced and one cut into wedges
- 2 tbsp olive oil
- 1 tsp chili powder
- 1 tsp cumin
- 1/2 tsp garlic powder
- Salt and pepper to taste
- Fresh cilantro for garnish

Instructions:
1. Preheat the oven to 400°F (200°C). Toss cauliflower and chickpeas with olive oil, chili powder, cumin, garlic powder, salt, and pepper.

2. Spread on a baking sheet and roast for 25 minutes until golden and tender.

3. Warm the tortillas in the oven for the last few minutes of roasting or on a skillet.

4. Assemble the tacos by placing a scoop of the cauliflower and chickpea mixture on each tortilla.

5. Top with avocado slices and a dollop of Greek yogurt. Drizzle with lime juice and garnish with fresh cilantro.

6. Serve with lime wedges on the side.

Benefits for Diabetics:

Cauliflower and chickpeas provide a hearty, low-GI base for these tacos, helping to manage blood sugar levels. The avocados add healthy fats and fiber for a satisfying and nutritious meal.

Roasted Cauliflower and Chickpea Tacos are a delicious, nutritious alternative to traditional tacos. They're easy to make and can be customized with your favorite toppings for a perfect vegetarian feast.

Per Serving:

Calories: 320 | Fat: 15g | Carbs: 40g | Fiber: 12g | Protein: 12g

Grilled Vegetable and Quinoa Salad

Serves: 4

Prep time: 20 minutes / Cook time: 15 minutes

Ingredients:

- 1 cup quinoa, cooked
- 1 zucchini, sliced lengthwise
- 1 bell pepper, sliced
- 1 eggplant, sliced into rounds
- 1/4 cup feta cheese, crumbled (optional or use a dairy-free alternative)
- 1/4 cup fresh basil, chopped
- 3 tbsp olive oil
- 2 tbsp lemon juice
- Salt and pepper to taste

Instructions:

1. Preheat the grill to medium-high heat. Brush zucchini, bell pepper, and eggplant with 1 tbsp olive oil and season with salt and pepper.
2. Grill vegetables until tender and charred, about 3-4 minutes per side. Let cool slightly and chop into bite-sized pieces.
3. In a large bowl, combine grilled vegetables with cooked quinoa and basil.
4. Whisk together remaining olive oil and lemon juice for the dressing. Pour over the salad and toss to combine.
5. Sprinkle with feta cheese before serving.

Benefits for Diabetics:

Quinoa is a complete protein and an excellent source of fiber, aiding in blood sugar regulation. The mix of grilled vegetables provides essential vitamins and antioxidants, while the lemon-herb dressing adds flavor without added sugars.

Per Serving:

Calories: 260 | Fat: 10g | Carbs: 35g | Fiber: 7g | Protein: 9g

Vegan Stuffed Portobello Mushrooms

Serves: 4

Prep time: 20 minutes / Cook time: 20 minutes

Ingredients:

- 4 large portobello mushroom caps, stems removed
- 1 cup cooked brown rice or breadcrumbs
- 1 small onion, diced
- 1/2 cup chopped walnuts
- 1/2 cup spinach, chopped
- 2 cloves garlic, minced
- 1 tsp thyme
- 2 tbsp nutritional yeast (optional for cheesy flavor)
- 2 tbsp olive oil
- Salt and pepper to taste

Instructions:

1. Preheat the oven to 375°F (190°C). Place mushroom caps on a baking sheet.
2. Heat 1 tbsp olive oil in a skillet. Sauté onion, garlic, and thyme until onion is translucent.
3. Add spinach and cook until wilted. Remove from heat and mix in brown rice or breadcrumbs, walnuts, and nutritional yeast.
4. Spoon the filling into each mushroom cap, pressing down gently.
5. Drizzle with remaining olive oil and season with salt and pepper.
6. Bake for 20 minutes or until mushrooms are tender and filling is golden.
7. Serve warm, garnished with fresh herbs if desired.

Benefits for Diabetics:

Portobello mushrooms are low in carbohydrates and calories, making them an excellent base for a diabetic-friendly dish. The filling provides fiber and protein, especially when using brown rice or nuts, contributing to a balanced meal.

Vegan Stuffed Portobello Mushrooms are a delicious, elegant dish that's easy to prepare and packed with flavor. They're perfect for impressing guests or enjoying a special meal at home.

Per Serving:

Calories: 220 | Fat: 15g | Carbs: 18g | Fiber: 4g | Protein: 6g

Creamy Coconut Lentil Curry

Serves: 4

Prep time: 10 minutes / Cook time: 25 minutes

Ingredients:

- 1 cup red lentils, rinsed
- 1 onion, diced
- 2 cloves garlic, minced
- 1 inch ginger, grated
- 1 can (14 oz) coconut milk
- 1 can (14 oz) diced tomatoes
- 1 tsp turmeric
- 1 tsp cumin
- 1/2 tsp chili powder
- 1/2 tsp garam masala
- 2 tbsp olive oil
- Salt and pepper to taste
- Fresh cilantro for garnish

Instructions:

1. Heat olive oil in a large pot over medium heat. Add onion, garlic, and ginger, sautéing until onion is translucent.
2. Add spices and cook for another minute until fragrant.
3. Stir in lentils, coconut milk, and diced tomatoes. Bring to a boil, then reduce heat and simmer for 20 minutes

until lentils are tender and curry has thickened.

4. Season with salt and pepper to taste.
5. Serve hot, garnished with fresh cilantro, alongside rice or naan.

Benefits for Diabetics:
Red lentils are a fantastic source of protein and fiber, helping to stabilize blood sugar levels. Coconut milk adds a creamy texture and healthy fats, making the dish both satisfying and nutritious.

Per Serving:
Calories: 350 | Fat: 18g | Carbs: 35g | Fiber: 15g | Protein: 14g

Ratatouille

Serves: 6
Prep time: 20 minutes / Cook time: 40 minutes

Ingredients:
- 1 eggplant, cut into cubes
- 2 zucchinis, sliced
- 1 red bell pepper, sliced
- 1 yellow bell pepper, sliced
- 1 onion, sliced
- 3 cloves garlic, minced
- 1 can (28 oz) crushed tomatoes
- 1 tsp thyme
- 1 tsp basil
- 1/4 cup olive oil
- Salt and pepper to taste
- Fresh basil for garnish

Instructions:
1. Heat olive oil in a large pot or Dutch oven over medium heat. Add onions and garlic, cooking until soft.
2. Add bell peppers, eggplant, and zucchini. Cook for 10 minutes until vegetables start to soften.
3. Stir in crushed tomatoes, thyme, and basil. Bring to a simmer.
4. Reduce heat, cover, and cook for 30 minutes, stirring occasionally.
5. Season with salt and pepper to taste.
6. Serve hot or at room temperature, garnished with fresh basil.

Benefits for Diabetics:
Ratatouille is packed with fiber from the variety of vegetables, aiding in digestion and blood sugar control. It's a low-calorie, nutrient-dense dish that's perfect for maintaining a healthy diet.

Per Serving:
Calories: 180 | Fat: 10g | Carbs: 22g | Fiber: 7g | Protein: 4g

Mediterranean Chickpea Salad

Serves: 4
Prep time: 15 minutes / Cook time: 0 minutes

Ingredients:
- 2 cans chickpeas, drained and rinsed
- 1 cucumber, diced
- 1 bell pepper, diced
- 1/2 red onion, thinly sliced
- 1/2 cup Kalamata olives, sliced
- 1/4 cup feta cheese, crumbled (or dairy-free alternative)
- 1/4 cup fresh parsley, chopped
- 3 tbsp olive oil
- 2 tbsp lemon juice
- 1 garlic clove, minced
- Salt and pepper to taste

Instructions:
1. In a large bowl, combine chickpeas, cucumber, bell pepper, red onion, olives, and parsley.
2. In a small bowl, whisk together olive oil, lemon juice, garlic, salt, and pepper to make the dressing.
3. Pour the dressing over the salad and toss to coat evenly.
4. Sprinkle feta cheese on top just before serving.
5. Serve chilled or at room temperature.

Benefits for Diabetics:
Chickpeas are an excellent source of protein and fiber, helping to regulate blood sugar levels. The salad's vegetables provide vital nutrients and antioxidants, while the olive oil contributes healthy fats.

Per Serving:
Calories: 320 | Fat: 14g | Carbs: 38g | Fiber: 10g | Protein: 12g

Spiced Lentil Soup

Serves: 6
Prep time: 10 minutes / Cook time: 40 minutes

Ingredients:
- 1 cup red lentils, rinsed
- 1 onion, diced
- 2 carrots, diced
- 2 stalks celery, diced
- 3 cloves garlic, minced
- 1 can (14 oz) diced tomatoes
- 6 cups vegetable broth
- 1 tsp cumin
- 1 tsp coriander
- 1/2 tsp turmeric
- 1/2 tsp smoked paprika
- 2 tbsp olive oil
- Salt and pepper to taste
- Fresh cilantro or parsley for garnish

Instructions:
1. Heat olive oil in a large pot over medium heat. Add onions, carrots, celery, and garlic, cooking until softened.
2. Stir in cumin, coriander, turmeric, and smoked paprika, cooking for another minute until fragrant.
3. Add lentils, diced tomatoes, and vegetable broth. Bring to a boil, then reduce heat and simmer for 30 minutes until lentils are tender.
4. Season with salt and pepper to taste.
5. Serve hot, garnished with fresh cilantro or parsley.

Benefits for Diabetics:
Lentils are a great source of fiber and protein, essential for blood sugar control and satiety. The variety of spices not only adds flavor but also offers anti-inflammatory benefits.

Per Serving:
Calories: 220 | Fat: 5g | Carbs: 32g | Fiber: 15g | Protein: 13g

Tomato and Basil Flatbread

Serves: 4

Prep time: 15 minutes / Cook time: 10 minutes

Ingredients:
- 4 whole wheat flatbreads
- 2 cups cherry tomatoes, halved
- 1/2 cup fresh basil leaves, torn
- 1 cup mozzarella cheese, shredded (or dairy-free alternative)
- 2 tbsp olive oil
- 1 garlic clove, minced
- Salt and pepper to taste
- Balsamic glaze for drizzling (optional)

Instructions:
1. Preheat the oven to 400°F (200°C).
2. Place flatbreads on a baking sheet. Brush each with olive oil and sprinkle minced garlic over the top.
3. Arrange cherry tomatoes and basil leaves on each flatbread. Sprinkle with mozzarella cheese.
4. Season with salt and pepper.
5. Bake for 10 minutes until the cheese is melted and bubbly.
6. Drizzle with balsamic glaze if desired and serve hot.

Benefits for Diabetics:
Whole wheat flatbreads provide a good source of fiber, while tomatoes and basil offer vitamins and antioxidants. Choosing a low-fat cheese or dairy-free alternative can help manage calorie and fat intake.

Per Serving:
Calories: 280 | Fat: 14g | Carbs: 28g | Fiber: 4g | Protein: 12g

Vegetable Paella

Serves: 6

Prep time: 20 minutes / Cook time: 30 minutes

Ingredients:
- 1 1/2 cups Arborio rice or short-grain rice
- 4 cups vegetable broth
- 1 onion, diced
- 1 red bell pepper, sliced
- 1 yellow bell pepper, sliced
- 1 cup green beans, trimmed and cut
- 1/2 cup frozen peas
- 1 can artichoke hearts, drained and quartered
- 2 tomatoes, diced
- 3 cloves garlic, minced
- 1 tsp smoked paprika
- 1/2 tsp saffron threads (optional)
- 2 tbsp olive oil
- Salt and pepper to taste
- Lemon wedges and fresh parsley for garnish

Instructions:
1. Heat olive oil in a large paella pan or wide skillet over medium heat. Add onions and garlic, cooking until soft.
2. Add bell peppers and green beans, cooking for a few more minutes until slightly tender.

3. Stir in rice, smoked paprika, and saffron, coating the rice in the oil and spices.
4. Pour in vegetable broth and bring to a simmer. Arrange tomatoes, peas, and artichoke hearts on top. Do not stir from this point.
5. Simmer for 20-25 minutes until rice is cooked and liquid is absorbed.
6. Remove from heat and cover with a towel for 10 minutes.
7. Serve garnished with lemon wedges and fresh parsley.

Benefits for Diabetics:
Vegetable Paella is full of fiber-rich vegetables and whole grains, making it a balanced, nutritious meal. The variety of vegetables provides essential vitamins and minerals while keeping the overall glycemic load moderate.

Per Serving:
Calories: 320 | Fat: 7g | Carbs: 55g | Fiber: 5g | Protein: 8g

Stuffed Acorn Squash with Wild Rice and Cranberries

Serves: 4

Prep time: 20 minutes / Cook time: 60 minutes

Ingredients:
- 2 acorn squashes, halved and seeds removed
- 1 cup wild rice blend, cooked
- 1/2 cup dried cranberries
- 1/2 cup pecans, chopped
- 1 onion, diced
- 2 stalks celery, diced
- 1 apple, diced
- 1 tsp thyme
- 1 tsp sage
- 2 tbsp maple syrup
- 2 tbsp olive oil
- Salt and pepper to taste

Instructions:
1. Preheat the oven to 375°F (190°C). Brush acorn squash halves with olive oil and season with salt and pepper. Place cut side down on a baking sheet and roast for 40 minutes until tender.
2. While squash is roasting, heat 1 tbsp olive oil in a skillet. Add onion and celery, cooking until soft. Add apple, cranberries, pecans, thyme, sage, and cooked wild rice. Cook for a few more minutes until everything is well combined and heated through. Season with salt and pepper.
3. Remove squash from oven and flip over. Fill each half with the wild rice mixture.
4. Drizzle maple syrup over each stuffed squash.
5. Return to the oven and bake for an additional 20 minutes.
6. Serve warm, garnished with additional herbs or nuts if desired.

Benefits for Diabetics:
Wild rice is a whole grain with more protein and fiber than white rice, aiding in blood sugar control. The combination of squash, cranberries, and apples provides antioxidants

and fiber, while pecans add healthy fats and texture.

Per Serving:
Calories: 340 | Fat: 15g | Carbs: 50g | Fiber: 6g | Protein: 6g

Kale and White Bean Soup

Serves: 6

Prep time: 15 minutes / Cook time: 30 minutes

Ingredients:
- 1 onion, diced
- 2 carrots, diced
- 2 stalks celery, diced
- 3 cloves garlic, minced
- 4 cups vegetable broth
- 2 cans white beans, drained and rinsed
- 4 cups kale, chopped
- 1 tsp thyme
- 1 bay leaf
- 2 tbsp olive oil
- Salt and pepper to taste
- Grated Parmesan cheese for garnish (optional)

Instructions:
1. Heat olive oil in a large pot over medium heat. Add onions, carrots, and celery, cooking until softened.
2. Add garlic, thyme, and bay leaf, cooking for another minute until fragrant.
3. Pour in vegetable broth and bring to a simmer.
4. Add white beans and kale. Simmer for 20 minutes until the vegetables are tender and flavors meld.
5. Season with salt and pepper to taste.
6. Serve hot, garnished with grated Parmesan cheese if desired.

Benefits for Diabetics:
Kale is a nutrient-dense vegetable high in vitamins and fiber, while white beans provide a good source of protein and more fiber, aiding in blood sugar control and satiety.

Per Serving:
Calories: 220 | Fat: 5g | Carbs: 35g | Fiber: 9g | Protein: 12g

Sweet Potato and Black Bean Enchiladas

Serves: 6

Prep time: 30 minutes / Cook time: 20 minutes

Ingredients:
- 2 large sweet potatoes, peeled and diced
- 1 can black beans, drained and rinsed
- 12 small whole wheat tortillas
- 2 cups enchilada sauce
- 1 cup shredded cheddar cheese (or dairy-free alternative)
- 1 onion, diced
- 2 cloves garlic, minced
- 1 tsp cumin
- 1 tsp smoked paprika
- 2 tbsp olive oil
- Salt and pepper to taste
- Fresh cilantro for garnish

Instructions:
1. Preheat the oven to 375°F (190°C).
2. Heat olive oil in a skillet over medium heat. Add onions

and cook until translucent. Add garlic, cumin, and paprika, cooking for another minute.
3. Add diced sweet potatoes and a splash of water. Cover and cook until tender, about 15 minutes.
4. Stir in black beans and cook for a few more minutes until heated through. Season with salt and pepper.
5. Spread a thin layer of enchilada sauce in the bottom of a baking dish.
6. Fill each tortilla with the sweet potato mixture, roll up, and place seam side down in the dish.
7. Pour the remaining enchilada sauce over the top and sprinkle with cheese.
8. Bake for 20 minutes until the cheese is melted and bubbly.
9. Serve hot, garnished with fresh cilantro.

Benefits for Diabetics:
Sweet potatoes are a source of complex carbohydrates with a lower glycemic index, and black beans provide protein and fiber, both helping in blood sugar management.

Per Serving:
Calories: 350 | Fat: 10g | Carbs: 55g | Fiber: 10g | Protein: 15g

Grilled Eggplant with Herbed Quinoa

Serves: 4

Prep time: 20 minutes / Cook time: 10 minutes

Ingredients:
- 2 large eggplants, sliced into rounds
- 1 cup quinoa, cooked
- 1/4 cup fresh basil, chopped
- 1/4 cup fresh parsley, chopped
- 2 tbsp olive oil
- 2 tbsp balsamic vinegar
- Salt and pepper to taste
- Lemon wedges for serving

Instructions:
1. Preheat the grill to medium-high heat. Brush eggplant slices with olive oil and season with salt and pepper.
2. Grill eggplant for 3-4 minutes on each side until tender and grill marks appear.
3. In a bowl, mix cooked quinoa with basil, parsley, salt, and pepper.
4. Arrange the grilled eggplant on a serving platter. Spoon herbed quinoa over the top.
5. Drizzle with balsamic vinegar and serve with lemon wedges.

Benefits for Diabetics:
Eggplant is a low-calorie vegetable that's high in fiber, while quinoa provides complete protein and additional fiber, aiding in overall blood sugar control and satiety.

Conclusion:
Grilled Eggplant with Herbed Quinoa is a delightful dish that's as healthy as it is flavorful. It's perfect for a light lunch or dinner, offering a delicious way to enjoy the benefits of whole grains and vegetables.

Per Serving:
Calories: 270 | Fat: 10g | Carbs: 38g | Fiber: 9g | Protein: 8g

Thai Peanut Veggie Stir-Fry

Serves: 4

Prep time: 15 minutes / Cook time: 10 minutes

Ingredients:

- 4 cups mixed vegetables (bell peppers, broccoli, carrots, snap peas)
- 1 onion, sliced
- 2 cloves garlic, minced
- 1/4 cup peanut butter
- 2 tbsp soy sauce
- 1 tbsp honey (or maple syrup for vegan option)
- 1 tbsp rice vinegar
- 1 tsp ginger, grated
- 1/2 tsp chili flakes (optional)
- 2 tbsp water
- 2 tbsp olive oil
- 2 tbsp roasted peanuts, chopped
- Fresh cilantro for garnish

Instructions:

1. Heat olive oil in a large skillet or wok over medium-high heat. Add onions and garlic, cooking until fragrant.
2. Add mixed vegetables and stir-fry until tender but still crisp.
3. In a small bowl, whisk together peanut butter, soy sauce, honey, rice vinegar, ginger, chili flakes, and water until smooth.
4. Pour the peanut sauce over the vegetables and stir to coat evenly.
5. Cook for a few more minutes until everything is heated through and well combined.
6. Serve hot, garnished with chopped peanuts and fresh cilantro.

Benefits for Diabetics:

This stir-fry is full of vegetables that provide fiber and nutrients, while the peanut sauce adds healthy fats and protein, contributing to a balanced meal that can help manage blood sugar levels.

Per Serving:

Calories: 280 | Fat: 18g | Carbs: 24g | Fiber: 6g | Protein: 10g

Caprese Stuffed Portobello Mushrooms

Serves: 4

Prep time: 15 minutes / Cook time: 15 minutes

Ingredients:

- 4 large portobello mushroom caps, stems removed
- 2 large tomatoes, sliced
- 1 ball fresh mozzarella cheese, sliced
- 1/4 cup fresh basil leaves
- 2 tbsp balsamic glaze
- 2 tbsp olive oil
- Salt and pepper to taste

Instructions:

1. Preheat the oven to 375°F (190°C). Place mushroom caps on a baking sheet, gill side up.
2. Brush each mushroom with olive oil and season with salt and pepper.
3. Layer tomato slices, mozzarella slices, and basil leaves inside each mushroom cap.
4. Drizzle with balsamic glaze.
5. Bake for 15 minutes until the cheese is melted and mushrooms are tender.
6. Serve warm, garnished with additional basil leaves if desired.

Benefits for Diabetics:

Portobello mushrooms are an excellent low-carb base for this dish, while tomatoes provide vitamins and antioxidants. Fresh mozzarella adds protein and calcium, making it a balanced and nutritious meal.

Per Serving:

Calories: 220 | Fat: 16g | Carbs: 10g | Fiber: 2g | Protein: 12g

Pesto Vegetable Tart

Serves: 6

Prep time: 20 minutes / Cook time: 20 minutes

Ingredients:

- 1 sheet puff pastry, thawed
- 1/2 cup pesto (homemade or store-bought)
- 2 zucchinis, thinly sliced
- 1 bell pepper, thinly sliced
- 1/2 red onion, thinly sliced
- 1/4 cup feta cheese, crumbled (optional)
- 1 egg (for egg wash, optional)
- Salt and pepper to taste
- Fresh basil leaves for garnish

Instructions:

1. Preheat the oven to 400°F (200°C). Roll out the puff pastry on a baking sheet lined with parchment paper.
2. Spread pesto evenly over the pastry, leaving a small border around the edges.
3. Arrange zucchini, bell pepper, and red onion slices on top of the pesto.
4. Sprinkle with feta cheese and season with salt and pepper.
5. If desired, brush the edges of the pastry with beaten egg for a golden finish.
6. Bake for 20 minutes until the pastry is puffed and golden.
7. Serve warm, garnished with fresh basil.

Benefits for Diabetics:

This tart provides a hearty serving of vegetables, offering fiber, vitamins, and minerals. The pesto adds healthy fats and flavor, making it a satisfying meal that's not heavy on carbs.

Per Serving:

Calories: 320 | Fat: 20g | Carbs: 28g | Fiber: 3g | Protein: 6g

Japanese Eggplant with Miso Glaze

Serves: 2

Prep time: 15 minutes / Cook time: 10 minutes

Ingredients:

- 2 medium Japanese eggplants, halved lengthwise
- 2 tbsp miso paste (ensure it's vegan)
- 1 tbsp rice vinegar

- 1 tbsp soy sauce
- 1 tsp sugar or sugar substitute
- 1 tsp sesame oil
- 1/2 tsp ginger, grated
- Sesame seeds and sliced green onions for garnish

Instructions:
1. Preheat your grill or broiler to medium-high heat.
2. Score the cut side of the eggplants in a crosshatch pattern.
3. In a small bowl, mix together miso paste, rice vinegar, soy sauce, sugar or substitute, sesame oil, and grated ginger to create the glaze.
4. Brush the eggplant halves with the miso glaze, making sure to get into the scored crevices.
5. Grill or broil the eggplants, cut side up, for about 8-10 minutes, or until the eggplant is tender and the glaze has caramelized.
6. Garnish with sesame seeds and green onions before serving.

Benefits for Diabetics:
Japanese eggplants are low in carbohydrates and high in fiber, which is beneficial for blood sugar management. The miso glaze provides a burst of flavor without the need for high-sugar sauces.

Per Serving:
Calories: 120 | Fat: 4g | Carbs: 18g | Fiber: 5g | Protein: 3g

Indian Spiced Roasted Cauliflower

Serves: 2
Prep time: 10 minutes / Cook time: 25 minutes

Ingredients:
- 1 large head of cauliflower, cut into florets
- 2 tbsp olive oil
- 1 tsp cumin seeds
- 1 tsp turmeric powder
- 1/2 tsp coriander powder
- 1/2 tsp garam masala
- 1/4 tsp chili powder (adjust to taste)
- Salt to taste
- Fresh cilantro for garnish

Instructions:
1. Preheat oven to 400°F (200°C).
2. In a large bowl, toss cauliflower florets with olive oil, cumin seeds, turmeric, coriander, garam masala, chili powder, and salt until well coated.
3. Spread the cauliflower in a single layer on a baking sheet.
4. Roast for 20-25 minutes, or until cauliflower is tender and edges are golden brown.
5. Garnish with fresh cilantro before serving.

Benefits for Diabetics:
Cauliflower is a low-carb vegetable that's high in fiber and nutrients. The spices used not only add flavor but also offer anti-inflammatory and antioxidant properties, which can be beneficial for overall health.

Per Serving:
Calories: 150 | Fat: 7g | Carbs: 18g | Fiber: 6g | Protein: 5g

Spanish Garlic Mushrooms (Champiñones al Ajillo)

Serves: 2
Prep time: 10 minutes / Cook time: 10 minutes

Ingredients:
- 2 cups mushrooms, cleaned and sliced
- 4 tbsp olive oil
- 4 garlic cloves, minced
- 2 tbsp sherry vinegar or dry sherry
- 1 tsp smoked paprika
- Salt and pepper to taste
- Fresh parsley, chopped for garnish

Instructions:
1. Heat olive oil in a large skillet over medium heat.
2. Add garlic and sauté for about 1 minute until fragrant but not browned.
3. Increase the heat to high, add mushrooms, and cook for 5-7 minutes, or until they are golden and have released their moisture.
4. Add sherry vinegar and smoked paprika, and stir well. Cook for an additional 2 minutes.
5. Season with salt and pepper to taste.
6. Garnish with fresh parsley before serving.

Benefits for Diabetics:
Mushrooms are a low-calorie and low-carb food that provide a good source of protein and fiber. Garlic and olive oil add heart-healthy benefits and bold flavors without needing to rely on high-sugar or high-carb ingredients.

Per Serving:
Calories: 190 | Fat: 14g | Carbs: 10g | Fiber: 2g | Protein: 6g

Korean Spicy Cucumber Salad (Oi Muchim)

Serves: 2
Prep time: 15 minutes / Cook time: 0 minutes

Ingredients:
- 2 medium cucumbers, thinly sliced
- 1 green onion, thinly sliced
- 2 tsp Korean red chili pepper flakes (gochugaru)
- 1 tbsp rice vinegar
- 1 tsp sesame oil
- 1 tsp soy sauce
- 1/2 tsp sugar or sugar substitute
- 1 garlic clove, minced
- Sesame seeds for garnish

Instructions:
1. In a mixing bowl, combine the sliced cucumbers and green onion.
2. In another small bowl, whisk together the Korean red chili pepper flakes, rice vinegar, sesame oil, soy sauce, sugar or substitute, and minced garlic to create the dressing.
3. Pour the dressing over the cucumbers and toss well to coat evenly.
4. Let the salad marinate for about 10 minutes for flavors to meld together.

5. Serve chilled or at room temperature, sprinkled with sesame seeds.

Benefits for Diabetics:
Cucumbers are low in carbohydrates and high in hydration. The dressing is carefully balanced with minimal sweeteners and healthy fats from sesame oil, providing a flavorful experience without a significant impact on blood sugar levels.

Per Serving:
Calories: 50 | Fat: 3g | Carbs: 6g | Fiber: 1g | Protein: 1g

Lebanese Roasted Eggplant Salad

Serves: 2
Prep time: 15 minutes / Cook time: 25 minutes

Ingredients:
- 2 medium eggplants
- 2 tomatoes, diced
- 1 small onion, finely chopped
- 1/4 cup fresh parsley, chopped
- 2 tbsp olive oil
- 1 tbsp lemon juice
- 1 garlic clove, minced
- Salt and pepper to taste

Instructions:
1. Preheat oven to 400°F (200°C).
2. Prick eggplants with a fork and place them on a baking sheet. Roast for 25-30 minutes or until the skin is charred and the inside is tender.
3. Once cooled, peel the skin off the eggplants and chop the flesh into small pieces.
4. In a mixing bowl, combine roasted eggplant, diced tomatoes, chopped onion, and parsley.
5. In a small bowl, whisk together olive oil, lemon juice, minced garlic, salt, and pepper to create the dressing.
6. Pour the dressing over the eggplant mixture and toss gently to combine.
7. Chill in the refrigerator for about 30 minutes before serving to allow flavors to develop.

Benefits for Diabetics:
Eggplant is a low-carb vegetable with a high fiber content, beneficial for blood sugar management. The additional vegetables and herbs provide nutrients and antioxidants, while the olive oil contributes healthy fats.

Per Serving:
Calories: 180 | Fat: 14g | Carbs: 14g | Fiber: 7g | Protein: 3g

Hungarian Roasted Pepper and Tomato Salad

Serves: 2
Prep time: 10 minutes / Cook time: 15 minutes

Ingredients:
- 2 bell peppers (any color), roasted and peeled
- 2 medium tomatoes, sliced
- 1 small red onion, thinly sliced
- 2 tbsp apple cider vinegar
- 1 tbsp olive oil
- Salt and pepper to taste
- Fresh parsley, chopped for garnish

Instructions:
1. Roast the bell peppers on a grill or under a broiler until the skin is charred. Place them in a bowl covered with plastic wrap for a few minutes, then peel off the skin and slice into strips.
2. Arrange the roasted pepper strips and sliced tomatoes on a serving dish.
3. Scatter the thinly sliced red onion over the top.
4. Drizzle with apple cider vinegar and olive oil. Season with salt and pepper.
5. Garnish with chopped parsley before serving.

Benefits for Diabetics:
Both bell peppers and tomatoes are low in carbohydrates and high in vitamins and antioxidants. The simple dressing of vinegar and olive oil adds flavor without unnecessary sugars or fats, making it a healthy choice for blood sugar management.

Per Serving:
Calories: 130 | Fat: 7g | Carbs: 15g | Fiber: 4g | Protein: 2g

Greek Roasted Vegetables (Briam)

Serves: 2
Prep time: 15 minutes / Cook time: 40 minutes

Ingredients:
- 1 zucchini, sliced
- 1 eggplant, sliced
- 1 bell pepper, sliced
- 1 potato, sliced (optional, can omit for lower carbs)
- 1 onion, sliced
- 2 tomatoes, sliced
- 3 tbsp olive oil
- 1 tsp dried oregano
- Salt and pepper to taste
- Fresh parsley, chopped for garnish

Instructions:
1. Preheat oven to 375°F (190°C).
2. In a large baking dish, arrange the sliced zucchini, eggplant, bell pepper, potato (if using), onion, and tomatoes.
3. Drizzle with olive oil and sprinkle with oregano, salt, and pepper.
4. Toss gently to coat all the vegetables evenly.
5. Roast in the preheated oven for about 40 minutes, or until vegetables are tender and lightly browned.
6. Garnish with fresh parsley before serving.

Benefits for Diabetics:
The variety of vegetables in Briam provides a wealth of nutrients, fibers, and antioxidants. Olive oil adds heart-healthy fats, while the herbs enhance the flavor without extra calories or carbs, supporting overall health and blood sugar control.

Per Serving:
Calories: 220 | Fat: 14g | Carbs: 24g (less if omitting potato) | Fiber: 7g | Protein: 5g

Chapter 4: Poultry Recipes

Welcome to Chapter 4, where we focus on poultry recipes that are flavorful, nutritious, and suitable for a diabetic-friendly diet. Poultry, such as chicken and turkey, is a staple protein source for many due to its versatility, lean protein content, and ability to absorb a variety of flavors from different cuisines. In this chapter, we present a collection of poultry recipes ranging from grilled and roasted to simmered and baked, all tailored to meet the dietary needs of those managing diabetes.

These dishes emphasize the use of herbs, spices, and healthy cooking methods to enhance flavor without excessive carbohydrates or unhealthy fats.

Each recipe is designed to provide a satisfying and balanced meal that supports stable blood sugar levels and overall health. Let's explore the delicious possibilities that poultry offers!

Lemon and Herb Grilled Chicken

Serves: 2

Prep time: 10 minutes (plus marination time) / Cook time: 15 minutes

Ingredients:
- 2 boneless, skinless chicken breasts
- 1 lemon, juice and zest • 1 tbsp olive oil
- 1 garlic clove, minced • 1 tsp rosemary, chopped
- 1 tsp thyme, chopped • Salt and pepper to taste

Instructions:
1. In a bowl, mix together lemon juice, lemon zest, olive oil, garlic, rosemary, thyme, salt, and pepper.
2. Marinate the chicken breasts in the lemon-herb mixture for at least 30 minutes in the refrigerator.
3. Preheat grill to medium-high heat.
4. Grill the chicken for about 7-8 minutes on each side, or until fully cooked and internal temperature reaches 165°F (74°C).
5. Serve hot with a side of grilled vegetables or a fresh salad.

Benefits for Diabetics:
Chicken is a great source of high-quality lean protein, essential for muscle maintenance and overall health. It's low in fat and carbohydrates, making it an ideal choice for managing blood sugar levels. The addition of lemon and herbs adds flavor without adding unnecessary sugars or carbs.

Per Serving:
Calories: 220 | Fat: 7g | Carbs: 3g | Fiber: 1g | Protein: 35g

Turkey and Vegetable Skillet

Serves: 2

Prep time: 10 minutes / Cook time: 20 minutes

Ingredients:
- 1/2 lb ground turkey • 1 bell pepper, diced
- 1 zucchini, diced • 1/2 onion, diced
- 2 cloves garlic, minced • 1 tomato, diced
- 1 tsp smoked paprika • 1 tsp cumin
- 2 tbsp olive oil • Salt and pepper to taste

Instructions:
1. Heat olive oil in a large skillet over medium heat. Add the onion and garlic, cooking until translucent.
2. Add the ground turkey, breaking it up with a spoon, and cook until browned.
3. Stir in bell pepper, zucchini, and tomato. Cook for an additional 10 minutes, or until the vegetables are tender.
4. Season with smoked paprika, cumin, salt, and pepper.
5. Serve hot, garnished with fresh herbs or a sprinkle of cheese if desired.

Benefits for Diabetics:
Ground turkey is a lean source of protein that helps maintain muscle mass and keeps you feeling full longer. The vegetables add essential nutrients and fiber, aiding in digestion and blood sugar regulation. This dish is low in carbohydrates and high in flavor, making it ideal for a diabetic diet.

Per Serving:
Calories: 320 | Fat: 18g | Carbs: 12g | Fiber: 3g | Protein: 28g

Baked Chicken with Spinach and Artichokes

Serves: 2

Prep time: 10 minutes / Cook time: 25 minutes

Ingredients:
- 2 boneless, skinless chicken breasts
- 1 cup spinach, chopped
- 1/2 cup canned artichoke hearts, chopped
- 1/2 cup low-fat cream cheese
- 1/4 cup grated Parmesan cheese
- 2 cloves garlic, minced
- 1 tbsp olive oil
- Salt and pepper to taste

Instructions:
1. Preheat the oven to 375°F (190°C).
2. In a skillet, heat olive oil over medium heat. Add garlic and sauté until fragrant.
3. Add spinach and artichokes, cooking until the spinach is wilted.
4. Stir in cream cheese and Parmesan until the mixture is creamy and well combined.
5. Place the chicken breasts in a baking dish. Spread the spinach and artichoke mixture over the chicken.
6. Bake for 25 minutes, or until the chicken is fully cooked and the topping is golden.
7. Serve hot, garnished with additional Parmesan or fresh herbs.

Benefits for Diabetics:
Chicken provides a high-quality protein source, which is crucial for blood sugar control and satiety. Spinach and artichokes add fiber, vitamins, and minerals, contributing

to a well-rounded meal. The low-fat cream cheese offers creaminess without excessive calories or unhealthy fats.

Per Serving:
Calories: 330 | Fat: 15g | Carbs: 8g | Fiber: 2g | Protein: 40g

Grilled Turkey Burgers with Avocado

Serves: 2
Prep time: 15 minutes / Cook time: 10 minutes

Ingredients:
- 1/2 lb ground turkey
- 1 ripe avocado, sliced
- 2 whole grain buns
- Lettuce, tomato, and onion for toppings
- 1 tsp garlic powder
- 1 tsp onion powder
- Salt and pepper to taste
- 1 tbsp olive oil (for grilling)

Instructions:
1. Preheat the grill to medium-high heat.
2. In a bowl, mix ground turkey with garlic powder, onion powder, salt, and pepper. Form into two patties.
3. Brush the grill with olive oil and cook the turkey burgers for about 5 minutes on each side, or until fully cooked and internal temperature reaches 165°F (74°C).
4. Serve the turkey burgers on whole grain buns, topped with avocado, lettuce, tomato, and onion.

Benefits for Diabetics:
Turkey is an excellent source of lean protein, helping to keep blood sugar levels stable and promote satiety. Avocado provides healthy monounsaturated fats, which are beneficial for heart health and can help in blood sugar management. Choosing whole grain buns adds fiber and nutrients, further supporting a healthy diet.

Per Serving:
Calories: 390 | Fat: 22g | Carbs: 24g | Fiber: 7g | Protein: 28g

Chicken and Broccoli Stir-Fry

Serves: 2
Prep time: 10 minutes / Cook time: 10 minutes

Ingredients:
- 2 boneless, skinless chicken breasts, thinly sliced
- 2 cups broccoli florets
- 1 bell pepper, sliced
- 1 onion, sliced
- 2 cloves garlic, minced
- 2 tbsp soy sauce
- 1 tbsp sesame oil
- 1 tsp cornstarch dissolved in 1 tbsp water
- 2 tbsp vegetable oil for frying
- Salt and pepper to taste

Instructions:
1. Heat vegetable oil in a large skillet or wok over medium-high heat. Add chicken slices and cook until browned and cooked through. Remove from skillet and set aside.
2. In the same skillet, add broccoli, bell pepper, and onion. Stir-fry until vegetables are tender-crisp.
3. Add garlic and cook for an additional minute until fragrant.
4. Return the chicken to the skillet. Add soy sauce, sesame oil, and the cornstarch mixture. Stir well to combine and cook until the sauce has thickened.

5. Serve hot, garnished with sesame seeds or green onions if desired.

Benefits for Diabetics:
This stir-fry provides a healthy balance of lean protein from chicken and nutrients from broccoli and other vegetables. The high protein content helps with blood sugar regulation, while the fiber from the vegetables aids in digestion and overall glycemic control.

Per Serving:
Calories: 320 | Fat: 16g | Carbs: 14g | Fiber: 3g | Protein: 32g

Herbed Chicken Piccata

Serves: 2
Prep time: 10 minutes / Cook time: 20 minutes

Ingredients:
- 2 boneless, skinless chicken breasts, pounded to even thickness
- 1 lemon, juice and zest
- 2 tbsp capers, rinsed
- 1/2 cup chicken broth
- 1 tbsp olive oil
- 2 garlic cloves, minced
- 1 tbsp fresh parsley, chopped
- 1 tsp dried oregano
- Salt and pepper to taste
- 1 tbsp all-purpose flour (for dredging, optional)

Instructions:
1. Season the chicken breasts with salt, pepper, and dried oregano. Dredge lightly in flour if desired.
2. Heat olive oil in a large skillet over medium-high heat. Add chicken and cook until golden and cooked through, about 4-5 minutes per side. Remove and set aside.
3. In the same skillet, add garlic and cook until fragrant. Pour in lemon juice, chicken broth, and capers. Bring to a simmer and let the sauce reduce slightly.
4. Return the chicken to the skillet, coating it with the sauce. Cook for an additional 2-3 minutes.
5. Serve the chicken drizzled with sauce and garnished with lemon zest and fresh parsley.

Benefits for Diabetics:
Chicken is a great source of lean protein, essential for maintaining muscle mass and controlling hunger. The high protein along with the low carbohydrate content of the dish helps in managing blood sugar levels. Lemon and herbs add flavor without adding sugar or excessive calories.

Per Serving:
Calories: 260 | Fat: 10g | Carbs: 6g | Fiber: 1g | Protein: 34g

Spicy Chicken and Veggie Lettuce Wraps

Serves: 2
Prep time: 15 minutes / Cook time: 10 minutes

Ingredients:
- 1/2 lb ground chicken
- 1 bell pepper, finely diced
- 1 carrot, grated
- 1/2 onion, finely diced
- 2 cloves garlic, minced
- 1 head iceberg or butter lettuce
- 2 tbsp soy sauce
- 1 tbsp olive oil
- 1 tbsp chili sauce (adjust to taste)
- Fresh cilantro or mint for garnish

Instructions:
1. Heat olive oil in a skillet over medium heat. Add onion

and garlic, sautéing until soft.
2. Add ground chicken and cook until browned and no longer pink.
3. Stir in bell pepper and carrot, cooking for a few more minutes until vegetables are tender.
4. Add soy sauce and chili sauce, stirring until everything is well combined and heated through.
5. Wash and separate the lettuce leaves, using them as cups for the chicken mixture.
6. Spoon the chicken and veggie mix into the lettuce leaves and garnish with fresh cilantro or mint.

Benefits for Diabetics:
Ground chicken is an excellent protein source, promoting satiety and aiding in blood sugar control. The vegetables add fiber and nutrients with minimal impact on blood sugar. Lettuce wraps offer a fresh, crunchy alternative to bread or tortillas, significantly reducing the carbohydrate content.

Per Serving:
Calories: 300 | Fat: 15g | Carbs: 12g | Fiber: 3g | Protein: 28g

Turkey Meatloaf with Hidden Veggies

Serves: 2
Prep time: 20 minutes / Cook time: 1 hour

Ingredients:
- 1/2 lb ground turkey   • 1/2 cup carrots, finely grated
- 1/2 cup zucchini, finely grated
- 1/2 onion, finely diced • 1/4 cup bell pepper, finely diced
- 1 egg
- 1/2 cup whole grain breadcrumbs
- 2 tbsp tomato paste   • 1 tsp garlic powder
- 1 tsp dried herbs (such as thyme or parsley)
- Salt and pepper to taste
- 1/4 cup low-sugar ketchup or tomato sauce for topping

Instructions:
1. Preheat the oven to 375°F (190°C). Line a loaf pan with parchment paper or lightly grease it.
2. In a large bowl, combine ground turkey, carrots, zucchini, onion, bell pepper, egg, breadcrumbs, tomato paste, garlic powder, dried herbs, salt, and pepper. Mix until well combined.
3. Press the mixture into the prepared loaf pan, smoothing the top with a spoon.
4. Spread low-sugar ketchup or tomato sauce over the top of the meatloaf.
5. Bake for about 1 hour or until the meatloaf is cooked through and the top is slightly caramelized.
6. Let it rest for a few minutes before slicing and serving.

Benefits for Diabetics:
Turkey meatloaf with added vegetables provides a high protein, low-fat meal option. The addition of carrots, zucchini, and bell peppers increases the fiber content, essential for blood sugar control and overall health. Using whole grain breadcrumbs adds nutrients and fiber compared to refined alternatives.

Per Serving:
Calories: 350 | Fat: 15g | Carbs: 24g | Fiber: 5g | Protein: 30g

Chicken Shawarma Salad

Serves: 2
Prep time: 20 minutes (plus marination time) / Cook time: 15 minutes

Ingredients:
- 2 boneless, skinless chicken thighs or breasts
- 4 cups mixed salad greens   • 1/2 cucumber, sliced
- 1/2 cup cherry tomatoes, halved
- 1/4 red onion, thinly sliced   • 2 tbsp olive oil
- 1 lemon, juice and zest   • 1 tsp cumin
- 1 tsp paprika   • 1/2 tsp turmeric
- 1 garlic clove, minced
- Salt and pepper to taste
- Tzatziki or Greek yogurt for serving (optional)

Instructions:
1. In a bowl, combine olive oil, lemon juice, cumin, paprika, turmeric, garlic, salt, and pepper to make the marinade.
2. Coat the chicken with the marinade and let it sit for at least 30 minutes or up to a few hours in the refrigerator.
3. Heat a grill or skillet over medium-high heat. Cook the chicken until golden and fully cooked, about 7 minutes per side. Let it rest, then slice thinly.
4. Assemble the salad with mixed greens, cucumber, cherry tomatoes, and red onion. Top with sliced chicken.
5. Serve the salad with a dollop of tzatziki or Greek yogurt if desired.

Benefits for Diabetics:
This salad is a great way to enjoy a high-protein, low-carbohydrate meal, which is essential for blood sugar management. The chicken provides lean protein, while the vegetables offer fiber, vitamins, and minerals. The spices not only add flavor but also contain antioxidants and anti-inflammatory properties.

Per Serving:
Calories: 330 | Fat: 18g | Carbs: 10g | Fiber: 3g | Protein: 30g

Honey Mustard Glazed Chicken Tenders

Serves: 2
Prep time: 10 minutes / Cook time: 15 minutes

Ingredients:
- 1 lb chicken tenders
- 2 tbsp honey (or a lower glycemic sweetener)
- 2 tbsp Dijon mustard   • 1 tbsp olive oil
- 1 tsp apple cider vinegar
- Salt and pepper to taste
- Fresh parsley for garnish

Instructions:
1. Preheat the oven to 375°F (190°C). Line a baking sheet with parchment paper.
2. In a bowl, whisk together honey, Dijon mustard, olive oil, apple cider vinegar, salt, and pepper to create the glaze.
3. Coat the chicken tenders in the honey mustard glaze and arrange them on the prepared baking sheet.
4. Bake for 15 minutes or until the chicken is cooked through and the glaze is caramelized.
5. Serve hot, garnished with fresh parsley.

Benefits for Diabetics:
Chicken tenders provide a lean source of protein, essential for maintaining stable blood sugar levels. Opting for a small amount of honey or a substitute sweetener helps keep the overall sugar content low while still enjoying the sweet and tangy flavors of the glaze.
Per Serving:
Calories: 300 | Fat: 8g | Carbs: 14g | Fiber: 0g | Protein: 44g

Turmeric Chicken with Cauliflower Rice

Serves: 2
Prep time: 15 minutes / Cook time: 20 minutes
Ingredients:
- 2 boneless, skinless chicken breasts, cut into bite-sized pieces
- 1 head cauliflower, grated into rice-like pieces
- 1 onion, finely diced • 2 cloves garlic, minced
- 1 tsp ground turmeric • 1/2 tsp ground cumin
- 1/2 tsp ground coriander
- 1/4 tsp chili powder (adjust to taste)
- 2 tbsp olive oil • Salt and pepper to taste
- Fresh cilantro for garnish

Instructions:
1. Heat one tablespoon of olive oil in a skillet over medium heat. Add onion and garlic, cooking until soft and fragrant.
2. Add chicken pieces to the skillet, seasoning with turmeric, cumin, coriander, chili powder, salt, and pepper. Cook until the chicken is golden and cooked through.
3. In another skillet, heat the remaining olive oil over medium heat. Add the cauliflower rice and sauté until it's tender and slightly crispy, about 5-7 minutes.
4. Serve the turmeric chicken over the cauliflower rice, garnished with fresh cilantro.

Benefits for Diabetics:
This dish is an excellent choice for diabetics due to its high protein and low carbohydrate content. Turmeric has been noted for its potential to improve insulin sensitivity, while cauliflower rice provides a nutritious, low-glycemic base for the meal.
Per Serving:
Calories: 320 | Fat: 15g | Carbs: 12g | Fiber: 4g | Protein: 35g

Chicken Vegetable Soup

Serves: 2
Prep time: 15 minutes / Cook time: 30 minutes
Ingredients:
- 2 cups chicken broth • 1/2 lb chicken breast, diced
- 1 carrot, diced • 1 celery stalk, diced
- 1/2 onion, diced • 1 garlic clove, minced
- 1/2 cup green beans, chopped
- 1/2 cup diced tomatoes (canned or fresh)
- 1 tsp dried thyme • 1 tbsp olive oil
- Salt and pepper to taste
- Fresh parsley for garnish

Instructions:
1. Heat olive oil in a large pot over medium heat. Add

onion, garlic, carrot, and celery, sautéing until the vegetables begin to soften.
2. Add the chicken pieces and cook until they are no longer pink.
3. Pour in chicken broth and add green beans, diced tomatoes, and thyme. Bring to a boil, then reduce heat and simmer for 20 minutes.
4. Season with salt and pepper to taste.
5. Serve hot, garnished with fresh parsley.

Benefits for Diabetics:
This soup offers a healthy balance of lean protein, fiber, and nutrients while being low in fat and carbohydrates. The variety of vegetables provides essential vitamins and minerals, supporting overall health and helping manage blood sugar levels.
Per Serving:
Calories: 240 | Fat: 8g | Carbs: 12g | Fiber: 3g | Protein: 30g

Mediterranean Stuffed Chicken Breast

Serves: 2
Prep time: 20 minutes / Cook time: 25 minutes
Ingredients:
- 2 boneless, skinless chicken breasts
- 1/4 cup sun-dried tomatoes, chopped
- 1/2 cup spinach, chopped
- 1/4 cup feta cheese, crumbled
- 1/2 tsp dried oregano • 2 tbsp olive oil
- Salt and pepper to taste • Fresh basil for garnish

Instructions:
1. Preheat the oven to 375°F (190°C).
2. Make a horizontal cut in each chicken breast to create a pocket. Be careful not to cut all the way through.
3. Stuff each chicken breast with sun-dried tomatoes, spinach, and feta cheese. Secure with toothpicks if necessary.
4. Season the outside of the chicken with oregano, salt, and pepper.
5. Heat olive oil in a skillet over medium-high heat. Sear the chicken on both sides until golden.
6. Transfer the chicken to a baking dish and bake for 20-25 minutes, or until fully cooked.
7. Serve hot, garnished with fresh basil.

Benefits for Diabetics:
The combination of chicken, vegetables, and feta provides a good balance of protein, healthy fats, and fiber. This dish is low in carbohydrates and high in flavor, making it an excellent choice for maintaining stable blood sugar levels and overall health.
Per Serving:
Calories: 330 | Fat: 18g | Carbs: 8g | Fiber: 2g | Protein: 35g

BBQ Chicken and Veggie Skewer

Serves: 2
Prep time: 20 minutes (plus marination time) / Cook time: 10 minutes
Ingredients:
- 1/2 lb chicken breast, cut into cubes
- 1 bell pepper, cut into chunks

- 1 zucchini, cut into chunks
- 1 red onion, cut into chunks
- 1/2 cup low-sugar BBQ sauce
- 1 tbsp olive oil
- Salt and pepper to taste
- Wooden or metal skewers

Instructions:
1. Preheat grill to medium-high heat.
2. Thread chicken, bell pepper, zucchini, and red onion alternately onto skewers.
3. Brush the skewers with olive oil and season with salt and pepper.
4. Grill the skewers, turning occasionally and basting with BBQ sauce, for about 10 minutes or until the chicken is fully cooked and vegetables are tender.
5. Serve hot, with extra BBQ sauce on the side if desired.

Benefits for Diabetics:
Grilling is a healthy cooking method that doesn't require added fats or carbohydrates. Chicken provides lean protein, while vegetables offer fiber and essential nutrients. Using a low-sugar BBQ sauce keeps the overall sugar content minimal, making these skewers a great choice for a diabetic diet.

Per Serving:
Calories: 300 | Fat: 10g | Carbs: 18g | Fiber: 3g | Protein: 35g

Thai Basil Chicken Stir-Fry

Serves: 2
Prep time: 10 minutes / Cook time: 10 minutes

Ingredients:
- 1/2 lb ground chicken
- 1 bell pepper, sliced
- 1 onion, sliced
- 2 cloves garlic, minced
- 1 tbsp ginger, grated
- 1 cup Thai basil leaves
- 2 tbsp soy sauce
- 1 tbsp fish sauce
- 1 tsp chili paste (adjust to taste)
- 2 tbsp vegetable oil
- Salt to taste

Instructions:
1. Heat vegetable oil in a large skillet or wok over medium-high heat. Add garlic and ginger, cooking until fragrant.
2. Add ground chicken and cook, breaking it apart with a spoon, until browned and cooked through.
3. Stir in bell pepper and onion, cooking until they are tender-crisp.
4. Add soy sauce, fish sauce, chili paste, and Thai basil. Cook for an additional minute until everything is well combined and the basil is wilted.
5. Serve hot, with a side of steamed cauliflower rice for a low-carb option.

Benefits for Diabetics:
This stir-fry is rich in protein and low in carbohydrates, making it ideal for blood sugar management. The addition of vegetables and herbs provides fiber and antioxidants, supporting overall health and well-being.

Per Serving:
Calories: 320 | Fat: 18g | Carbs: 10g | Fiber: 2g | Protein: 28g

Rosemary Roasted Chicken Thighs

Serves: 2
Prep time: 10 minutes / Cook time: 35 minutes

Ingredients:
- 4 chicken thighs, bone-in and skin-on
- 2 tbsp olive oil
- 2 garlic cloves, minced
- 1 tbsp fresh rosemary, chopped
- Salt and pepper to taste

Instructions:
1. Preheat the oven to 375°F (190°C).
2. Rub the chicken thighs with olive oil, garlic, rosemary, salt, and pepper.
3. Place the chicken in a roasting pan, skin-side up.
4. Roast for 35 minutes, or until the chicken is golden brown and the internal temperature reaches 165°F (74°C).
5. Serve hot, garnished with additional rosemary if desired.

Benefits for Diabetics:
Chicken thighs offer a higher fat content than breasts, providing a rich flavor while still being a good source of protein. The use of olive oil adds healthy fats, and rosemary provides antioxidants, making this a nutritious choice that's low in carbohydrates.

Per Serving:
Calories: 370 | Fat: 28g | Carbs: 1g | Fiber: 0g | Protein: 27g

Turkey Stuffed Bell Peppers

Serves: 2
Prep time: 20 minutes / Cook time: 30 minutes

Ingredients:
- 2 large bell peppers, halved and seeded
- 1/2 lb ground turkey
- 1/2 onion, diced
- 1 garlic clove, minced
- 1/2 cup cooked quinoa or brown rice
- 1/2 cup diced tomatoes
- 1 tsp cumin
- 1 tsp paprika
- 2 tbsp olive oil
- Salt and pepper to taste
- 1/4 cup shredded low-fat cheese (optional)

Instructions:
1. Preheat the oven to 375°F (190°C).
2. In a skillet, heat 1 tablespoon of olive oil over medium heat. Add onion and garlic, sautéing until soft.
3. Add ground turkey, cooking until browned. Drain any excess fat.
4. Stir in cooked quinoa or rice, diced tomatoes, cumin, and paprika. Season with salt and pepper.
5. Stuff each bell pepper half with the turkey mixture and place in a baking dish.
6. Drizzle with the remaining olive oil and cover with foil.
7. Bake for 25 minutes. Remove the foil, top with cheese if using, and bake for an additional 5 minutes, or until the cheese is melted and peppers are tender.
8. Serve hot, garnished with fresh herbs or a side salad.

Benefits for Diabetics:
Lean ground turkey is an excellent protein source, helping to maintain muscle mass and control hunger. The combination of high-fiber quinoa or brown rice and bell peppers adds vitamins, minerals, and antioxidants,

supporting overall health and blood sugar management.
Per Serving:
Calories: 350 | Fat: 18g | Carbs: 22g | Fiber: 5g | Protein: 27g

Chicken Caesar Salad Wrap

Serves: 2
Prep time: 15 minutes / Cook time: 10 minutes

Ingredients:
- 2 whole grain tortillas
- 2 boneless, skinless chicken breasts, grilled and sliced
- 2 cups romaine lettuce, chopped
- 1/4 cup low-fat Caesar dressing
- 2 tbsp Parmesan cheese, grated
- Salt and pepper to taste

Instructions:
1. Lay out the whole grain tortillas on a flat surface.
2. Toss the chopped romaine lettuce with Caesar dressing and Parmesan cheese. Season with salt and pepper.
3. Divide the salad between the two tortillas, laying it in a line down the center.
4. Top the salad with grilled chicken slices.
5. Roll up the tortillas tightly, tucking in the ends to secure the filling.
6. Cut in half and serve immediately or wrap for an on-the-go meal.

Benefits for Diabetics:
Using whole grain tortillas provides a source of complex carbohydrates and fiber, which are important for blood sugar management. The lean protein from the chicken and the nutrients from the lettuce make this wrap a well-rounded choice that's filling and low in unhealthy fats.
Per Serving:
Calories: 320 | Fat: 12g | Carbs: 24g | Fiber: 4g | Protein: 30g

Spicy Asian Chicken Lettuce Cups

Serves: 2
Prep time: 15 minutes / Cook time: 10 minutes

Ingredients:
- 1/2 lb ground chicken
- 1 head of lettuce (such as Bibb or iceberg), leaves separated
- 1 bell pepper, finely diced   • 1 carrot, grated
- 1/2 onion, finely diced • 2 cloves garlic, minced
- 2 tbsp soy sauce   • 1 tbsp hoisin sauce
- 1 tsp chili sauce (adjust to taste)
- 1 tsp sesame oil   • 2 tbsp vegetable oil
- Fresh cilantro for garnish

Instructions:
1. Heat vegetable oil in a skillet over medium-high heat. Add onion and garlic, sautéing until fragrant.
2. Add ground chicken, breaking it apart as it cooks until browned and fully cooked.
3. Stir in bell pepper and carrot, cooking for a few more minutes until slightly softened.
4. Add soy sauce, hoisin sauce, chili sauce, and sesame oil, stirring well to combine all the ingredients. Cook for an additional 2-3 minutes.

5. Spoon the chicken mixture into the center of the lettuce leaves.
6. Garnish with fresh cilantro and serve immediately.
Benefits for Diabetics:
This dish is an excellent choice for individuals with diabetes, as it provides a high protein, low carbohydrate meal option. The lettuce cups act as a fresh, crunchy alternative to bread or other carb-heavy wrappers, while the chicken and vegetables provide essential nutrients and fiber.
Per Serving:
Calories: 300 | Fat: 18g | Carbs: 10g | Fiber: 3g | Protein: 26g

Pesto Chicken Zoodles

Serves: 2
Prep time: 20 minutes / Cook time: 10 minutes

Ingredients:
- 2 medium zucchini, spiralized into noodles
- 2 boneless, skinless chicken breasts, grilled and sliced
- 1/4 cup homemade or store-bought pesto sauce
- 1 tbsp olive oil
- Salt and pepper to taste
- Parmesan cheese for garnish (optional)

Instructions:
1. Heat olive oil in a large skillet over medium heat. Add the spiralized zucchini noodles and sauté for 2-3 minutes, just until tender. Be careful not to overcook.
2. Remove from heat and toss the zoodles with pesto sauce until well coated.
3. Divide the zoodles between two plates and top with grilled chicken slices.
4. Garnish with Parmesan cheese if desired and serve immediately.

Benefits for Diabetics:
Zoodles provide a fantastic low-carb alternative to traditional pasta, significantly reducing the dish's overall carbohydrate content. Chicken is an excellent source of lean protein, and the pesto adds healthy fats from olive oil and nuts, making this dish well-rounded and diabetic-friendly.
Per Serving:
Calories: 330 | Fat: 18g | Carbs: 8g | Fiber: 2g | Protein: 35g

Sesame Ginger Turkey Meatballs

Serves: 2
Prep time: 20 minutes / Cook time: 20 minutes

Ingredients:
- 1/2 lb ground turkey
- 1/4 cup breadcrumbs (whole grain if available)
- 1 egg   • 2 tbsp sesame seeds
- 1 tbsp fresh ginger, grated
- 2 cloves garlic, minced • 2 tbsp soy sauce
- 1 tsp sesame oil
- Green onions and additional sesame seeds for garnish

Instructions:
1. Preheat the oven to 375°F (190°C).
2. In a large bowl, combine ground turkey, breadcrumbs, egg, sesame seeds, ginger, garlic, soy sauce, and

sesame oil. Mix until well combined.
3. Form the mixture into small meatballs and place on a baking sheet lined with parchment paper.
4. Bake for 20 minutes, or until the meatballs are cooked through and slightly golden.
5. Serve hot, garnished with sliced green onions and a sprinkle of sesame seeds.

Benefits for Diabetics:
Ground turkey is an excellent lean protein choice, which helps with blood sugar control and satiety. The sesame and ginger add a burst of flavor and potential anti-inflammatory benefits without adding unnecessary carbohydrates, making these meatballs a healthy addition to any meal.

Per Serving:
Calories: 290 | Fat: 14g | Carbs: 12g | Fiber: 1g | Protein: 28g

Chicken and Asparagus Lemon Stir Fry

Serves: 2
Prep time: 15 minutes / Cook time: 10 minutes

Ingredients:
- 2 boneless, skinless chicken breasts, thinly sliced
- 2 cups asparagus, trimmed and cut into pieces
- 1 lemon, juice and zest • 1 tbsp olive oil
- 2 cloves garlic, minced• 1 tbsp soy sauce
- 1 tsp honey or a low-calorie sweetener
- Salt and pepper to taste

Instructions:
1. Heat olive oil in a large skillet over medium-high heat. Add chicken slices and cook until golden and nearly cooked through. Remove and set aside.
2. In the same skillet, add asparagus and cook until tender-crisp.
3. Return the chicken to the skillet. Add garlic, lemon juice, lemon zest, soy sauce, and honey or sweetener. Cook for an additional 2-3 minutes, until everything is heated through and coated with the sauce.
4. Season with salt and pepper to taste.
5. Serve hot, garnished with additional lemon zest if desired.

Benefits for Diabetics:
The combination of chicken and asparagus provides a high-protein, low-carbohydrate meal, ideal for blood sugar control. Asparagus is rich in fiber and nutrients, while lemon adds a dose of vitamin C and a fresh flavor, enhancing the dish's overall health benefits.

Per Serving:
Calories: 260 | Fat: 10g | Carbs: 10g | Fiber: 3g | Protein: 35g

Balsamic Glazed Chicken Drumsticks

Serves: 2
Prep time: 10 minutes / Cook time: 45 minutes

Ingredients:
- 4 chicken drumsticks • 1/4 cup balsamic vinegar
- 2 tbsp olive oil
- 1 tbsp honey or a suitable sweetener
- 2 cloves garlic, minced

- Salt and pepper to taste
- Fresh herbs for garnish (such as rosemary or thyme)

Instructions:
1. Preheat the oven to 375°F (190°C).
2. In a small saucepan, heat balsamic vinegar over medium heat until it reduces to a thicker glaze. Stir in honey or sweetener and garlic.
3. Rub the chicken drumsticks with olive oil, salt, and pepper. Place them in a baking dish.
4. Brush the balsamic glaze over the chicken drumsticks.
5. Bake for 45 minutes, or until the chicken is cooked through and the glaze has caramelized.
6. Serve hot, garnished with fresh herbs.

Benefits for Diabetics:
Chicken drumsticks are a good source of protein, which is essential for blood sugar management and maintaining lean muscle mass. The balsamic glaze provides a flavorful coating without a significant amount of sugar, especially when a low-calorie sweetener is used.

Per Serving:
Calories: 320 | Fat: 18g | Carbs: 12g | Fiber: 0g | Protein: 28g

Garlic Herb Roasted Turkey Breast

Serves: 2
Prep time: 20 minutes / Cook time: 1 hour

Ingredients:
- 1 bone-in turkey breast (about 2 lbs)
- 2 tbsp olive oil
- 4 cloves garlic, minced
- 1 tbsp fresh rosemary, chopped
- 1 tbsp fresh thyme, chopped
- Salt and pepper to taste

Instructions:
1. Preheat the oven to 350°F (175°C).
2. Rub the turkey breast with olive oil, then season with minced garlic, rosemary, thyme, salt, and pepper.
3. Place the turkey breast in a roasting pan and cover loosely with foil.
4. Roast for about 1 hour, or until the internal temperature reaches 165°F (74°C). Remove the foil in the last 15 minutes of cooking to brown the top.
5. Let the turkey rest for 10 minutes before slicing.
6. Serve hot, garnished with additional herbs if desired.

Benefits for Diabetics:
Turkey breast is an excellent source of lean protein, helping to regulate blood sugar levels and promote fullness. The use of herbs and garlic adds flavor without additional carbohydrates or sugars, making this dish both healthy and delicious.

Per Serving:
Calories: 330 | Fat: 10g | Carbs: 2g | Fiber: 1g | Protein: 55g

Grilled Chicken Kabobs with Vegetables

Serves: 2
Prep time: 20 minutes/ Cook time: 10 minutes

Ingredients:
- 1/2 lb chicken breast, cut into cubes

- 1 bell pepper, cut into chunks
- 1 zucchini, cut into chunks
- 1 red onion, cut into chunks
- 2 tbsp olive oil   • 1 lemon, juice and zest
- 1 tsp dried oregano   • Salt and pepper to taste
- Wooden or metal skewers

Instructions:

1. In a bowl, mix together olive oil, lemon juice, lemon zest, oregano, salt, and pepper. Add chicken cubes and let marinate for at least 30 minutes in the refrigerator.
2. Preheat grill to medium-high heat.
3. Thread marinated chicken, bell pepper, zucchini, and red onion alternately onto skewers.
4. Grill the kabobs, turning occasionally, for about 10 minutes, or until the chicken is fully cooked and vegetables are tender.
5. Serve hot, with a side of tzatziki sauce or a fresh salad.

Benefits for Diabetics:

Grilled Chicken Kabobs provide a great source of lean protein from the chicken and a variety of nutrients from the vegetables. The dish is low in carbohydrates and high in fiber, making it ideal for blood sugar management and overall health.

Per Serving:

Calories: 310 | Fat: 15g | Carbs: 12g | Fiber: 3g | Protein: 35g

Smoky Paprika Chicken Tenders

Serves: 2

Prep time: 10 minutes / Cook time: 20 minutes

Ingredients:

- 1 lb chicken tenders   • 1 tbsp smoked paprika
- 1/2 tsp garlic powder   • 1/2 tsp onion powder
- 1 tbsp olive oil   • Salt and pepper to taste

Instructions:

1. Preheat the oven to 400°F (200°C).
2. In a large bowl, mix together smoked paprika, garlic powder, onion powder, salt, and pepper.
3. Add chicken tenders and olive oil to the bowl, tossing until they are well coated with the seasoning.
4. Arrange the chicken tenders on a baking sheet lined with parchment paper.
5. Bake for 20 minutes or until the chicken is cooked through and the outside is crispy.
6. Serve hot, perhaps with a side of steamed vegetables or a light salad.

Benefits for Diabetics:

Chicken tenders are an excellent source of lean protein, crucial for managing blood sugar levels and maintaining muscle mass. The smoky paprika and other spices add a burst of flavor without additional sugar or carbohydrates.

Per Serving:

Calories: 260 | Fat: 9g | Carbs: 1g | Fiber: 0g | Protein: 42g

Herb-Brined Turkey Cutlets

Serves: 2

Prep time: 30 minutes (plus brining time) / Cook time: 15 minutes

Ingredients:

- 2 turkey breast cutlets • 2 cups water
- 2 tbsp salt   • 1 tbsp sugar or a sugar substitute
- 1 garlic clove, minced   • 1 tsp rosemary, chopped
- 1 tsp thyme, chopped   • 1 tbsp olive oil

Instructions:

1. In a large bowl, dissolve salt and sugar or substitute in water to make the brine. Add garlic, rosemary, and thyme.
2. Submerge the turkey cutlets in the brine and let them soak for at least 1 hour in the refrigerator.
3. Preheat a skillet or grill pan over medium-high heat. Remove the turkey from the brine and pat dry.
4. Brush the turkey cutlets with olive oil and cook for about 7 minutes on each side or until fully cooked and golden brown.
5. Serve hot, garnished with additional fresh herbs if desired.

Benefits for Diabetics:

Turkey is a lean source of protein, which is essential for blood sugar control and satiety. The herb brine adds depth of flavor without the need for high-carb sauces or seasonings, making it a suitable choice for those looking to manage their carbohydrate intake.

Per Serving:

Calories: 220 | Fat: 7g | Carbs: 2g | Fiber: 0g | Protein: 35g

Spiced Rubbed Chicken and Veggie Skillet

Serves: 2

Prep time: 15 minutes / Cook time: 20 minutes

Ingredients:

- 2 boneless, skinless chicken breasts
- 1 zucchini, sliced   • 1 bell pepper, sliced
- 1 small red onion, sliced
- 1 tsp chili powder   • 1/2 tsp cumin
- 1/2 tsp garlic powder • 1/2 tsp paprika
- 2 tbsp olive oil   • Salt and pepper to taste

Instructions:

1. In a small bowl, mix together chili powder, cumin, garlic powder, paprika, salt, and pepper.
2. Rub the spice mixture over the chicken breasts.
3. Heat 1 tablespoon of olive oil in a large skillet over medium-high heat. Add the chicken and cook until golden on both sides and cooked through. Remove from skillet and set aside.
4. In the same skillet, heat the remaining olive oil. Add zucchini, bell pepper, and red onion. Sauté until the vegetables are tender-crisp.
5. Slice the cooked chicken and return it to the skillet with the vegetables. Stir to combine and heat through.
6. Serve hot, with a garnish of fresh herbs or a squeeze of lemon if desired.

Benefits for Diabetics:

This dish is an excellent source of lean protein from the chicken and provides a serving of healthy vegetables, which are high in fiber and nutrients. The combination helps regulate blood sugar levels while satisfying hunger with a variety of textures and flavors.

Per Serving:

Calories: 300 | Fat: 15g | Carbs: 12g | Fiber: 3g | Protein: 30g

Lemon Garlic Chicken Thighs

Serves: 2

Prep time: 10 minutes / Cook time: 30 minutes

Ingredients:
- 4 chicken thighs, bone-in and skin-on
- 1 lemon, juice and zest
- 4 cloves garlic, minced
- 2 tbsp olive oil
- Salt and pepper to taste
- Fresh parsley for garnish

Instructions:
1. In a large bowl, combine lemon juice, lemon zest, minced garlic, olive oil, salt, and pepper.
2. Add the chicken thighs to the bowl, coating them thoroughly with the marinade. Let them marinate for at least 30 minutes in the refrigerator.
3. Preheat the oven to 400°F (200°C) or prepare a grill for medium-high heat.
4. Arrange the chicken thighs on a baking sheet or grill them, cooking until the skin is crispy and the chicken is cooked through (internal temperature should reach 165°F or 74°C).
5. Serve hot, garnished with fresh parsley and additional lemon wedges if desired.

Benefits for Diabetics:
Chicken thighs provide a higher fat content for more flavor while still being a good source of protein. The lemon and garlic add a significant amount of flavor without carbohydrates, making this dish flavorful and suitable for those monitoring their blood sugar levels.

Per Serving:
Calories: 380 | Fat: 28g | Carbs: 3g | Fiber: 0g | Protein: 30g

Tandoori Spiced Turkey Kebabs

Serves: 2

Prep time: 20 minutes / Cook time: 15 minutes

Ingredients:
- 1/2 lb ground turkey
- 1 tbsp tandoori spice mix (store-bought or homemade)
- 1/4 cup Greek yogurt
- 1 tbsp lemon juice
- 1 tbsp fresh cilantro, chopped
- Salt to taste
- Wooden or metal skewers

Instructions:
1. In a bowl, combine ground turkey, tandoori spice mix, Greek yogurt, lemon juice, cilantro, and salt. Mix until well combined.
2. Divide the mixture and form it around skewers into kebab shapes.
3. Preheat the grill to medium-high heat or the oven to 375°F (190°C).
4. Grill the kebabs for about 7-8 minutes on each side or bake for 15 minutes, turning halfway through, until fully cooked and slightly charred on the outside.
5. Serve hot, garnished with additional cilantro and lemon wedges on the side.

Benefits for Diabetics:
Turkey is an excellent source of lean protein, which is beneficial for blood sugar management. The tandoori spices add a depth of flavor without extra sugar or fat, and the Greek yogurt provides a creamy texture and additional protein, making these kebabs both nutritious and satisfying.

Conclusion:
Tandoori Spiced Turkey Kebabs are a flavorful and exotic way to enjoy lean protein. They're perfect for a family dinner or entertaining guests, offering a healthy meal option that doesn't sacrifice taste or enjoyment.

Per Serving:
Calories: 250 | Fat: 12g | Carbs: 4g | Fiber: 1g | Protein: 30g

Cilantro Lime Chicken

Serves: 2

Prep time: 15 minutes / Cook time: 20 minutes

Ingredients:
- 2 boneless, skinless chicken breasts
- 1/4 cup fresh cilantro, finely chopped
- 2 limes, juice and zest
- 2 cloves garlic, minced
- 1 tbsp olive oil
- Salt and pepper to taste

Instructions:
1. In a bowl, mix together lime juice, lime zest, cilantro, garlic, olive oil, salt, and pepper.
2. Marinate the chicken breasts in the cilantro lime mixture for at least 30 minutes in the refrigerator.
3. Preheat a grill or skillet over medium-high heat.
4. Grill or cook the chicken for 10 minutes on each side, or until fully cooked and the juices run clear.
5. Serve the chicken garnished with extra cilantro and lime wedges on the side.

Benefits for Diabetics:
Chicken is a great source of lean protein, which is essential for blood sugar control and maintaining a healthy weight. The addition of lime and cilantro provides a burst of flavor without added sugars or unhealthy fats, making this dish both nutritious and delicious.

Per Serving:
Calories: 230 | Fat: 8g | Carbs: 4g | Fiber: 1g | Protein: 35g

Turkey and Spinach Stuffed Peppers

Serves: 2

Prep time: 20 minutes / Cook time: 30 minutes

Ingredients:
- 2 large bell peppers, halved and seeded
- 1/2 lb ground turkey
- 1 cup spinach, chopped
- 1/2 onion, finely chopped
- 2 cloves garlic, minced
- 1/2 cup canned diced tomatoes, drained
- 1 tsp dried oregano
- 1 tbsp olive oil
- Salt and pepper to taste
- 1/4 cup shredded low-fat cheese (optional)

Instructions:

1. Preheat the oven to 375°F (190°C).
2. In a skillet, heat olive oil over medium heat. Add onion and garlic, cooking until translucent.
3. Add ground turkey and cook until browned. Stir in spinach, diced tomatoes, and oregano. Cook until the spinach is wilted and the mixture is well combined. Season with salt and pepper.
4. Stuff each bell pepper half with the turkey mixture. Place in a baking dish.
5. Bake for 25-30 minutes, or until the peppers are tender and the filling is heated through. If using cheese, sprinkle it on top in the last 5 minutes of baking.
6. Serve the stuffed peppers hot.

Benefits for Diabetics:

This dish is rich in protein from the turkey and contains a good amount of fiber from the vegetables, particularly the bell peppers and spinach. These nutrients are key in managing blood sugar levels and keeping you full and satisfied.

Per Serving:

Calories: 290 | Fat: 12g | Carbs: 15g | Fiber: 4g | Protein: 32g

Baked Pesto Parmesan Chicken

Serves: 2

Prep time: 10 minutes / Cook time: 25 minutes

Ingredients:

- 2 boneless, skinless chicken breasts
- 1/4 cup pesto sauce
- 1/4 cup grated Parmesan cheese
- Salt and pepper to taste

Instructions:

1. Preheat the oven to 375°F (190°C).
2. Season the chicken breasts with salt and pepper, then spread pesto sauce evenly over each piece.
3. Sprinkle grated Parmesan cheese on top of the pesto.
4. Place the chicken breasts in a baking dish and bake for 25 minutes, or until the chicken is fully cooked and the cheese is golden.
5. Serve hot, accompanied by a side of steamed vegetables or a fresh salad.

Benefits for Diabetics:

Chicken provides a high-quality protein source, crucial for controlling hunger and maintaining muscle mass. The addition of pesto and Parmesan adds flavor without significantly increasing the carbohydrate content, making this dish a flavorful and healthful choice.

Per Serving:

Calories: 320 | Fat: 18g | Carbs: 3g | Fiber: 0g | Protein: 35g

Slow Cooker Chicken Cacciatore

Serves: 2

Prep time: 15 minutes / Cook time: 4 hours on high or 8 hours on low

Ingredients:

- 2 boneless, skinless chicken breasts
- 1 can diced tomatoes
- 1 bell pepper, sliced
- 1 onion, sliced
- 2 cloves garlic, minced
- 1 tsp dried basil
- 1 tsp dried oregano
- 1/2 cup chicken broth
- Salt and pepper to taste
- Fresh parsley for garnish

Instructions:

1. Place the chicken breasts at the bottom of the slow cooker.
2. Add diced tomatoes, bell pepper, onion, garlic, basil, oregano, and chicken broth over the chicken.
3. Season with salt and pepper.
4. Cover and cook on high for 4 hours or on low for 8 hours, until the chicken is tender and the flavors have melded together.
5. Serve hot, garnished with fresh parsley.

Benefits for Diabetics:

Chicken Cacciatore made in a slow cooker is an excellent low-carb, high-protein meal. The vegetables add fiber and nutrients, while the slow cooking process ensures that the chicken remains moist and tender, providing a satisfying and nutritious dish.

Per Serving:

Calories: 240 | Fat: 3g | Carbs: 15g | Fiber: 4g | Protein: 35g

Grilled Chicken and Mango Salsa

Serves: 2

Prep time: 20 minutes / Cook time: 10 minutes

Ingredients:

- 2 boneless, skinless chicken breasts
- 1 ripe mango, diced
- 1/2 red bell pepper, diced
- 1/4 red onion, finely chopped
- 1 jalapeno, seeded and minced (optional)
- 2 tbsp fresh cilantro, chopped
- 1 lime, juice and zest
- Salt and pepper to taste
- 1 tbsp olive oil for grilling

Instructions:

1. Season the chicken breasts with salt and pepper.
2. Preheat a grill or grill pan over medium-high heat. Brush the chicken with olive oil and grill for about 5 minutes on each side, or until fully cooked and marked by the grill.
3. To make the mango salsa, combine diced mango, red bell pepper, red onion, jalapeno (if using), cilantro, lime juice, and zest in a bowl. Season with salt and mix well.
4. Serve the grilled chicken topped with a generous scoop of mango salsa.

Benefits for Diabetics:

Grilled chicken is a lean protein source that's excellent for blood sugar control. The mango salsa provides a healthy dose of vitamins and antioxidants, while the overall dish remains low in carbohydrates, making it suitable for a diabetic diet.

Per Serving:

Calories: 310 | Fat: 8g | Carbs: 25g | Fiber: 3g | Protein: 35g

Chapter 5: Fish and Seafood Recipes

Introduction to Fish and Seafood Recipes
Welcome to Chapter 5, dedicated to fish and seafood recipes that are both delicious and suitable for a diabetic-friendly diet. Fish and seafood are excellent sources of high-quality protein and omega-3 fatty acids, known for their heart-healthy benefits and importance in maintaining overall well-being.

This chapter offers a variety of dishes, from simple grilled fish to flavorful seafood stews, all designed with health and taste in mind. These recipes focus on incorporating fresh ingredients, herbs, and spices to enhance the natural flavors of the seafood while keeping the dishes nutritious and low in unhealthy fats and carbohydrates.

Enjoy exploring these ocean-inspired recipes, perfect for adding diversity and delight to your meal planning.

Lemon Garlic Baked Cod

Serves: 2
Prep time: 10 minutes / Cook time: 15 minutes

Ingredients:
- 2 cod fillets
- 1 lemon, juice and zest
- Salt and pepper to taste
- 2 tbsp olive oil
- 2 cloves garlic, minced
- Fresh parsley for garnish

Instructions:
1. Preheat the oven to 400°F (200°C).
2. Place cod fillets in a baking dish.
3. In a small bowl, mix together olive oil, lemon juice, lemon zest, and minced garlic.
4. Pour the lemon garlic mixture over the cod, ensuring the fillets are well coated.
5. Season with salt and pepper.
6. Bake for 15 minutes, or until the fish flakes easily with a fork.
7. Serve hot, garnished with fresh parsley and additional lemon slices if desired.

Benefits for Diabetics:
Cod is an excellent source of lean protein and contains vital nutrients, making it a great choice for blood sugar management. The use of lemon and garlic adds flavor without additional sugars or carbs, while olive oil provides healthy fats beneficial for heart health.

Per Serving:
Calories: 200 | Fat: 10g | Carbs: 2g | Fiber: 0g | Protein: 25g

Spicy Shrimp and Broccoli Stir-Fry

Serves: 2
Prep time: 15 minutes / Cook time: 10 minutes

Ingredients:
- 1/2 lb shrimp, peeled and deveined
- 2 cups broccoli florets
- 2 cloves garlic, minced
- 1 tsp chili sauce or paste (adjust to taste)
- 1 tsp sesame oil
- Salt to taste
- 1 bell pepper, sliced
- 1 tbsp soy sauce
- 2 tbsp vegetable oil

- Sesame seeds and green onions for garnish

Instructions:
1. Heat vegetable oil in a large skillet or wok over medium-high heat. Add garlic and stir-fry until fragrant.
2. Add shrimp and cook until they turn pink and are nearly cooked through. Remove from the skillet and set aside.
3. In the same skillet, add broccoli and bell pepper, stir-frying until tender-crisp.
4. Return the shrimp to the skillet. Add soy sauce, chili sauce, and sesame oil, stirring well to combine all ingredients and coat evenly.
5. Cook for an additional 2-3 minutes until everything is heated through and the sauce is slightly thickened.
6. Serve hot, garnished with sesame seeds and green onions.

Benefits for Diabetics:
Shrimp is a low-fat, high-protein food that's excellent for a diabetic diet. Broccoli adds fiber and an array of vitamins and minerals. The overall low carbohydrate content and high nutrient density of this dish make it an excellent choice for blood sugar management.

Per Serving:
Calories: 250 | Fat: 12g | Carbs: 10g | Fiber: 3g | Protein: 25g

Herb-Crusted Salmon with Spinach Salad

Serves: 2
Prep time: 15 minutes / Cook time: 15 minutes

Ingredients:
- 2 salmon fillets
- 1/4 cup mixed fresh herbs (such as dill, parsley, and chives), finely chopped
- 1/4 cup almond flour or breadcrumbs
- 1 lemon, juice and zest • 2 tbsp olive oil
- Salt and pepper to taste • 4 cups spinach leaves
- 1/2 red onion, thinly sliced
- Additional lemon wedges for serving

Instructions:
1. Preheat the oven to 400°F (200°C).
2. In a small bowl, mix together the chopped herbs, almond flour or breadcrumbs, lemon zest, salt, and pepper.
3. Brush the salmon fillets with lemon juice and olive oil. Press the herb mixture onto the top of each fillet to form a crust.
4. Place the salmon on a lined baking sheet and bake for 12-15 minutes or until the crust is golden and the salmon is cooked through.
5. While the salmon is baking, toss spinach leaves and red onion with a bit of olive oil and lemon juice for the salad.
6. Serve the herb-crusted salmon over the spinach salad, accompanied by additional lemon wedges.

Benefits for Diabetics:
Salmon is rich in omega-3 fatty acids, which are known for their heart-healthy benefits and potential to improve insulin

sensitivity. The high protein content and healthy fats in salmon help with blood sugar regulation, while the spinach provides fiber and essential nutrients.

Per Serving:
Calories: 370 | Fat: 22g | Carbs: 8g | Fiber: 3g | Protein: 35g

Grilled Tuna Steaks with Avocado Salsa

Serves: 2
Prep time: 20 minutes / Cook time: 10 minutes

Ingredients:
- 2 tuna steaks
- 1 ripe avocado, diced
- 1/2 cup cherry tomatoes, quartered
- 1/4 red onion, finely chopped
- 1 jalapeno, seeded and minced (optional)
- 1 lime, juice and zest
- 2 tbsp olive oil
- Salt and pepper to taste
- Fresh cilantro for garnish

Instructions:
1. Preheat the grill to medium-high heat.
2. Brush the tuna steaks with 1 tablespoon of olive oil and season with salt and pepper.
3. Grill the tuna for about 4-5 minutes on each side, or until desired doneness is reached.
4. Meanwhile, in a bowl, combine avocado, cherry tomatoes, red onion, jalapeno, lime juice, lime zest, and the remaining olive oil. Season with salt and mix gently to combine.
5. Serve the grilled tuna steaks topped with a generous scoop of avocado salsa.
6. Garnish with fresh cilantro before serving.

Benefits for Diabetics:
Tuna is an excellent source of protein and omega-3 fatty acids, contributing to cardiovascular health and aiding in blood sugar control. Avocado adds healthy fats and fiber, making the salsa not only flavorful but also beneficial for maintaining stable blood glucose levels.

Per Serving:
Calories: 400 | Fat: 24g | Carbs: 12g | Fiber: 6g | Protein: 35g

Pan-Seared Scallops with Lemon Butter Sauce

Serves: 2
Prep time: 10 minutes / Cook time: 10 minutes

Ingredients:
- 1/2 lb scallops, patted dry
- 2 tbsp butter
- 1 lemon, juice and zest
- 1 tbsp fresh parsley, chopped
- Salt and pepper to taste
- Olive oil for searing

Instructions:
1. Heat a bit of olive oil in a large skillet over medium-high heat.
2. Season the scallops with salt and pepper. Sear them for about 2 minutes on each side or until they have a golden crust and are just cooked through.
3. Remove scallops from the skillet and set aside.
4. In the same skillet, reduce heat to low and add butter, lemon juice, and lemon zest. Stir to combine and cook until the butter is melted and the sauce has slightly thickened.
5. Return the scallops to the skillet, coating them in the lemon butter sauce.
6. Serve the scallops drizzled with the sauce and garnished with fresh parsley.

Benefits for Diabetics:
Scallops are a low-fat, high-protein seafood option that's excellent for blood sugar control. The lemon butter sauce adds a touch of indulgence without a significant amount of carbohydrates, making this dish a luxurious yet health-conscious choice.

Per Serving:
Calories: 240 | Fat: 12g | Carbs: 5g | Fiber: 0g | Protein: 28g

Spicy Grilled Shrimp

Serves: 2
Prep time: 15 minutes (plus marination time) / Cook time: 5 minutes

Ingredients:
- 1/2 lb large shrimp, peeled and deveined
- 2 tbsp olive oil
- 1 tbsp paprika
- 1 tsp garlic powder
- Salt to taste
- 1/2 tsp cayenne pepper (adjust to taste)
- 1/2 lemon, juice and zest

Instructions:
1. In a bowl, combine olive oil, paprika, garlic powder, cayenne pepper, lemon juice, lemon zest, and salt. Add shrimp and toss to coat. Marinate for at least 30 minutes in the refrigerator.
2. Preheat grill to medium-high heat.
3. Thread shrimp onto skewers and grill for 2-3 minutes on each side, or until shrimp are pink and slightly charred.
4. Serve hot, garnished with additional lemon wedges and fresh herbs if desired.

Benefits for Diabetics:
Shrimp is a great source of protein and essential nutrients while being low in fat and carbohydrates, making it ideal for blood sugar control. The spices add flavor without extra calories or sugar, enhancing the dish's overall taste and health benefits.

Per Serving:
Calories: 200 | Fat: 10g | Carbs: 2g | Fiber: 0g | Protein: 24g

Baked Tilapia with Dill Sauce

Serves: 2
Prep time: 10 minutes / Cook time: 15 minutes

Ingredients:
- 2 tilapia fillets
- 1/4 cup Greek yogurt
- 1 tbsp fresh dill, chopped
- 1 tsp lemon juice
- 1 clove garlic, minced
- Salt and pepper to taste
- 1 tbsp olive oil

Instructions:
1. Preheat the oven to 375°F (190°C).
2. Place tilapia fillets in a baking dish and season with salt and pepper.
3. In a small bowl, mix together Greek yogurt, dill, lemon juice, and garlic. Spread the dill sauce evenly over the

tilapia fillets.

4. Drizzle olive oil over the top of the fillets.

5. Bake for 15 minutes, or until the fish flakes easily with a fork.

6. Serve hot, with extra lemon wedges on the side if desired.

Benefits for Diabetics:

Tilapia is a lean source of protein, which helps in maintaining blood sugar levels and promoting satiety. The addition of Greek yogurt provides a creamy texture and healthy fats without a significant amount of carbohydrates, while dill adds a burst of flavor and potential digestive benefits.

Per Serving:

Calories: 220 | Fat: 10g | Carbs: 3g | Fiber: 0g | Protein: 30g

Poached Salmon in Tomato Basil Sauce

Serves: 2

Prep time: 10 minutes / Cook time: 20 minutes

Ingredients:

- 2 salmon fillets
- 1 can diced tomatoes
- 1/4 cup fresh basil, chopped
- 2 cloves garlic, minced
- 1/2 onion, chopped
- 1 tbsp olive oil
- Salt and pepper to taste

Instructions:

1. Heat olive oil in a large skillet over medium heat. Add garlic and onion, cooking until translucent.

2. Add diced tomatoes and half of the basil to the skillet. Bring to a simmer.

3. Season the salmon fillets with salt and pepper, then place them in the skillet with the tomato basil sauce.

4. Cover and let the salmon poach for 12-15 minutes, or until cooked through and flaky.

5. Serve the salmon topped with the tomato basil sauce and garnished with the remaining fresh basil.

Benefits for Diabetics:

Salmon is well-known for its omega-3 fatty acids, which are beneficial for heart health and inflammation reduction. The tomatoes provide lycopene and other antioxidants, while the overall low carbohydrate content of the dish helps maintain stable blood sugar levels.

Per Serving:

Calories: 350 | Fat: 20g | Carbs: 8g | Fiber: 2g | Protein: 35g

Garlic Butter Scallops with Herbs

Serves: 2

Prep time: 10 minutes / Cook time: 10 minutes

Ingredients:

- 1/2 lb scallops
- 2 tbsp butter
- 2 cloves garlic, minced
- 1 tbsp fresh parsley, chopped
- 1 tbsp fresh chives, chopped
- Salt and pepper to taste
- Lemon wedges for serving

Instructions:

1. Pat the scallops dry and season with salt and pepper.

2. Heat butter in a large skillet over medium-high heat. Add garlic and cook until fragrant.

3. Add the scallops to the skillet, searing for about 2 minutes on each side or until they have a golden crust and are just cooked through.

4. Sprinkle the scallops with parsley and chives, tossing

gently to coat.

5. Serve hot, with lemon wedges on the side for an extra zesty flavor.

Benefits for Diabetics:

Scallops are a great source of lean protein and B vitamins, essential for energy and metabolism. The dish is low in carbohydrates, and the herbs add additional flavor without the need for sugary sauces or seasonings.

Per Serving:

Calories: 250 | Fat: 12g | Carbs: 5g | Fiber: 0g | Protein: 30g

Asian-Style Steamed Mussels

Serves: 2

Prep time: 15 minutes / Cook time: 10 minutes

Ingredients:

- 1 lb mussels, cleaned and debearded
- 2 cloves garlic, minced
- 1 inch piece of ginger, minced
- 1/4 cup soy sauce
- 1/4 cup water
- 1 tbsp sesame oil
- 1 green onion, chopped
- 1/2 red chili, sliced (optional)
- Fresh cilantro for garnish

Instructions:

1. In a large pot, heat sesame oil over medium heat. Add garlic and ginger, sautéing until fragrant.

2. Add soy sauce, water, and red chili if using. Bring to a simmer.

3. Add the mussels to the pot, cover, and steam for about 5-7 minutes or until the mussels have opened. Discard any that do not open.

4. Once cooked, sprinkle the mussels with chopped green onions and fresh cilantro.

5. Serve hot, with the aromatic broth and extra soy sauce on the side for dipping.

Benefits for Diabetics:

Mussels are a lean source of protein and omega-3 fatty acids, which are beneficial for heart health and maintaining healthy blood sugar levels. The dish is low in carbohydrates, focusing on the natural flavors of the seafood and spices to create a satisfying meal.

Per Serving:

Calories: 290 | Fat: 10g | Carbs: 10g | Fiber: 0g | Protein: 38g

Chili Lime Fish Tacos

Serves: 2

Prep time: 20 minutes / Cook time: 10 minutes

Ingredients:

- 2 white fish fillets (such as cod or tilapia)
- 1 tbsp olive oil
- 1 tsp chili powder
- 1 lime, juice and zest
- 4 small whole grain or low-carb tortillas
- 1 cup cabbage, shredded
- 1/4 cup fresh cilantro, chopped
- Salt and pepper to taste
- Additional lime wedges for serving

Instructions:

1. Season the fish fillets with chili powder, lime zest, salt, and pepper.

2. Heat olive oil in a skillet over medium heat. Cook the fish for 4-5 minutes on each side or until flaky and cooked through.
3. Break the cooked fish into chunks.
4. Warm the tortillas according to package instructions.
5. Assemble the tacos by placing fish chunks on each tortilla, topped with shredded cabbage and a drizzle of lime juice.
6. Garnish with fresh cilantro and serve with lime wedges on the side.

Benefits for Diabetics:
White fish is an excellent source of lean protein, which is beneficial for blood sugar management. Whole grain or low-carb tortillas provide a healthier alternative to traditional tortillas, and the fresh vegetables add fiber and essential nutrients.

Per Serving:
Calories: 300 | Fat: 12g | Carbs: 24g | Fiber: 6g | Protein: 25g

Mediterranean Grilled Swordfish

Serves: 2

Prep time: 15 minutes (plus marination time) / Cook time: 10 minutes

Ingredients:
- 2 swordfish steaks
- 2 tbsp olive oil
- 1 lemon, juice and zest
- 2 cloves garlic, minced
- 1 tsp dried oregano
- 1 tsp dried basil
- Salt and pepper to taste
- Fresh parsley for garnish

Instructions:
1. In a bowl, combine olive oil, lemon juice, lemon zest, garlic, oregano, basil, salt, and pepper. Marinate the swordfish steaks in this mixture for at least 30 minutes in the refrigerator.
2. Preheat the grill to medium-high heat.
3. Grill the swordfish for about 5 minutes on each side, or until the fish is cooked through and grill marks appear.
4. Serve hot, garnished with fresh parsley and additional lemon wedges on the side.

Benefits for Diabetics:
Swordfish is a high-protein, low-carbohydrate option that's also rich in omega-3 fatty acids, known for their heart-healthy benefits. The herbs and lemon add flavor without extra carbs, making this dish both nutritious and delicious.

Per Serving:
Calories: 370 | Fat: 18g | Carbs: 3g | Fiber: 1g | Protein: 45g

Honey Soy Glazed Salmon

Serves: 2

Prep time: 10 minutes / Cook time: 15 minutes

Ingredients:
- 2 salmon fillets
- 2 tbsp soy sauce
- 1 tbsp honey or a suitable sweetener
- 1 garlic clove, minced
- 1 tsp ginger, grated
- 1 tbsp olive oil
- Sesame seeds for garnish

Instructions:
1. Preheat the oven to 400°F (200°C).

2. In a small bowl, whisk together soy sauce, honey or sweetener, garlic, and ginger to create the glaze.
3. Place salmon fillets on a lined baking sheet and brush them with olive oil.
4. Spoon the honey soy glaze over the salmon, ensuring they are well coated.
5. Bake for 12-15 minutes, or until the salmon is cooked through and the glaze has caramelized.
6. Serve hot, sprinkled with sesame seeds.

Benefits for Diabetics:
Salmon is an excellent source of omega-3 fatty acids and protein, aiding in cardiovascular health and blood sugar regulation. The honey soy glaze provides a touch of sweetness without a significant sugar load, especially when a suitable sweetener is used.

Per Serving:
Calories: 330 | Fat: 15g | Carbs: 10g | Fiber: 0g | Protein: 35g

Coconut Curry Shrimp

Serves: 2

Prep time: 15 minutes / Cook time: 20 minutes

Ingredients:
- 1/2 lb shrimp, peeled and deveined
- 1 can coconut milk
- 1 tbsp curry powder
- 1/2 onion, chopped
- 1 bell pepper, sliced
- 1 tomato, diced
- 2 cloves garlic, minced
- 1 tsp ginger, grated
- 1 tbsp olive oil
- Salt and pepper to taste
- Fresh cilantro for garnish

Instructions:
1. Heat olive oil in a large skillet over medium heat. Add onion, garlic, and ginger, cooking until softened.
2. Stir in curry powder and cook for an additional minute until fragrant.
3. Pour in coconut milk and bring the mixture to a simmer.
4. Add the shrimp, bell pepper, and tomato to the skillet. Simmer for 10-15 minutes, or until the shrimp are cooked through and the sauce has thickened.
5. Season with salt and pepper to taste.
6. Serve hot, garnished with fresh cilantro.

Benefits for Diabetics:
Shrimp is a lean protein source, making it great for blood sugar control. The coconut milk provides healthy fats and the curry spices offer anti-inflammatory benefits, while the overall dish remains relatively low in carbohydrates.

Per Serving:
Calories: 400 | Fat: 28g | Carbs: 12g | Fiber: 2g | Protein: 25g

Seared Scallops with Asparagus

Serves: 2

Prep time: 10 minutes / Cook time: 10 minutes

Ingredients:
- 1/2 lb scallops
- 1 lb asparagus, trimmed
- 2 tbsp olive oil
- 1 lemon, juice and zest
- Salt and pepper to taste
- Fresh herbs for garnish (such as parsley or chives)

Instructions:
1. Pat the scallops dry and season with salt and pepper.

2. Heat 1 tablespoon of olive oil in a skillet over medium-high heat. Sear the scallops for about 2 minutes on each side or until they have a golden crust and are just cooked through. Remove from the skillet and set aside.
3. In the same skillet, add the remaining olive oil and asparagus. Cook until the asparagus is tender-crisp, about 5-7 minutes. Season with lemon juice and zest.
4. Serve the seared scallops over the asparagus, garnished with fresh herbs.

Benefits for Diabetics:
Scallops provide a high-quality, lean protein source that's excellent for maintaining stable blood sugar levels. Asparagus is rich in fiber, vitamins, and minerals, contributing to a nutritious meal that's low in carbohydrates and high in taste.

Per Serving:
Calories: 250 | Fat: 14g | Carbs: 10g | Fiber: 4g | Protein: 24g

Blackened Catfish with Avocado Slaw

Serves: 2
Prep time: 20 minutes / Cook time: 10 minutes

Ingredients:
- 2 catfish fillets
- 1 tbsp blackening seasoning
- 1 avocado, diced
- 2 cups cabbage slaw mix
- 1/4 cup cilantro, chopped
- 2 tbsp lime juice
- 1 tbsp olive oil
- Salt and pepper to taste

Instructions:
1. Generously coat the catfish fillets with blackening seasoning.
2. Heat olive oil in a skillet over medium-high heat. Add the catfish and cook for about 4-5 minutes on each side, or until the outside is crispy and the fish is cooked through.
3. In a bowl, combine the cabbage slaw mix, diced avocado, cilantro, and lime juice. Season with salt and pepper and toss gently.
4. Serve the blackened catfish over a bed of avocado slaw.

Benefits for Diabetics:
Catfish is a good source of lean protein, which is beneficial for blood sugar control. The avocado provides healthy fats and fiber, aiding in satiety and cardiovascular health. The overall dish is low in carbohydrates, focusing on flavors and nutrients beneficial for diabetes management.

Per Serving:
Calories: 350 | Fat: 20g | Carbs: 12g | Fiber: 6g | Protein: 30g

Lemon Herb Haddock Packets

Serves: 2
Prep time: 10 minutes / Cook time: 15 minutes

Ingredients:
- 2 haddock fillets
- 1 lemon, thinly sliced
- 1 zucchini, thinly sliced
- 1 carrot, thinly sliced
- 1 tbsp fresh dill, chopped
- 1 tbsp olive oil
- Salt and pepper to taste
- Parchment paper

Instructions:
1. Preheat the oven to 400°F (200°C).
2. Cut two large pieces of parchment paper, enough to wrap each fillet and vegetables.
3. Place a haddock fillet on each piece of parchment, top with lemon slices, zucchini, carrot, and dill. Drizzle with olive oil and season with salt and pepper.
4. Fold the parchment paper over the fish and vegetables, crimping the edges to seal the packets.
5. Place the packets on a baking sheet and bake for 15 minutes, or until the fish is cooked through and vegetables are tender.
6. Serve directly in the parchment for an easy and elegant presentation.

Benefits for Diabetics:
Haddock is a low-fat, high-protein fish, making it an excellent choice for a diabetic diet. The inclusion of vegetables adds fiber and nutrients, while the cooking method preserves the moisture and flavor of the fish without the need for extra fats or carbohydrates.

Per Serving:
Calories: 220 | Fat: 8g | Carbs: 8g | Fiber: 2g | Protein: 30g

Spicy Thai Seafood Soup

Serves: 2
Prep time: 20 minutes / Cook time: 20 minutes

Ingredients:
- 1/2 lb mixed seafood (shrimp, scallops, mussels)
- 4 cups seafood or vegetable broth
- 1 stalk lemongrass, finely chopped
- 1 inch piece ginger, sliced
- 2 hot peppers, sliced (adjust to taste)
- 1/2 cup mushrooms, sliced
- 1 tomato, diced
- 1 lime, juice and zest
- 1 tbsp fish sauce
- Fresh cilantro and basil for garnish

Instructions:
1. In a large pot, bring the broth to a boil. Add lemongrass, ginger, and hot peppers. Simmer for 10 minutes to infuse the broth.
2. Add the mixed seafood, mushrooms, and tomato to the pot. Cook until the seafood is cooked through and the mussels have opened, about 5-7 minutes.
3. Stir in lime juice and fish sauce, adjusting the seasoning to taste.
4. Serve the soup hot, garnished with fresh cilantro and basil leaves.

Benefits for Diabetics:
The variety of seafood in this soup provides high-quality protein and omega-3 fatty acids, beneficial for heart health and blood sugar regulation. The spicy broth helps boost metabolism and adds rich flavor without added sugars or unhealthy fats.

Per Serving:
Calories: 250 | Fat: 6g | Carbs: 15g | Fiber: 2g | Protein: 35g

Cajun-Style Grilled Oysters

Serves: 2
Prep time: 15 minutes / Cook time: 10 minutes

Ingredients:
- 12 fresh oysters, shucked
- 4 tbsp butter, melted
- 1 tsp Cajun seasoning
- 1 garlic clove, minced

- 1/2 lemon, juice and zest
- Fresh parsley, chopped for garnish
- Lemon wedges for serving

Instructions:
1. Preheat your grill to medium-high heat.
2. In a small bowl, combine melted butter, Cajun seasoning, garlic, lemon juice, and lemon zest to make the Cajun butter sauce.
3. Place the shucked oysters on the half shell directly on the grill.
4. Spoon a small amount of Cajun butter sauce onto each oyster.
5. Grill the oysters for about 5-6 minutes, or until the edges of the oysters start to curl slightly and they are heated through.
6. Remove from the grill and serve hot, garnished with chopped parsley and lemon wedges on the side.

Benefits for Diabetics:
Oysters are an excellent source of zinc and other essential minerals, while being low in carbohydrates. The Cajun-style preparation adds a wealth of flavor without relying on sugary sauces or breading, making this a suitable and exciting option for those managing diabetes.

Per Serving:
Calories: 150 | Fat: 10g | Carbs: 4g | Fiber: 0g | Protein: 10g

Lemon Garlic Shrimp Skewers

Serves: 2
Prep time: 15 minutes / Cook time: 10 minutes

Ingredients:
- 12 large shrimp, peeled and deveined
- 2 tablespoons olive oil
- Juice and zest of 1 lemon
- 2 garlic cloves, minced
- Salt and pepper to taste
- Fresh parsley, chopped for garnish

Instructions:
1. Preheat your grill or grill pan to medium-high heat.
2. In a bowl, combine olive oil, lemon juice and zest, minced garlic, salt, and pepper.
3. Add shrimp to the marinade and let sit for 10 minutes.
4. Thread the shrimp onto skewers.
5. Grill for 2-3 minutes on each side or until shrimp are pink and opaque.
6. Garnish with fresh parsley and serve immediately.

Benefits for Diabetics:
Shrimp is a high-protein, low-fat option that's excellent for blood sugar management. The addition of lemon and garlic adds flavor without adding carbs, making it a perfect dish for maintaining a balanced diabetic diet.

Per Serving:
Calories: 200 | Fat: 10g | Carbs: 3g | Fiber: 0g | Protein: 24g

Herb-Crusted Cod with Zucchini Noodles

Serves: 2
Prep time: 20 minutes / Cook time: 15 minutes

Ingredients:
- 2 cod fillets (about 6 ounces each)

- 1/4 cup almond flour
- 1 tablespoon fresh parsley, finely chopped
- 1 teaspoon fresh thyme, finely chopped
- 1 garlic clove, minced
- Salt and pepper to taste
- 2 tablespoons olive oil
- 2 medium zucchinis, spiralized

Instructions:
1. Preheat your oven to 400°F (200°C).
2. In a bowl, combine almond flour, parsley, thyme, garlic, salt, and pepper.
3. Brush each cod fillet with olive oil and press the herb mixture onto the top of each fillet.
4. Place fillets on a baking tray and bake for 12-15 minutes or until the crust is golden and fish flakes easily.
5. While the fish is baking, heat a non-stick pan over medium heat and sauté the spiralized zucchini in olive oil until tender.
6. Serve the herb-crusted cod over a bed of zucchini noodles.

Benefits for Diabetics:
Cod is a low-fat protein source, and when paired with fiber-rich zucchini noodles, it makes for a meal that's filling without spiking blood sugar levels. The herbs add a burst of flavor without extra calories or carbohydrates.

Per Serving:
Calories: 290 | Fat: 16g | Carbs: 8g | Fiber: 3g | Protein: 30g

Mediterranean Tuna Salad

Serves: 2
Prep time: 15 minutes

Ingredients:
- 1 can (6 ounces) tuna in water, drained
- 1/4 cup diced red bell pepper
- 1/4 cup diced cucumber
- 1/4 cup cherry tomatoes, halved
- 2 tablespoons sliced olives
- 1 tablespoon capers
- 2 tablespoons olive oil
- 1 tablespoon red wine vinegar
- Salt and pepper to taste
- Mixed greens for serving

Instructions:
1. In a large bowl, mix together the tuna, red bell pepper, cucumber, cherry tomatoes, olives, and capers.
2. In a small bowl, whisk together olive oil, red wine vinegar, salt, and pepper.
3. Pour the dressing over the tuna mixture and toss to coat evenly.
4. Serve the tuna salad over a bed of mixed greens.

Benefits for Diabetics:
This salad is rich in omega-3 fatty acids from the tuna and loaded with antioxidants from the fresh vegetables. It's a balanced meal that's low in carbohydrates and high in nutrients, ideal for blood sugar management.

Per Serving:
Calories: 230 | Fat: 15g | Carbs: 6g | Fiber: 2g | Protein: 20g

Spicy Grilled Salmon with Avocado Salsa

Serves: 2

Prep time: 20 minutes / Cook time: 10 minutes

Ingredients:

- 2 salmon fillets (about 6 ounces each)
- 1 teaspoon chili powder
- 1/2 teaspoon cumin
- Salt and pepper to taste
- 1 ripe avocado, diced
- 1/4 cup diced tomato
- 1/4 cup diced red onion
- Juice of 1 lime
- Fresh cilantro for garnish

Instructions:

1. Preheat your grill to medium-high heat.
2. Season the salmon fillets with chili powder, cumin, salt, and pepper.
3. Grill the salmon for 5 minutes on each side or until desired doneness is reached.
4. In a bowl, combine avocado, tomato, red onion, and lime juice.
5. Serve the grilled salmon topped with avocado salsa and garnished with fresh cilantro.

Benefits for Diabetics:

Salmon is an excellent source of omega-3 fatty acids, which are beneficial for heart health. The avocado adds healthy fats and fiber, making this dish a nutrient-dense option that supports blood sugar regulation.

Per Serving:

Calories: 360 | Fat: 22g | Carbs: 9g | Fiber: 7g | Protein: 34g

Sesame Ginger Seared Scallops

Serves: 2

Prep time: 10 minutes / Cook time: 10 minutes

Ingredients:

- 12 large scallops
- 1 tablespoon sesame oil
- 1 teaspoon grated ginger
- 1 garlic clove, minced
- 2 tablespoons low-sodium soy sauce
- 1 teaspoon honey or a sugar-free sweetener
- Sesame seeds and sliced green onions for garnish

Instructions:

1. Rinse scallops and pat dry with a paper towel.
2. Heat sesame oil in a large skillet over medium-high heat.
3. Add scallops to the skillet, searing for about 2 minutes on each side or until a golden crust forms.
4. Remove scallops and set aside.
5. In the same skillet, add ginger, garlic, soy sauce, and honey. Cook for 1 minute until the sauce is slightly thickened.
6. Return scallops to the skillet and toss them in the sauce.
7. Serve scallops garnished with sesame seeds and sliced green onions.

Benefits for Diabetics:

Scallops are a lean protein source, making them ideal for blood sugar management. The sesame and ginger add a burst of flavor without significant carbs, while the soy sauce provides umami depth with minimal impact on glucose levels.

Per Serving:

Calories: 210 | Fat: 8g | Carbs: 10g | Fiber: 0g | Protein: 24g

Baked Halibut with Lemon Caper Sauce

Serves: 2

Prep time: 15 minutes / Cook time: 15 minutes

Ingredients:

- 2 halibut fillets (about 6 ounces each)
- 1 tablespoon olive oil
- Salt and pepper to taste
- 2 tablespoons capers, drained
- Juice of 1 lemon
- 1 garlic clove, minced
- 1 tablespoon fresh parsley, chopped

Instructions:

1. Preheat oven to 375°F (190°C).
2. Place halibut fillets on a greased baking sheet. Drizzle with olive oil and season with salt and pepper.
3. Bake for 12-15 minutes or until fish flakes easily with a fork.
4. While the fish is baking, prepare the sauce by combining capers, lemon juice, and minced garlic in a small bowl.
5. Remove halibut from the oven and spoon lemon caper sauce over the fillets.
6. Garnish with fresh parsley before serving.

Benefits for Diabetics:

Halibut is a great source of high-quality protein and omega-3 fatty acids, beneficial for overall health and blood sugar control. The lemon and capers add a high-impact flavor without additional carbs or calories.

Per Serving:

Calories: 280 | Fat: 12g | Carbs: 3g | Fiber: 0g | Protein: 38g

Chili Lime Tilapia with Avocado Crema

Serves: 2

Prep time: 15 minutes / Cook time: 10 minutes

Ingredients:

- 2 tilapia fillets (about 6 ounces each)
- 1 teaspoon chili powder • Juice and zest of 1 lime
- Salt and pepper to taste • 1 ripe avocado
- 1/4 cup Greek yogurt • Fresh cilantro for garnish

Instructions:

1. Preheat your grill or grill pan to medium-high heat.
2. Season the tilapia fillets with chili powder, lime zest, salt, and pepper.
3. Grill the tilapia for about 3-4 minutes on each side or until fully cooked.
4. Meanwhile, mash the avocado and mix with Greek yogurt, lime juice, and a pinch of salt to make the avocado crema.
5. Serve the grilled tilapia topped with a dollop of avocado crema and garnished with fresh cilantro.

Benefits for Diabetics:

Tilapia is a lean source of protein, while avocado provides healthy fats and fiber, contributing to a slower digestion and more stable blood sugar levels. The chili and lime add a pop of flavor without extra sugar or carbs.

Per Serving:

Calories: 320 | Fat: 18g | Carbs: 8g | Fiber: 5g | Protein: 34g

Pesto Grilled Scallops

Serves: 2

Prep time: 10 minutes / Cook time: 6 minutes

Ingredients:
- 12 large scallops
- 2 tablespoons homemade or store-bought pesto
- 1 tablespoon olive oil • Salt and pepper to taste
- Lemon wedges for serving

Instructions:
1. Preheat your grill or grill pan to medium-high heat.
2. Toss scallops with olive oil, salt, and pepper.
3. Grill scallops for about 2-3 minutes on each side, until they have a nice sear and are cooked through.
4. Remove from grill and coat each scallop with pesto.
5. Serve immediately with lemon wedges on the side.

Benefits for Diabetics:
Scallops are a lean protein source, excellent for blood sugar management. The pesto adds flavor without unnecessary sugars, and the healthy fats in the olive oil contribute to satiety.

Per Serving:
Calories: 220 | Fat: 10g | Carbs: 5g | Fiber: 0g | Protein: 26g

Curried Coconut Shrimp

Serves: 2

Prep time: 15 minutes / Cook time: 15 minutes

Ingredients:
- 12 large shrimp, peeled and deveined
- 1 tablespoon coconut oil
- 1 tablespoon curry powder
- 1 teaspoon grated ginger
- 1/2 cup coconut milk
- 1 garlic clove, minced
- Salt to taste
- Fresh cilantro for garnish

Instructions:
1. Heat coconut oil in a large skillet over medium heat.
2. Add garlic and ginger, sautéing until fragrant.
3. Stir in curry powder and then add the coconut milk, bringing the mixture to a simmer.
4. Add shrimp to the skillet, cooking until they are pink and cooked through, about 5 minutes.
5. Season with salt to taste.
6. Garnish with fresh cilantro and serve.

Benefits for Diabetics:
This dish provides a hearty dose of protein from the shrimp and healthy fats from the coconut milk, aiding in satiety and blood sugar control. The curry spices add a depth of flavor without significant carbohydrates.

Per Serving:
Calories: 300 | Fat: 18g | Carbs: 8g | Fiber: 1g | Protein: 28g

Smoked Salmon and Avocado Salad

Serves: 2

Prep time: 10 minutes

Ingredients:
- 4 ounces smoked salmon
- 1 ripe avocado, sliced
- 2 cups mixed salad greens
- 1/4 red onion, thinly sliced
- 2 tablespoons olive oil
- 1 tablespoon lemon juice
- Salt and pepper to taste
- Capers for garnish (optional)

Instructions:
1. Arrange mixed greens on two plates.
2. Top with smoked salmon, sliced avocado, and red onion.
3. Whisk together olive oil, lemon juice, salt, and pepper to create a dressing.
4. Drizzle the dressing over the salad.
5. Garnish with capers if desired and serve.

Benefits for Diabetics:
Smoked salmon is an excellent source of omega-3 fatty acids and protein, while avocado adds healthy fats and fiber, contributing to steady blood sugar levels and heart health.

Per Serving:
Calories: 320 | Fat: 25g | Carbs: 9g | Fiber: 7g | Protein: 15g

Garlic Butter Baked Trout

Serves: 2

Prep time: 10 minutes / Cook time: 15 minutes

Ingredients:
- 2 trout fillets (about 6 ounces each)
- 2 tablespoons butter, melted
- 2 garlic cloves, minced
- 1 tablespoon parsley, chopped
- Lemon slices for garnish
- Salt and pepper to taste

Instructions:
1. Preheat oven to 375°F (190°C).
2. Place trout fillets on a baking sheet lined with parchment paper.
3. Mix melted butter with minced garlic and parsley. Brush over trout fillets.
4. Season with salt and pepper.
5. Bake for 12-15 minutes or until fish flakes easily with a fork.
6. Garnish with lemon slices and additional parsley before serving.

Benefits for Diabetics:
Trout is a great source of lean protein and omega-3 fatty acids, which are essential for heart health and blood sugar management. The garlic butter adds flavor without excessive carbohydrates.

Per Serving:
Calories: 280 | Fat: 16g | Carbs: 1g | Fiber: 0g | Protein: 31g

Spicy Cajun Crab Cakes

Serves: 2

Prep time: 20 minutes / Cook time: 10 minutes

Ingredients:
- 8 ounces lump crab meat
- 1/4 cup almond flour
- 1 egg, beaten
- 2 tablespoons mayonnaise
- 1 teaspoon Cajun seasoning
- 1 green onion, finely chopped

- 1 teaspoon Dijon mustard
- Olive oil for frying
- Lemon wedges for serving

Instructions:
1. In a bowl, mix together crab meat, almond flour, beaten egg, mayonnaise, Cajun seasoning, green onion, and Dijon mustard until well combined.
2. Form the mixture into small patties.
3. Heat olive oil in a skillet over medium heat.
4. Fry crab cakes for about 4-5 minutes on each side or until golden and crispy.
5. Serve hot with lemon wedges.

Benefits for Diabetics:
Crab is an excellent low-fat protein source. These crab cakes are made with almond flour instead of traditional breadcrumbs, reducing the carbohydrate content significantly and making them a diabetic-friendly choice.

Per Serving:
Calories: 280 | Fat: 18g | Carbs: 8g | Fiber: 3g | Protein: 24g

Asian-Style Steamed Mussels

Serves: 2
Prep time: 15 minutes / Cook time: 10 minutes

Ingredients:
- 1 pound mussels, cleaned and de-bearded
- 1 tablespoon sesame oil
- 2 garlic cloves, minced
- 1 inch piece of ginger, minced
- 1/4 cup low-sodium soy sauce
- 1/4 cup water
- 1 green onion, sliced
- Fresh cilantro for garnish

Instructions:
1. In a large pot, heat sesame oil over medium heat.
2. Add garlic and ginger, sautéing until fragrant.
3. Add mussels, soy sauce, and water to the pot. Cover and steam for about 5-7 minutes until mussels have opened.
4. Discard any mussels that do not open.
5. Serve hot, garnished with green onion and fresh cilantro.

Benefits for Diabetics:
Mussels are a high-protein, low-fat seafood option, making them excellent for blood sugar control. The aromatic flavors from the ginger and garlic provide depth without adding sugar or excess carbs.

Per Serving:
Calories: 240 | Fat: 10g | Carbs: 10g | Fiber: 0g | Protein: 28g

Grilled Octopus with Olive Tapenade

Serves: 2
Prep time: 20 minutes / Cook time: 10 minutes

Ingredients:
- 1 medium-sized octopus, cleaned and tentacles separated
- 2 tablespoons olive oil • 1 cup mixed olives, pitted
- 1 garlic clove • 1 teaspoon capers
- 1 tablespoon lemon juice
- Fresh parsley for garnish

Instructions:
1. Preheat grill to medium-high heat.

2. Boil the octopus in a pot of water for about 40-60 minutes until tender, then drain and let cool.
3. Once cooled, toss the octopus tentacles with 1 tablespoon of olive oil and place on the grill. Cook for about 3-4 minutes on each side until charred.
4. For the tapenade, blend olives, garlic, capers, and lemon juice in a food processor until smooth. Drizzle in the remaining olive oil as you blend.
5. Serve the grilled octopus topped with olive tapenade and garnished with fresh parsley.

Benefits for Diabetics:
Octopus is an excellent source of lean protein, important for blood sugar management. The olive tapenade provides healthy fats and adds a burst of flavor without added sugars.

Per Serving:
Calories: 310 | Fat: 18g | Carbs: 8g | Fiber: 3g | Protein: 30g

Lime-Cilantro Tilapia with Mango Salsa

Serves: 2
Prep time: 20 minutes / Cook time: 10 minutes

Ingredients:
- 2 tilapia fillets (about 6 ounces each)
- Juice of 2 limes • 1 tablespoon olive oil
- 1/4 cup chopped cilantro • Salt and pepper to taste
- 1 mango, diced • 1/4 red bell pepper, diced
- 1/4 red onion, diced • 1 jalapeno, minced (optional)
- Additional lime wedges for serving

Instructions:
1. Marinate the tilapia fillets in lime juice, olive oil, half of the cilantro, salt, and pepper for 15 minutes.
2. Preheat your grill or grill pan to medium heat.
3. Grill tilapia for about 4-5 minutes on each side or until fully cooked.
4. For the mango salsa, combine diced mango, red bell pepper, red onion, jalapeno, and the remaining cilantro in a bowl.
5. Serve the grilled tilapia topped with mango salsa and additional lime wedges on the side.

Benefits for Diabetics:
Tilapia is a lean protein, ideal for weight management and blood sugar control. The mango adds a natural sweetness to the dish, providing essential vitamins without excessive sugar when consumed in moderation.

Per Serving:
Calories: 280 | Fat: 10g | Carbs: 18g | Fiber: 2g | Protein: 34g

Pan-Seared Sole with Asparagus

Serves: 2
Prep time: 10 minutes / Cook time: 12 minutes

Ingredients:
- 2 sole fillets (about 6 ounces each)
- 1 bunch asparagus, trimmed
- 2 tablespoons olive oil
- 1 lemon, juice, and zest
- Salt and pepper to taste
- Fresh dill for garnish

Instructions:
1. Heat 1 tablespoon of olive oil in a pan over medium heat.

2. Season the sole fillets with salt and pepper, then place them in the pan. Cook for about 2-3 minutes on each side or until golden and flaky.
3. In another pan, heat the remaining olive oil and sauté the asparagus until tender-crisp, about 5 minutes.
4. Drizzle lemon juice over the cooked sole and asparagus.
5. Serve the sole fillets with asparagus on the side, garnished with lemon zest and fresh dill.

Benefits for Diabetics:
Sole is a low-fat, high-protein fish that's excellent for a diabetic diet. Asparagus is a nutrient-rich vegetable that's high in fiber and low in carbohydrates, supporting stable blood sugar levels.

Per Serving:
Calories: 250 | Fat: 14g | Carbs: 6g | Fiber: 2g | Protein: 26g

Poached Salmon in Dill Sauce

Serves: 2

Prep time: 15 minutes / Cook time: 10 minutes

Ingredients:
- 2 salmon fillets (about 6 ounces each)
- 1 cup water or fish stock
- 1/2 cup Greek yogurt
- 2 tablespoons fresh dill, chopped
- 1 teaspoon lemon zest
- Salt and pepper to taste
- Lemon slices for garnish

Instructions:
1. In a skillet, bring water or fish stock to a simmer.
2. Add the salmon fillets, cover, and poach for about 6-8 minutes, until cooked through.
3. In a bowl, mix Greek yogurt, dill, lemon zest, salt, and pepper to make the dill sauce.
4. Remove the salmon from the skillet and plate.
5. Spoon the dill sauce over the salmon and garnish with lemon slices.

Benefits for Diabetics:
Salmon is high in omega-3 fatty acids and protein, supporting cardiovascular health and helping manage blood sugar. The Greek yogurt in the sauce provides a healthy, creamy texture without the added fat and carbs of traditional cream sauces.

Per Serving:
Calories: 360 | Fat: 22g | Carbs: 3g | Fiber: 0g | Protein: 34g

Roasted Monkfish with Mediterranean Vegetables

Serves: 2

Prep time: 15 minutes / Cook time: 25 minutes

Ingredients:
- 2 monkfish tails (about 6 ounces each)
- 1 zucchini, sliced
- 1 small eggplant, sliced
- 3 tablespoons olive oil
- 1 teaspoon dried oregano
- Salt and pepper to taste
- 1 bell pepper, sliced
- 1 red onion, sliced
- Fresh basil for garnish

Instructions:
1. Preheat oven to 400°F (200°C).
2. Place the sliced vegetables on a baking sheet, drizzle with 2 tablespoons of olive oil, sprinkle with oregano, salt, and pepper, and toss to coat.
3. Roast the vegetables for about 15 minutes.
4. Meanwhile, season the monkfish tails with salt and pepper.
5. Heat the remaining olive oil in a skillet over medium heat and sear the monkfish on all sides until golden.
6. Place the seared monkfish on top of the vegetables and return to the oven. Roast for an additional 10 minutes or until the fish is cooked through.
7. Serve the monkfish with the roasted vegetables, garnished with fresh basil.

Benefits for Diabetics:
Monkfish is a low-fat, high-protein choice that's excellent for maintaining blood sugar levels. The medley of Mediterranean vegetables provides vitamins, minerals, and fiber, promoting overall health and aiding in blood sugar control.

Per Serving:
Calories: 340 | Fat: 18g | Carbs: 14g | Fiber: 5g | Protein: 30g

Shrimp and Broccoli Stir-Fry

Serves: 2

Prep time: 10 minutes / Cook time: 10 minutes

Ingredients:
- 12 large shrimp, peeled and deveined
- 2 cups broccoli florets
- 1 tablespoon olive oil
- 2 garlic cloves, minced
- 1 teaspoon grated ginger
- 2 tablespoons low-sodium soy sauce
- 1 teaspoon sesame oil
- 1 teaspoon honey or a sugar-free sweetener
- Sesame seeds for garnish

Instructions:
1. Heat olive oil in a large skillet or wok over medium-high heat.
2. Add garlic and ginger, sautéing until fragrant.
3. Add broccoli and stir-fry for about 3-4 minutes until it begins to soften.
4. Add shrimp and continue to stir-fry until they are pink and cooked through.
5. In a small bowl, whisk together soy sauce, sesame oil, and honey. Pour over the shrimp and broccoli, tossing to coat evenly.
6. Cook for an additional 1-2 minutes, then remove from heat.
7. Garnish with sesame seeds before serving.

Benefits for Diabetics:
This stir-fry is a great source of protein and fiber, helping to maintain stable blood sugar levels. Broccoli is a nutrient-dense vegetable with a low glycemic index, and shrimp provides lean protein for energy without a significant carbohydrate load.

Per Serving:
Calories: 250 | Fat: 12g | Carbs: 10g | Fiber: 3g | Protein: 28g

Chapter 6: Pork, Beef, and Lamb

Rosemary Garlic Grilled Lamb Chops

Serves: 2

Prep time: 20 minutes / Cook time: 15 minutes

Ingredients:
- 4 lamb chops
- 2 tbsp olive oil
- 2 cloves garlic, minced
- 2 tsp fresh rosemary, chopped
- Salt and pepper to taste

Instructions:
1. Marinate the lamb chops with olive oil, garlic, rosemary, salt, and pepper. Let it sit for at least 15 minutes.
2. Preheat the grill to medium-high heat.
3. Place the lamb chops on the grill and cook for about 6-7 minutes on each side for medium-rare, or until desired doneness.
4. Remove from grill and let rest for a few minutes.

Benefits for Diabetics:
Lamb is a great source of high-quality protein and essential vitamins and minerals, particularly vitamin B12 and zinc, vital for maintaining health in a diabetic diet. The use of herbs and spices adds flavor without adding carbs, making it a delicious and diabetes-friendly choice.

Per Serving:
Calories: 400 | Fat: 30g | Carbs: 0g | Fiber: 0g | Protein: 30g

Herb-Crusted Pork Tenderloin

Serves: 2

Prep time: 10 minutes / Cook time: 25 minutes

Ingredients:
- 1 pork tenderloin (about 1 lb)
- 1 tbsp olive oil
- 2 tsp dried thyme
- 2 tsp dried rosemary
- Salt and pepper to taste

Instructions:
1. Preheat your oven to 375°F (190°C).
2. Rub the pork tenderloin with olive oil, thyme, rosemary, salt, and pepper.
3. Place in a roasting pan and cook for 25-30 minutes, or until the internal temperature reaches 145°F (63°C).
4. Let rest for 5 minutes, slice, and serve.

Benefits for Diabetics:
Pork tenderloin is an excellent source of lean protein, essential for blood sugar management. The herbs provide flavor without adding extra carbs or sugars, making this dish a healthy choice for those with diabetes.

Per Serving:
Calories: 240 | Fat: 8g | Carbs: 0g | Fiber: 0g | Protein: 36g

Mediterranean Beef Kabobs

Serves: 2

Prep time: 25 minutes / Cook time: 10 minutes

Ingredients:
- 1/2 lb beef cubes (preferably sirloin)
- 1 red bell pepper, cut into chunks
- 1 zucchini, sliced
- 1/2 red onion, cut into chunks
- 2 tbsp olive oil
- 1 tsp dried oregano
- 1 tsp garlic powder
- Salt and pepper to taste

Instructions:
1. In a bowl, mix the beef with olive oil, oregano, garlic powder, salt, and pepper. Let marinate for at least 30 minutes.
2. Preheat the grill to medium-high heat.
3. Thread the beef and vegetables alternately onto skewers.
4. Grill for about 10 minutes, turning occasionally, until the beef is cooked to your liking and vegetables are tender.

Benefits for Diabetics:
Beef provides high-quality protein and iron, while the vegetables add fiber and essential nutrients without many carbs. The Mediterranean spices offer health benefits and elevate the taste without extra sugar or fat.

Per Serving:
Calories: 300 | Fat: 15g | Carbs: 8g | Fiber: 2g | Protein: 34g

Spicy Lamb Meatballs with Yogurt Sauce

Serves: 2

Prep time: 20 minutes / Cook time: 20 minutes

Ingredients:
- 1/2 lb ground lamb
- 1 tsp cumin
- 1 tsp paprika
- 1/2 tsp chili flakes
- 1/4 cup fresh cilantro, chopped
- 1/2 cup Greek yogurt
- 1 tbsp lemon juice
- Salt and pepper to taste

Instructions:
1. Preheat your oven to 375°F (190°C).
2. Mix the lamb with cumin, paprika, chili flakes, cilantro, salt, and pepper. Form into small meatballs.
3. Place on a lined baking sheet and bake for 20 minutes or until cooked through.
4. Combine Greek yogurt with lemon juice, salt, and pepper to make the sauce.
5. Serve meatballs with yogurt sauce drizzled over or on the side.

Benefits for Diabetics:
Lamb is a good source of protein and vital nutrients, while yogurt provides healthy fat and probiotics for a balanced diet. The spices enhance the flavor without adding unnecessary carbs or sugars.

Per Serving:
Calories: 320 | Fat: 18g | Carbs: 6g | Fiber: 1g | Protein: 35g

Balsamic Glazed Pork Chops

Serves: 2

Prep time: 10 minutes / Cook time: 15 minutes

Ingredients:
- 2 pork chops
- 1/4 cup balsamic vinegar
- 1 tbsp olive oil
- 1 garlic clove, minced
- Salt and pepper to taste

Instructions:
1. Season the pork chops with salt and pepper.
2. Heat olive oil in a pan over medium-high heat. Add pork chops and cook until browned on both sides.
3. Reduce the heat to medium, add garlic and balsamic vinegar. Cook for an additional 5-7 minutes, basting the chops with the glaze until cooked through.
4. Serve the chops drizzled with the remaining glaze.

Benefits for Diabetics:
Pork chops provide a high-quality protein source, essential for muscle maintenance and overall health. The balsamic glaze offers a burst of flavor without the need for sugary sauces or marinades.

Per Serving:
Calories: 290 | Fat: 16g | Carbs: 5g | Fiber: 0g | Protein: 30g

Lemon and Herb Roast Beef

Serves: 2

Prep time: 15 minutes / Cook time: 1 hour

Ingredients:
- 1 lb beef roast (such as sirloin or rump)
- 1 lemon, zest and juice
- 2 tsp mixed dried herbs (such as thyme, rosemary, and oregano)
- 2 cloves garlic, minced
- Salt and pepper to taste

Instructions:
1. Preheat your oven to 375°F (190°C).
2. Rub the beef with lemon zest, lemon juice, herbs, garlic, salt, and pepper.
3. Place in a roasting pan and cook in the oven for about 1 hour or until the desired level of doneness is reached.
4. Let the beef rest for 10 minutes before slicing.

Benefits for Diabetics:
Roast beef is an excellent source of protein and essential nutrients, making it a hearty and healthy option for individuals managing diabetes. The lemon and herbs add a powerful flavor punch without added sugars or carbs.

Per Serving:
Calories: 340 | Fat: 14g | Carbs: 3g | Fiber: 1g | Protein: 50g

Garlic Butter Beef Tips

Serves: 2

Prep time: 10 minutes / Cook time: 20 minutes

Ingredients:
- 1/2 lb beef tips or stew meat
- 2 tbsp butter
- 3 cloves garlic, minced
- Salt and pepper to taste

Instructions:
1. Season the beef tips with salt and pepper.
2. In a skillet over medium-high heat, melt the butter and add the garlic.
3. Add the beef tips and cook until browned and cooked to your liking.
4. Serve hot, drizzled with the garlic butter from the pan.

Benefits for Diabetics:
Beef tips provide a substantial amount of protein and are

low in carbohydrates, making them an excellent option for blood sugar management. The garlic butter adds flavor and healthy fats without unnecessary carbs.

Per Serving:
Calories: 300 | Fat: 18g | Carbs: 2g | Fiber: 0g | Protein: 32g

Spiced Lamb Shank Stew

Serves: 2

Prep time: 20 minutes / Cook time: 2 hours

Ingredients:
- 2 lamb shanks
- 2 carrots, chopped
- 2 cloves garlic, minced
- 1 tsp cumin
- 1/2 tsp cinnamon
- Salt and pepper to taste
- 1 onion, chopped
- 2 celery stalks, chopped
- 1 tsp coriander
- 4 cups low-sodium beef broth

Instructions:
1. Season the lamb shanks with salt, pepper, cumin, coriander, and cinnamon.
2. In a large pot, brown the lamb shanks on all sides. Remove and set aside.
3. In the same pot, sauté onion, carrots, celery, and garlic until softened.
4. Return the lamb to the pot, add beef broth, and bring to a simmer.
5. Cover and cook on low heat for about 2 hours, or until the lamb is tender.
6. Serve hot, garnished with fresh herbs if desired.

Benefits for Diabetics:
Lamb is rich in protein and essential nutrients, making it an excellent choice for maintaining muscle health and overall well-being. The stew's blend of spices adds depth of flavor without the need for added sugars or carbs.

Per Serving:
Calories: 300 | Fat: 15g | Carbs: 10g | Fiber: 3g | Protein: 35g

Spicy Beef Stir-Fry with Broccoli

Serves: 2

Prep time: 15 minutes / Cook time: 10 minutes

Ingredients:
- 8 oz lean beef, thinly sliced
- 2 cups broccoli florets
- 1 tbsp olive oil
- 2 garlic cloves, minced
- 1 tsp ginger, minced
- 1 tbsp low-sodium soy sauce
- 1 tsp chili flakes (adjust to taste)
- 1/2 tsp sesame oil

Instructions:
1. Heat olive oil in a large skillet over medium-high heat.
2. Add garlic and ginger, sautéing until fragrant.
3. Increase heat, add the beef slices, and stir-fry until they are nearly cooked through.
4. Add the broccoli, soy sauce, chili flakes, and stir well to combine.
5. Continue to cook until broccoli is tender-crisp and beef is fully cooked.
6. Drizzle with sesame oil before serving.

Benefits for Diabetics:
Lean beef provides a high-quality protein source, crucial for a balanced diabetic diet. Broccoli adds fiber and nutrients without unwanted sugars, while the spicy elements stimulate metabolism.
Per Serving:
Calories: 250 | Fat: 10g | Carbs: 10g | Fiber: 3g | Protein: 28g

Herbed Pork Tenderloin with Zucchini

Serves: 2
Prep time: 20 minutes / Cook time: 25 minutes
Ingredients:
- 1 pork tenderloin (about 1 lb)
- 2 medium zucchinis, sliced
- 1 tbsp olive oil
- 1 tsp thyme
- 1 tsp rosemary
- Salt and pepper to taste

Instructions:
1. Preheat oven to 375°F (190°C).
2. Rub the pork tenderloin with olive oil, then season with thyme, rosemary, salt, and pepper.
3. Place the tenderloin in a baking dish and roast for 25-30 minutes or until the desired doneness is reached.
4. Meanwhile, sauté the sliced zucchini in a pan with a bit of olive oil until tender and lightly browned.
5. Slice the pork and serve with the sautéed zucchini.

Benefits for Diabetics:
Pork tenderloin is a lean cut of meat, high in protein and low in fat, making it a good choice for a stable blood sugar level. Zucchini is a low-carb vegetable, rich in vitamins and fiber, enhancing the dish's nutritional value without adding sugars.
Per Serving:
Calories: 310 | Fat: 14g | Carbs: 8g | Fiber: 2g | Protein: 38g

Beef and Mushroom Stuffed Peppers

Serves: 2
Prep time: 20 minutes / Cook time: 25 minutes
Ingredients:
- 2 large bell peppers, halved and seeded
- 8 oz lean ground beef
- 1 cup mushrooms, chopped
- 1 small onion, diced
- 1 garlic clove, minced
- 1 tsp olive oil
- 1/2 tsp each of dried oregano and basil
- Salt and pepper to taste

Instructions:
1. Preheat the oven to 350°F (175°C).
2. In a skillet, heat olive oil over medium heat and sauté onion, garlic, and mushrooms until soft.
3. Add ground beef, oregano, basil, salt, and pepper, cooking until the beef is browned.
4. Spoon the beef and mushroom mixture into the halved bell peppers.
5. Place the stuffed peppers in a baking dish and bake for 25 minutes, or until the peppers are tender.
6. Serve hot.

Benefits for Diabetics:

Lean beef and mushrooms provide a high-quality protein and fiber source, ideal for maintaining stable blood sugar levels. Bell peppers are a low-calorie, nutrient-rich vegetable that adds volume and nutrients without many carbs.
Per Serving:
Calories: 310 | Fat: 14g | Carbs: 16g | Fiber: 4g | Protein: 28g

Lamb and Feta Burgers

Serves: 2
Prep time: 15 minutes / Cook time: 10 minutes
Ingredients:
- 8 oz ground lamb
- 1/4 cup feta cheese, crumbled
- 1 tsp dried oregano
- Salt and pepper to taste
- Lettuce leaves for serving

Instructions:
1. Preheat the grill to medium-high heat.
2. In a bowl, mix together ground lamb, feta cheese, oregano, salt, and pepper.
3. Form the mixture into two patties.
4. Grill the patties for about 5 minutes on each side or until cooked to your preference.
5. Serve each patty wrapped in lettuce leaves.

Benefits for Diabetics:
Ground lamb is a rich source of protein, while feta adds a tangy flavor without excessive calories or carbs. Wrapping the burgers in lettuce instead of a bun significantly reduces the carbohydrate content, making it a keto-friendly and diabetic-conscious meal.
Per Serving:
Calories: 320 | Fat: 25g | Carbs: 2g | Fiber: 0g | Protein: 22g

Pork Loin with Ginger-Peach Glaze

Serves: 2
Prep time: 15 minutes / Cook time: 1 hour
Ingredients:
- 1 lb pork loin
- 1/2 cup peach preserves (sugar-free)
- 1 tbsp fresh ginger, minced
- 1 garlic clove, minced
- Salt and pepper to taste

Instructions:
1. Preheat the oven to 350°F (175°C).
2. Season the pork loin with salt and pepper and place it in a baking dish.
3. In a small bowl, mix together peach preserves, ginger, and garlic.
4. Brush the ginger-peach glaze over the pork loin.
5. Roast in the oven for about 1 hour or until the pork is cooked through and the glaze is caramelized.
6. Slice and serve the pork loin with the glaze.

Benefits for Diabetics:
Pork loin is a lean cut of meat, providing a substantial amount of protein with minimal fat. The sugar-free peach preserves allow for a hint of sweetness without adding a sugar load, complemented by the zesty flavor of ginger.
Per Serving:
Calories: 350 | Fat: 14g | Carbs: 10g | Fiber: 0g | Protein: 42g

Seared Beef Steak with Cauliflower Mash

Serves: 2

Prep time: 10 minutes / Cook time: 20 minutes

Ingredients:
- 2 beef steaks (sirloin or ribeye)
- 1 head of cauliflower, cut into florets
- 2 tbsp olive oil
- 1/4 cup milk (or almond milk for lower carbs)
- Salt and pepper to taste
- Fresh chives, chopped for garnish

Instructions:
1. Season the steaks with salt and pepper.
2. Heat 1 tbsp of olive oil in a skillet over medium-high heat and sear the steaks for 4-5 minutes on each side or until desired doneness.
3. Steam the cauliflower until tender, then blend in a food processor with milk, remaining olive oil, salt, and pepper until smooth.
4. Serve the steaks with a side of creamy cauliflower mash and garnish with chives.

Benefits for Diabetics:
Beef steaks provide a high-quality protein source, essential for a balanced diet. Cauliflower mash is an excellent low-carb alternative to traditional mashed potatoes, offering the same creamy texture without the high sugar content.

Per Serving:
Calories: 380 | Fat: 22g | Carbs: 8g | Fiber: 3g | Protein: 38g

Citrus-Herb Marinated Pork Tenderloin

Serves: 2

Prep time: 30 minutes + marinating / Cook time: 20 minutes

Ingredients:
- 1 pork tenderloin (about 1 lb)
- Juice of 1 orange
- Juice of 1 lemon
- 2 tbsp olive oil
- 2 garlic cloves, minced
- 1 tsp rosemary, chopped
- 1 tsp thyme, chopped
- Salt and pepper to taste

Instructions:
1. In a bowl, whisk together orange juice, lemon juice, olive oil, garlic, rosemary, thyme, salt, and pepper.
2. Pour the marinade over the pork tenderloin and let it marinate for at least 1 hour in the refrigerator.
3. Preheat the oven to 375°F (190°C).
4. Place the marinated pork in a baking dish and roast for 20 minutes, or until the internal temperature reaches 145°F (63°C).
5. Let the pork rest for a few minutes before slicing and serving.

Benefits for Diabetics:
Pork tenderloin is a lean cut, providing high-quality protein without excess fat. The citrus fruits add a natural sweetness and brightness to the dish without the need for added sugars, making it a balanced choice for blood sugar management.

Per Serving:
Calories: 310 | Fat: 15g | Carbs: 6g | Fiber: 1g | Protein: 35g

Savory Beef Brisket

Serves: 2

Prep time: 15 minutes / Cook time: 3 hours

Ingredients:
- 1 lb beef brisket
- 1 onion, sliced
- 2 garlic cloves, minced
- 1 cup beef broth
- 1 tbsp Worcestershire sauce
- 1 tsp smoked paprika
- Salt and pepper to taste

Instructions:
1. Preheat the oven to 300°F (150°C).
2. Season the beef brisket with salt, pepper, and smoked paprika.
3. In a large oven-proof pot, sauté onion and garlic until softened.
4. Add the brisket to the pot and pour in beef broth and Worcestershire sauce.
5. Cover and cook in the oven for about 3 hours or until the brisket is tender.
6. Slice the brisket and serve with the cooking juices.

Benefits for Diabetics:
Beef brisket is a rich source of protein and nutrients. Slow cooking it with spices and a small amount of liquid enhances the flavor without adding unnecessary sugars or carbohydrates.

Per Serving:
Calories: 380 | Fat: 24g | Carbs: 5g | Fiber: 1g | Protein: 36g

Grilled Lamb Kofta Kebabs

Serves: 2

Prep time: 20 minutes / Cook time: 10 minutes

Ingredients:
- 8 oz ground lamb
- 1 small onion, finely chopped
- 2 garlic cloves, minced
- 1 tsp cumin
- 1 tsp paprika
- 1/2 tsp cinnamon
- Salt and pepper to taste
- Fresh parsley, chopped for garnish

Instructions:
1. In a bowl, mix together ground lamb, onion, garlic, cumin, paprika, cinnamon, salt, and pepper.
2. Form the mixture into elongated shapes around skewers.
3. Preheat the grill to medium-high heat and grill the koftas for 4-5 minutes on each side or until cooked through.
4. Serve hot, garnished with chopped parsley.

Benefits for Diabetics:
Lamb is a great source of protein and essential vitamins and minerals. The spices in the dish add depth and richness without contributing extra carbs, making these kebabs a tasty and healthy choice.

Per Serving:
Calories: 320 | Fat: 22g | Carbs: 4g | Fiber: 1g | Protein: 28g

Slow-Cooked Pulled Pork with Smoky Rub

Serves: 2

Prep time: 15 minutes / Cook time: 8 hours

Ingredients:
- 1 lb pork shoulder
- 1 tbsp smoked paprika
- 1 tsp garlic powder
- 1 tsp onion powder
- 1/2 tsp cayenne pepper
- Salt and pepper to taste

Instructions:

1. Mix smoked paprika, garlic powder, onion powder, cayenne pepper, salt, and pepper to create the smoky rub.
2. Rub the mixture all over the pork shoulder.
3. Place the pork in a slow cooker and cook on low for 8 hours or until tender.
4. Shred the pork with two forks and serve.

Benefits for Diabetics:

Pulled pork provides a hearty, satisfying source of protein. The smoky rub adds a burst of flavor without needing sugary sauces, making this dish a smart choice for maintaining blood sugar levels.

Per Serving:

Calories: 340 | Fat: 20g | Carbs: 1g | Fiber: 0g | Protein: 36g

Beef and Spinach Stuffed Mushrooms

Serves: 2

Prep time: 20 minutes / Cook time: 15 minutes

Ingredients:

- 8 large mushrooms, stems removed
- 8 oz lean ground beef • 1 cup spinach, chopped
- 1/4 cup parmesan cheese, grated
- 1 garlic clove, minced • 1 tsp olive oil
- Salt and pepper to taste

Instructions:

1. Preheat the oven to 375°F (190°C).
2. In a skillet, heat the olive oil over medium heat and cook the ground beef and garlic until the beef is browned.
3. Add the spinach and cook until wilted. Season with salt and pepper.
4. Stir in the parmesan cheese until well combined.
5. Stuff the mixture into the mushroom caps and place them on a baking sheet.
6. Bake for 15 minutes or until the mushrooms are tender and the filling is golden.
7. Serve hot.

Benefits for Diabetics:

This dish is a fantastic way to enjoy a high-protein, low-carb meal. The beef provides essential nutrients, while the spinach offers fiber and vitamins without adding excess sugar.

Per Serving:

Calories: 270 | Fat: 15g | Carbs: 6g | Fiber: 2g | Protein: 28g

Peppered Beef Sirloin with Roasted Vegetables

Serves: 2

Prep time: 15 minutes / Cook time: 25 minutes

Ingredients:

- 1 lb beef sirloin steak
- 2 tbsp coarse black pepper
- 1 tbsp olive oil
- 1 cup cherry tomatoes
- 1 cup asparagus, trimmed
- 1 small red onion, cut into wedges
- Salt to taste

Instructions:

1. Preheat the oven to 425°F (220°C).
2. Rub the beef sirloin with black pepper and salt.
3. Heat olive oil in a skillet over high heat and sear the sirloin on both sides.
4. Transfer the sirloin to a baking tray. Surround it with cherry tomatoes, asparagus, and red onion wedges.
5. Roast in the oven for 15-20 minutes or until the vegetables are tender and the beef is cooked to your liking.
6. Slice the beef and serve with the roasted vegetables.

Benefits for Diabetics:

Beef sirloin is a lean protein source that's excellent for a stable blood sugar level. The roasted vegetables provide necessary vitamins and fiber without adding significant carbs, making this a balanced and nutritious meal.

Per Serving:

Calories: 360 | Fat: 18g | Carbs: 12g | Fiber: 3g | Protein: 38g

Garlic-Herb Roasted Lamb Shanks

Serves: 2

Prep time: 15 minutes / Cook time: 2 hours

Ingredients:

- 2 lamb shanks
- 4 garlic cloves, minced
- 1 tbsp fresh rosemary, chopped
- 1 tbsp fresh thyme, chopped
- 2 tbsp olive oil
- Salt and pepper to taste

Instructions:

1. Preheat the oven to 325°F (160°C).
2. Rub the lamb shanks with olive oil, then season with garlic, rosemary, thyme, salt, and pepper.
3. Place the lamb shanks in a roasting pan and cover with foil.
4. Roast in the oven for about 2 hours or until the meat is tender and falls off the bone.
5. Serve the lamb shanks with their juices.

Benefits for Diabetics:

Lamb is a rich protein source with essential vitamins and minerals. The use of herbs and garlic adds immense flavor without the need for carb-heavy sauces or marinades.

Conclusion:

Per Serving:

Calories: 380 | Fat: 24g | Carbs: 5g | Fiber: 1g | Protein: 36g

Smoky Chipotle Pork Tacos

Serves: 2

Prep time: 20 minutes / Cook time: 1 hour

Ingredients:

- 8 oz pork shoulder, thinly sliced
- 2 low-carb tortillas
- 1 chipotle in adobo sauce, minced
- 1/2 onion, sliced • 1 bell pepper, sliced
- 1 tsp cumin • 1/2 tsp smoked paprika
- 1 tbsp olive oil • Fresh cilantro for garnish
- Lime wedges for serving

Instructions:

1. In a skillet, heat olive oil over medium-high heat

and cook the pork with cumin, smoked paprika, and chipotle until browned and tender.

2. In the same skillet, sauté onion and bell pepper until softened.
3. Warm the low-carb tortillas according to package instructions.
4. Assemble the tacos by placing the pork, onion, and bell pepper mixture into each tortilla.
5. Garnish with fresh cilantro and serve with lime wedges on the side.

Benefits for Diabetics:
Pork is a great protein source, and when paired with low-carb tortillas, it makes for a filling meal without the high blood sugar spike. The smoky chipotle and spices add depth and heat without the need for sugary sauces.

Per Serving:
Calories: 300 | Fat: 18g | Carbs: 12g | Fiber: 5g | Protein: 22g

Mediterranean Beef and Eggplant Casserole

Serves: 2
Prep time: 20 minutes / Cook time: 40 minutes

Ingredients:
- 8 oz lean ground beef
- 1 large eggplant, sliced and roasted
- 1 cup tomato sauce (sugar-free)
- 1 onion, diced
- 1 garlic clove, minced
- 1/2 cup feta cheese, crumbled
- 1 tsp olive oil
- 1 tsp dried oregano
- Salt and pepper to taste

Instructions:
1. Preheat the oven to 375°F (190°C).
2. In a skillet, heat olive oil over medium heat and cook the ground beef, onion, and garlic until the beef is browned.
3. Layer the bottom of a casserole dish with roasted eggplant slices.
4. Top with the cooked beef mixture, then pour the tomato sauce over it.
5. Sprinkle feta cheese and oregano on top.
6. Bake for 30 minutes or until the casserole is bubbly and the cheese is slightly golden.
7. Serve hot.

Benefits for Diabetics:
Lean beef and eggplant provide a high-protein, high-fiber meal, essential for stable blood sugar management. The tomato sauce and feta cheese add flavor without excessive carbs, making this casserole a comforting yet healthy choice.

Per Serving:
Calories: 350 | Fat: 20g | Carbs: 15g | Fiber: 6g | Protein: 28g

Rosemary and Garlic Braised Lamb Shanks

Serves: 2
Prep time: 20 minutes / Cook time: 2 hours

Ingredients:
- 2 lamb shanks
- 2 sprigs rosemary
- 1 onion, sliced
- Salt and pepper to taste
- 1 cup beef broth
- 3 garlic cloves, minced
- 1 tbsp olive oil

Instructions:
1. Season the lamb shanks with salt and pepper.
2. In a large pot, heat olive oil over medium-high heat and brown the lamb shanks on all sides.
3. Add the onion and garlic to the pot and sauté until softened.
4. Add beef broth and rosemary sprigs, bring to a boil, then reduce to a simmer.
5. Cover and cook on low heat for about 2 hours or until the lamb is tender and falls off the bone.
6. Serve the lamb shanks with the braising liquid as a sauce.

Benefits for Diabetics:
Lamb shanks are an excellent source of protein and nutrients. The slow cooking process allows the flavors to develop fully without the need for high-carb thickeners or sweeteners.

Per Serving:
Calories: 380 | Fat: 22g | Carbs: 8g | Fiber: 2g | Protein: 38g

Pork Loin Roast with Mustard Crust

Serves: 2
Prep time: 15 minutes / Cook time: 1 hour

Ingredients:
- 1 lb pork loin roast
- 1 tbsp olive oil
- 1 tsp rosemary, chopped
- 2 tbsp Dijon mustard
- 1 tsp thyme, chopped
- Salt and pepper to taste

Instructions:
1. Preheat the oven to 375°F (190°C).
2. Mix Dijon mustard, olive oil, thyme, rosemary, salt, and pepper to create a paste.
3. Rub the mustard mixture all over the pork loin.
4. Place the pork loin in a roasting pan and roast for about 1 hour or until the internal temperature reaches 145°F (63°C).
5. Let the pork rest for 10 minutes before slicing and serving.

Benefits for Diabetics:
Pork loin is a lean, high-protein meat that helps maintain stable blood sugar levels. The mustard crust adds flavor and zest without additional carbs, creating a dish that's as nutritious as it is delicious.

Per Serving:
Calories: 360 | Fat: 20g | Carbs: 2g | Fiber: 0g | Protein: 40g

Spiced Lamb Gyros with Tzatziki

Serves: 2
Prep time: 20 minutes / Cook time: 10 minutes

Ingredients:
- 8 oz ground lamb
- 1/2 cup Greek yogurt
- 1/2 cucumber, grated and drained
- 1 garlic clove, minced
- 1 tsp paprika
- 2 low-carb pitas
- 1 tsp cumin
- Salt and pepper to taste

- Fresh lettuce and tomatoes for serving

Instructions:

1. In a bowl, mix ground lamb with cumin, paprika, salt, and pepper.
2. Form the lamb mixture into thin patties or strips and cook in a skillet over medium-high heat until browned and cooked through.
3. For the tzatziki, mix Greek yogurt, grated cucumber, minced garlic, and a pinch of salt.
4. Warm the low-carb pitas and assemble the gyros with cooked lamb, lettuce, tomatoes, and a generous dollop of tzatziki.
5. Serve immediately.

Benefits for Diabetics:

The lamb provides a high-quality source of protein, while the low-carb pitas allow for a satisfying meal without a significant increase in blood sugar. Tzatziki adds a refreshing element without added sugars.

Per Serving:

Calories: 330 | Fat: 22g | Carbs: 12g | Fiber: 2g | Protein: 24g

Balsamic and Thyme Beef Skewers

Serves: 2

Prep time: 15 minutes + marinating / Cook time: 10 minutes

Ingredients:

- 8 oz beef tenderloin, cut into cubes
- 1/4 cup balsamic vinegar
- 2 tbsp olive oil
- 1 tsp fresh thyme, chopped
- Salt and pepper to taste

Instructions:

1. In a bowl, mix balsamic vinegar, olive oil, thyme, salt, and pepper.
2. Add the beef cubes to the marinade and let them marinate for at least 1 hour in the refrigerator.
3. Thread the beef onto skewers.
4. Preheat the grill to medium-high and cook the skewers for about 4-5 minutes on each side or until desired doneness.
5. Serve hot, straight off the grill.

Benefits for Diabetics:

Beef is an excellent source of protein, vital for a diabetic diet. The balsamic vinegar provides a touch of sweetness and acidity without needing additional sugar, and thyme adds a fresh, aromatic flavor.

Per Serving:

Calories: 320 | Fat: 20g | Carbs: 4g | Fiber: 0g | Protein: 30g

Lemon-Thyme Roasted Lamb Shoulder

Serves: 2

Prep time: 20 minutes / Cook time: 2 hours

Ingredients:

- 1 lb lamb shoulder
- 2 tbsp olive oil
- 2 garlic cloves, minced
- Salt and pepper to taste
- Juice of 1 lemon
- 1 tbsp fresh thyme leaves

Instructions:

1. Preheat the oven to 325°F (165°C).
2. In a small bowl, mix together lemon juice, olive oil, thyme, garlic, salt, and pepper.
3. Rub the mixture all over the lamb shoulder.
4. Place the lamb in a roasting pan and roast for about 2 hours or until tender.
5. Let the lamb rest before slicing and serving.

Benefits for Diabetics:

Lamb is a great source of high-quality protein and essential nutrients, important for maintaining steady blood sugar levels. The addition of lemon and thyme offers a flavorful experience without the need for high-carb sauces or marinades.

Per Serving:

Calories: 360 | Fat: 24g | Carbs: 3g | Fiber: 1g | Protein: 33g

Smoky Chipotle Pork Tacos

Serves: 2

Prep time: 20 minutes + marinating / Cook time: 10 minutes

Ingredients:

- 8 oz pork loin, thinly sliced
- 2 chipotle peppers in adobo sauce, minced
- 1 tbsp adobo sauce
- 1/2 tsp smoked paprika
- 1/2 tsp cumin
- 2 low-carb tortillas
- Fresh cilantro, lime wedges for garnish

Instructions:

1. In a bowl, mix together chipotle peppers, adobo sauce, smoked paprika, and cumin.
2. Add the pork slices to the marinade and let sit for at least 30 minutes.
3. Heat a skillet over medium-high heat and cook the pork until tender and slightly charred.
4. Warm the tortillas and fill them with the cooked pork.
5. Garnish with fresh cilantro and serve with lime wedges.

Benefits for Diabetics:

Pork is a nutritious source of protein, and when prepared with low-carb ingredients, it makes for a meal that's both satisfying and diabetic-friendly. The spices and chipotle add a depth of flavor without relying on sugar or high-carb additions.

Per Serving:

Calories: 280 | Fat: 12g | Carbs: 10g | Fiber: 4g | Protein: 32g

Mediterranean Beef Kabobs

Serves: 2

Prep time: 25 minutes / Cook time: 10 minutes

Ingredients:

- 8 oz beef sirloin, cut into cubes
- 1 zucchini, sliced into rounds
- 1 red bell pepper, cut into chunks
- 1 tbsp olive oil
- 1 tsp oregano
- 1 tsp garlic powder
- 1/2 tsp paprika
- Salt and pepper to taste

Instructions:

1. In a bowl, mix together olive oil, oregano, garlic powder, paprika, salt, and pepper.

2. Add the beef cubes to the marinade and toss to coat.
3. Thread the beef, zucchini, and bell pepper onto skewers.
4. Preheat the grill to medium-high heat and grill the kabobs for about 4-5 minutes on each side or until the beef is cooked to your liking.
5. Serve hot.

Benefits for Diabetics:
Beef is an excellent protein source, crucial for a balanced diabetic diet. The vegetables add fiber and nutrients without significant carbohydrates, and the Mediterranean spices offer robust flavor without added sugar.

Per Serving:
Calories: 310 | Fat: 16g | Carbs: 9g | Fiber: 2g | Protein: 33g

Garlic Butter Beef Tenderloin

Serves: 2

Prep time: 15 minutes / Cook time: 45 minutes

Ingredients:
- 1 lb beef tenderloin
- 4 tbsp butter
- 3 garlic cloves, minced
- Salt and pepper to taste
- Fresh parsley, chopped for garnish

Instructions:
1. Preheat the oven to 400°F (200°C).
2. Season the beef tenderloin with salt and pepper.
3. In a skillet over medium heat, melt the butter and add the minced garlic, cooking until fragrant.
4. Sear the tenderloin in the skillet on all sides until golden brown.
5. Transfer the skillet to the oven and roast the tenderloin for 20-25 minutes or until it reaches the desired doneness.
6. Let the tenderloin rest before slicing, then serve with the garlic butter drizzled over the top and garnished with parsley.

Benefits for Diabetics:
Beef tenderloin is a lean, premium cut of meat that provides plenty of protein without unnecessary carbs. The garlic butter adds a lot of flavors and can be used sparingly to enhance taste without adding too much fat.

Per Serving:
Calories: 380 | Fat: 26g | Carbs: 2g | Fiber: 0g | Protein: 35g

Spiced Pork Ribs with Low-Carb BBQ Sauce

Serves: 2

Prep time: 15 minutes / Cook time: 1 hour 30 minutes

Ingredients:
- 1 lb pork ribs
- 1 tbsp paprika
- 1 tsp garlic powder
- 1 tsp onion powder
- 1/2 tsp cayenne pepper
- Salt and pepper to taste
- Low-carb BBQ sauce (store-bought or homemade)

Instructions:
1. Preheat the oven to 275°F (135°C).
2. Mix together paprika, garlic powder, onion powder, cayenne pepper, salt, and pepper to create the spice rub.
3. Rub the mixture all over the pork ribs.
4. Place the ribs in a baking dish, cover with foil, and bake for about 1.5 hours or until tender.

5. In the last 10 minutes of cooking, remove the foil and brush the ribs with low-carb BBQ sauce.
6. Finish cooking uncovered, then serve with additional BBQ sauce if desired.

Benefits for Diabetics:
Pork ribs are a flavorful source of protein, and when prepared with a low-carb rub and sauce, they make a satisfying meal that won't spike blood sugar levels.

Per Serving:
Calories: 400 | Fat: 30g | Carbs: 3g | Fiber: 1g | Protein: 30g

Classic Beef Stroganoff with Zoodles

Serves: 2

Prep time: 15 minutes / Cook time: 20 minutes

Ingredients:
- 8 oz beef sirloin, thinly sliced
- 1 cup mushrooms, sliced
- 1 small onion, diced
- 1 garlic clove, minced
- 1/2 cup sour cream
- 1 tbsp olive oil
- 2 zucchinis, spiralized into noodles
- Salt and pepper to taste

Instructions:
1. Heat olive oil in a skillet over medium-high heat. Add the beef and cook until browned. Remove and set aside.
2. In the same skillet, add the onion and garlic, sautéing until soft. Add the mushrooms and cook until they're tender.
3. Reduce the heat to low and stir in the sour cream. Add the cooked beef back into the skillet, stirring to combine. Season with salt and pepper.
4. In another skillet, sauté the spiralized zucchini in a bit of olive oil until tender.
5. Serve the beef stroganoff over the zoodles.

Benefits for Diabetics:
This dish offers a hearty, satisfying meal without the heavy carbs found in traditional noodles. Beef provides high-quality protein, while zucchini noodles are an excellent low-carb, low-calorie substitute for pasta.

Per Serving:
Calories: 370 | Fat: 22g | Carbs: 8g | Fiber: 2g | Protein: 34g

Moroccan Lamb Stew

Serves: 2

Prep time: 20 minutes / Cook time: 2 hours

Ingredients:
- 1 lb lamb shoulder, cut into chunks
- 1/2 cup dried apricots, chopped
- 1 onion, chopped
- 2 garlic cloves, minced
- 1 tsp cumin
- 1 tsp coriander
- 1/2 tsp cinnamon
- 2 cups beef broth
- 1 tbsp olive oil
- Salt and pepper to taste

Instructions:
1. Heat olive oil in a large pot over medium-high heat. Add the lamb and brown on all sides.
2. Add the onion and garlic, cooking until softened.
3. Stir in the spices, apricots, and beef broth. Bring to

a boil, then reduce the heat and simmer covered for about 2 hours or until the lamb is tender.

4. Season with salt and pepper to taste, and serve hot.

Benefits for Diabetics:

Lamb is an excellent protein source, essential for a diabetic diet. The apricots add a natural sweetness without the need for added sugars, and the spices create a depth of flavor that makes this dish incredibly satisfying.

Per Serving:

Calories: 390 | Fat: 24g | Carbs: 18g | Fiber: 4g | Protein: 28g

Pork Tenderloin with Apple-Cider Glaze

Serves: 2

Prep time: 20 minutes / Cook time: 30 minutes

Ingredients:

- 1 pork tenderloin (about 1 lb)
- Salt and pepper, to taste
- 1 tbsp olive oil
- 1/2 cup unsweetened apple cider
- 1 tsp fresh thyme, chopped
- 1/2 tsp cinnamon
- 1 apple, sliced into wedges

Instructions:

1. Preheat your oven to 375°F (190°C).
2. Season the pork tenderloin with salt and pepper.
3. In a large ovenproof skillet, heat olive oil over medium-high heat. Add the pork and sear until golden brown on all sides, about 5-7 minutes total.
4. Remove the pork from the skillet and set aside. In the same skillet, add apple cider, thyme, and cinnamon, scraping up any browned bits from the pork.
5. Return the pork to the skillet and add apple slices around it.
6. Transfer the skillet to the oven and roast for about 20-25 minutes or until the pork reaches an internal temperature of 145°F (63°C).
7. Let the pork rest for 5 minutes before slicing. Serve with the apple slices and drizzle with the apple-cider glaze from the skillet.

Benefits for Diabetics:

This dish is a hearty, low-carb option rich in protein and essential nutrients. The apple-cider glaze provides a natural sweetness without added sugars, and the cinnamon is known for its potential blood sugar regulating properties. Enjoy the savory and slightly sweet flavors that make this dish a comforting yet healthy option for diabetics.

Per Serving:

Calories: 320 | Fat: 14g | Carbs: 10g | Fiber: 2g | Protein: 35g

Spiced Pork Chops with Vegetable Stir Fry

Serves: 2

Prep time: 15 minutes / Cook time: 20 minutes

Ingredients:

- 2 boneless pork chops • 1 tbsp olive oil
- 1 tsp smoked paprika • 1/2 tsp garlic powder
- Salt and pepper to taste • 2 cups mixed vegetables (bell peppers, broccoli, carrots) • 1 tsp sesame oil
- 1 tbsp low-sodium soy sauce

Instructions:

1. Season pork chops with smoked paprika, garlic powder, salt, and pepper.
2. Heat olive oil in a pan over medium heat and cook pork chops for about 4-5 minutes on each side or until fully cooked.
3. Remove pork chops and set aside. In the same pan, add the mixed vegetables, soy sauce, and sesame oil, and stir-fry until vegetables are tender-crisp.
4. Serve the pork chops with the vegetable stir-fry on the side.

Benefits for Diabetics:

This meal is low in carbs and high in fiber, aiding in blood sugar control. The lean protein from pork along with the nutrients from the vegetables make it a balanced meal that won't spike blood sugar levels.

Per Serving:

Calories: 260 | Fat: 15g | Carbs: 8g | Fiber: 3g | Protein: 25g

Spiced Pork Chops with Vegetable Stir Fry

Serves: 2

Prep time: 15 minutes / Cook time: 20 minutes

Ingredients:

- 2 boneless pork chops • 1 tbsp olive oil
- 1 tsp smoked paprika • 1/2 tsp garlic powder
- Salt and pepper to taste
- 2 cups mixed vegetables (bell peppers, broccoli, carrots)
- 1 tbsp low-sodium soy sauce
- 1 tsp sesame oil

Instructions:

1. Season pork chops with smoked paprika, garlic powder, salt, and pepper.
2. Heat olive oil in a pan over medium heat and cook pork chops for about 4-5 minutes on each side or until fully cooked.
3. Remove pork chops and set aside. In the same pan, add the mixed vegetables, soy sauce, and sesame oil, and stir-fry until vegetables are tender-crisp.
4. Serve the pork chops with the vegetable stir-fry on the side.

Benefits for Diabetics:

This meal is low in carbs and high in fiber, aiding in blood sugar control. The lean protein from pork along with the nutrients from the vegetables make it a balanced meal that won't spike blood sugar levels.

Per Serving:

Calories: 260 | Fat: 15g | Carbs: 8g | Fiber: 3g | Protein: 25g

Lemon-Herb Grilled Pork and Zucchini

Serves: 2

Prep time: 10 minutes / Cook time: 15 minutes

Ingredients:

- 2 pork loin steaks
- 2 medium zucchinis, sliced lengthwise
- 2 tbsp olive oil
- 1 lemon, juice and zest

- 1 tbsp mixed herbs (such as thyme, oregano, and parsley)
- Salt and pepper to taste

Instructions:
1. Preheat grill to medium-high heat.
2. Season pork loin steaks and zucchini slices with salt and pepper.
3. In a small bowl, combine olive oil, lemon juice, lemon zest, and mixed herbs.
4. Brush the pork and zucchini with the lemon-herb mixture.
5. Grill pork for about 6-7 minutes per side or until fully cooked. Grill zucchini for about 3-4 minutes per side or until tender.
6. Serve the grilled pork and zucchini with extra lemon wedges on the side.

Benefits for Diabetics:
Grilled pork and zucchini offer a meal high in protein and low in carbohydrates, ideal for blood sugar management. The added lemon and herbs provide a burst of flavor without added sugar or fat.

Per Serving:
Calories: 280 | Fat: 16g | Carbs: 6g | Fiber: 2g | Protein: 30g

Maple-Dijon Pork Tenderloin with Cauliflower Mash

Serves: 2
Prep time: 15 minutes / Cook time: 25 minutes

Ingredients:
- 1 pork tenderloin (about 1 lb)
- 2 tbsp Dijon mustard
- 1 tbsp maple syrup (sugar-free)
- 1 head cauliflower, cut into florets
- 2 tbsp olive oil
- Salt and pepper to taste

Instructions:
1. Preheat oven to 375°F (190°C).
2. Season the pork tenderloin with salt and pepper. In a small bowl, mix together Dijon mustard and maple syrup. Brush the mixture over the pork.
3. Roast the pork in the oven for 20-25 minutes or until cooked to desired doneness.
4. While the pork is roasting, steam the cauliflower florets until tender. Mash the cauliflower with olive oil, salt, and pepper until smooth.
5. Slice the pork tenderloin and serve with a side of cauliflower mash.

Benefits for Diabetics:
This meal offers a low-glycemic load, crucial for blood sugar control. The cauliflower mash is a nutritious substitute for high-carb sides, and the pork tenderloin is an excellent source of lean protein.

Per Serving:
Calories: 330 | Fat: 15g | Carbs: 10g | Fiber: 4g | Protein: 40g

Smoky BBQ Pork Skewers with Avocado Salad

Serves: 2
Prep time: 20 minutes (plus marinating) / Cook time: 10 minutes

Ingredients:
- 1 lb pork shoulder, cut into 1-inch cubes
- 2 tbsp sugar-free BBQ sauce
- 1 tbsp olive oil
- 1 tsp smoked paprika
- Salt and pepper to taste
- 1 avocado, diced
- 1 cup cherry tomatoes, halved
- 1/4 red onion, thinly sliced
- 1 lime, juice and zest
- Fresh cilantro for garnish

Instructions:
1. In a bowl, mix pork cubes with BBQ sauce, olive oil, smoked paprika, salt, and pepper. Marinate for at least 30 minutes.
2. Thread the marinated pork onto skewers.
3. Preheat grill to medium-high and grill skewers for 4-5 minutes on each side or until fully cooked.
4. For the salad, combine diced avocado, cherry tomatoes, red onion, lime juice, and zest. Toss gently.
5. Serve BBQ pork skewers with a side of avocado salad and garnish with fresh cilantro.

Benefits for Diabetics:
Pork provides a high-quality protein source, while the avocado salad offers healthy fats and fiber, promoting satiety and supporting blood sugar control. The use of sugar-free BBQ sauce ensures a lower carbohydrate content.

Per Serving:
Calories: 350 | Fat: 22g | Carbs: 12g | Fiber: 6g | Protein: 28g

Garlic and Rosemary Pork Medallions with Green Beans

Serves: 2
Prep time: 10 minutes / Cook time: 15 minutes

Ingredients:
- 1 lb pork tenderloin, sliced into medallions
- 2 tbsp olive oil
- 2 garlic cloves, minced
- 1 tbsp fresh rosemary, chopped
- 2 cups green beans, trimmed
- Salt and pepper to taste

Instructions:
1. Season pork medallions with salt and pepper.
2. In a large skillet, heat olive oil over medium heat. Add garlic and rosemary, and sauté for 1 minute.
3. Add pork medallions to the skillet and cook for 3-4 minutes on each side or until golden and cooked through.
4. In another pan, blanch the green beans in boiling water for 2-3 minutes, then drain.
5. Serve the pork medallions with a side of green beans.

Benefits for Diabetics:
This meal is a great source of lean protein from the pork, while the green beans provide a good amount of fiber, important for blood sugar regulation. The garlic and rosemary not only add flavor but also offer potential health benefits.

Per Serving:
Calories: 310 | Fat: 16g | Carbs: 8g | Fiber: 3g | Protein: 35g

Chapter 7: Legumes and Pulses - Powerhouses of Nutrition

Welcome to Chapter 7, where we dive into the world of legumes and pulses, the unsung heroes of the culinary world. These nutrient-dense foods are not only versatile and delicious but also incredibly beneficial for those managing diabetes. From lentils and beans to chickpeas and peas, legumes and pulses are packed with fiber, protein, and essential nutrients, making them an excellent choice for blood sugar management and overall health.

In this chapter, you'll discover a variety of ways to incorporate these powerhouses into your daily meals. We'll explore recipes that transform these humble ingredients into delectable dishes that will please your palate and support your health. Whether you're looking for hearty soups, refreshing salads, or innovative main courses, legumes and pulses provide a solid foundation for countless culinary creations.

As you embark on this journey through the world of legumes and pulses, you'll learn not only how to cook them to perfection but also understand their health benefits, including their role in stabilizing blood sugar, improving digestion, and supporting heart health. So, let's get ready to unlock the potential of these nutritional gems and bring a new level of flavor and nourishment to your table. Welcome to the wholesome world of legumes and pulses!

Mexican Lentil Stew

Serves: 2
Prep time: 10 minutes / Cook time: 45 minutes

Ingredients:
- 1 cup dried green lentils, rinsed
- 4 cups low-sodium vegetable broth
- 1 small onion, chopped
- 2 cloves garlic, minced
- 1 bell pepper, chopped
- 1 small carrot, diced
- 1 tsp ground cumin
- 1/2 tsp chili powder
- 1/2 tsp smoked paprika
- Salt and pepper to taste
- Fresh cilantro for garnish

Instructions:
1. In a large pot, sauté onion, garlic, bell pepper, and carrot until softened.
2. Add lentils, vegetable broth, cumin, chili powder, and smoked paprika.
3. Bring to a boil, then reduce heat and simmer uncovered for about 30-35 minutes, or until lentils are tender.
4. Season with salt and pepper to taste.
5. Serve hot, garnished with fresh cilantro.

Benefits for Diabetics:
Lentils are an excellent source of fiber and protein, helping to manage blood sugar levels. The vegetables and spices add flavor and nutrients without excess carbohydrates.

Per Serving:
Calories: 240 | Fat: 2g | Carbs: 40g | Fiber: 19g | Protein: 18g

Italian White Bean and Spinach Soup

Serves: 2
Prep time: 10 minutes / Cook time: 30 minutes

Ingredients:
- 1 can (15 oz) white beans, drained and rinsed
- 4 cups low-sodium chicken or vegetable broth
- 1 small onion, chopped
- 2 cloves garlic, minced
- 2 cups fresh spinach leaves
- 1 tsp dried oregano
- Salt and pepper to taste
- Parmesan cheese for garnish (optional)

Instructions:
1. In a large pot, sauté onion and garlic until translucent.
2. Add broth, beans, and oregano, bringing to a simmer.
3. Cook for about 20 minutes, then add spinach and cook until wilted.
4. Season with salt and pepper to taste.
5. Serve hot, garnished with Parmesan cheese if desired.

Benefits for Diabetics:
White beans are a great low-GI option, providing sustained energy and fiber. Spinach adds a wealth of vitamins and minerals, supporting overall health.

Per Serving:
Calories: 200 | Fat: 1g | Carbs: 35g | Fiber: 8g | Protein: 14g

Moroccan Chickpea Salad

Serves: 2
Prep time: 15 minutes / Cook time: 0 minutes

Ingredients:
- 1 can (15 oz) chickpeas, drained and rinsed
- 1/2 cucumber, diced
- 1 red bell pepper, diced
- 1/4 cup fresh parsley, chopped
- 1/4 cup fresh mint, chopped
- Juice of 1 lemon
- 2 tbsp olive oil
- 1 tsp cumin
- 1/2 tsp paprika
- Salt to taste

Instructions:
1. In a large bowl, combine chickpeas, cucumber, bell pepper, parsley, and mint.
2. In a small bowl, whisk together lemon juice, olive oil, cumin, paprika, and salt.

3. Pour the dressing over the salad and toss to coat evenly.
4. Refrigerate for at least 30 minutes before serving to allow flavors to meld.

Benefits for Diabetics:
Chickpeas are an excellent source of fiber and protein, aiding in blood sugar stabilization. The added herbs and spices provide anti-inflammatory benefits and a boost of flavor.

Per Serving:
Calories: 280 | Fat: 10g | Carbs: 38g | Fiber: 10g | Protein: 12g

Indian Dal Tadka

Serves: 2
Prep time: 10 minutes / Cook time: 30 minutes

Ingredients:
- 1 cup yellow lentils (Toor dal), rinsed
- 4 cups water
- 1 tsp turmeric
- 1 small onion, finely chopped
- 2 cloves garlic, minced
- 1 tsp grated ginger
- 1 green chili, finely chopped (optional)
- 1 tsp cumin seeds
- 1/2 tsp mustard seeds
- 1/2 tsp garam masala
- 2 tbsp cilantro, chopped for garnish
- 1 tbsp olive oil
- Salt to taste

Instructions:
1. In a pot, boil lentils with water and turmeric until soft and mushy.
2. In a separate pan, heat olive oil and add cumin seeds, mustard seeds, onion, garlic, ginger, and green chili. Sauté until onions are golden.
3. Add the cooked lentils to the sautéed mixture, adding garam masala and salt.
4. Simmer for an additional 10 minutes.
5. Garnish with cilantro before serving.

Benefits for Diabetics:
Lentils are a low-glycemic index food, excellent for blood sugar control. The spices used in tadka are known for their anti-inflammatory properties and health benefits.

Per Serving:
Calories: 260 | Fat: 7g | Carbs: 38g | Fiber: 16g | Protein: 14g

Brazilian Black Bean Soup

Serves: 2
Prep time: 10 minutes / Cook time: 2 hours

Ingredients:
- 1 cup dried black beans, soaked overnight and drained
- 4 cups low-sodium chicken or vegetable broth
- 1 bay leaf
- 1 onion, chopped
- 2 cloves garlic, minced
- 1 carrot, diced
- 1/2 tsp cumin
- 1/2 tsp coriander
- 1 small orange, zest and juice
- Salt and pepper to taste
- Fresh cilantro for garnish

Instructions:
1. In a large pot, combine black beans, broth, bay leaf, onion, garlic, and carrot. Bring to a boil.
2. Reduce heat and simmer for 1.5 to 2 hours, or until beans are tender.
3. Remove bay leaf, and blend soup to desired consistency.
4. Stir in cumin, coriander, orange zest, and juice. Season with salt and pepper.
5. Serve hot, garnished with cilantro.

Benefits for Diabetics:
Black beans are an excellent source of fiber and protein, supporting steady blood sugar levels. The addition of spices and citrus provides antioxidants and a unique flavor profile.

Per Serving:
Calories: 210 | Fat: 1g | Carbs: 40g | Fiber: 15g | Protein: 14g

Lebanese Lentil & Spinach Soup

Serves: 2
Prep time: 10 minutes / Cook time: 45 minutes

Ingredients:
- 1 cup red lentils, rinsed
- 4 cups low-sodium vegetable broth
- 1 onion, chopped
- 2 cloves garlic, minced
- 2 cups fresh spinach, chopped
- 1 lemon, juice and zest
- 1 tsp cumin
- 1/2 tsp coriander
- Salt and pepper to taste
- Olive oil for cooking

Instructions:
1. In a large pot, heat olive oil over medium heat and sauté onion and garlic until soft.
2. Add lentils, vegetable broth, cumin, and coriander. Bring to a boil, then reduce heat and simmer for about 30 minutes.
3. Add spinach and cook until wilted.
4. Stir in lemon zest and juice, season with salt and pepper.
5. Serve hot, with a drizzle of olive oil if desired.

Benefits for Diabetics:
Red lentils are a great source of protein and fiber, helping to maintain stable blood sugar. Spinach is rich in iron and vitamins, making this soup both nourishing and low in glycemic impact.

Per Serving:
Calories: 220 | Fat: 3g | Carbs: 35g | Fiber: 17g | Protein: 15g

Ethiopian Red Lentil Stew (Misir Wot)

Serves: 2
Prep time: 15 minutes / Cook time: 45 minutes

Ingredients:
- 1 cup red lentils, rinsed
- 4 cups water
- 1 onion, finely chopped
- 2 cloves garlic, minced
- 1 tbsp berbere spice mix
- 1 tbsp tomato paste
- 1 tsp ginger, grated
- 2 tbsp olive oil
- Salt to taste
- Fresh cilantro for garnish

Instructions:
1. In a pot, heat olive oil and cook onion, garlic, and

ginger until soft.
2. Add berbere spice and tomato paste, stirring for a minute until fragrant.
3. Add lentils and water, bring to a boil, then reduce to a simmer.
4. Cook uncovered for about 30-35 minutes, or until lentils are soft and stew has thickened.
5. Season with salt to taste.
6. Serve hot, garnished with fresh cilantro.

Benefits for Diabetics:
Red lentils are a low-GI food, rich in fiber and protein, ideal for managing blood sugar. The berbere spice mix adds a depth of flavor without sugar or unhealthy fats.

Per Serving:
Calories: 270 | Fat: 7g | Carbs: 40g | Fiber: 18g | Protein: 16g

Turkish Red Lentil Soup (Mercimek Çorbası)

Serves: 2
Prep time: 10 minutes / Cook time: 30 minutes

Ingredients:
- 1 cup red lentils, rinsed and drained
- 4 cups low-sodium vegetable broth
- 1 onion, chopped   • 1 carrot, diced
- 1 potato, peeled and diced
- 1 tsp dried mint   • 1 tsp paprika
- Salt and pepper to taste
- 1 tbsp olive oil
- Lemon wedges for serving

Instructions:
1. In a large pot, heat olive oil and sauté onion, carrot, and potato until slightly softened.
2. Add red lentils, vegetable broth, dried mint, and paprika.
3. Bring to a boil, then reduce heat and simmer for about 25-30 minutes until lentils and vegetables are tender.
4. Blend the soup until smooth.
5. Season with salt and pepper to taste.
6. Serve hot with a lemon wedge on the side.

Benefits for Diabetics:
Red lentils are a great source of dietary fiber and protein, helping in blood sugar management. The soup is filling yet low in calories, making it an ideal choice for a diabetic diet.

Per Serving:
Calories: 230 | Fat: 4g | Carbs: 38g | Fiber: 16g | Protein: 13g

Cuban Black Bean Dip

Serves: 2
Prep time: 10 minutes / Cook time: 10 minutes

Ingredients:
- 1 can (15 oz) black beans, drained and rinsed
- 1 small onion, chopped
- 2 cloves garlic, minced • 1 tsp cumin
- 1/2 tsp oregano   • 2 tbsp olive oil
- Juice of 1 lime   • Salt and pepper to taste
- Fresh cilantro, chopped for garnish

Instructions:
1. In a skillet, heat olive oil and sauté onion and garlic until fragrant.
2. Add black beans, cumin, and oregano, cooking for a few minutes.
3. Remove from heat and let cool slightly.
4. In a food processor, blend the bean mixture with lime juice until smooth.
5. Season with salt and pepper to taste.
6. Garnish with fresh cilantro before serving.

Benefits for Diabetics:
Black beans are rich in fiber and protein, providing slow-releasing energy and aiding in blood sugar control. The dip is a tasty way to include legumes in a diabetic diet.

Per Serving:
Calories: 210 | Fat: 7g | Carbs: 29g | Fiber: 10g | Protein: 11g

Thai Green Curry Lentils

Serves: 2
Prep time: 10 minutes / Cook time: 25 minutes

Ingredients:
- 1 cup green lentils, rinsed and drained
- 1 can (14 oz) coconut milk
- 2 tbsp green curry paste
- 1 bell pepper, sliced
- 1 small zucchini, sliced
- 1 tbsp fish sauce (optional)
- 1 tsp brown sugar or a suitable diabetic-friendly sweetener
- Basil leaves for garnish
- 1 tbsp vegetable oil

Instructions:
1. In a pot, heat vegetable oil and sauté green curry paste until fragrant.
2. Add coconut milk, lentils, bell pepper, and zucchini.
3. Bring to a boil, then reduce heat and simmer until lentils are tender, about 20 minutes.
4. Stir in fish sauce and sweetener, adjusting to taste.
5. Garnish with fresh basil leaves before serving.

Benefits for Diabetics:
Lentils are a low glycemic index food, helping in blood sugar control. Coconut milk provides healthy fats, while the green curry adds flavor without the need for additional sugars.

Per Serving:
Calories: 280 | Fat: 14g | Carbs: 30g | Fiber: 14g | Protein: 12g

South African Samp and Beans

Serves: 2
Prep time: 8 hours (soaking) / Cook time: 2 hours

Ingredients:
- 1/2 cup dried samp (hominy)
- 1/2 cup dried beans (such as kidney or navy), soaked overnight
- 1 onion, chopped   • 1 tomato, diced
- 1 tsp curry powder   • 1 garlic clove, minced

- Salt and pepper to taste   • 2 tbsp vegetable oil

Instructions:

1. Soak samp and beans overnight in water.
2. Drain and rinse samp and beans, then place them in a large pot with enough water to cover.
3. Bring to a boil, reduce heat, and simmer until both are tender (about 2 hours).
4. In a separate pan, heat oil and sauté onion, garlic, and curry powder.
5. Add the sautéed mixture and diced tomato to the cooked samp and beans.
6. Cook for an additional 10 minutes. Season with salt and pepper to taste.
7. Serve warm.

Benefits for Diabetics:

Beans and samp provide a good balance of protein and fiber, essential for blood sugar management. The dish is hearty and satisfying while being low in fat and sugar.

Per Serving:

Calories: 300 | Fat: 7g | Carbs: 50g | Fiber: 13g | Protein: 15g

French Lentil Salad with Dijon Vinaigrette

Serves: 2

Prep time: 10 minutes / Cook time: 25 minutes

Ingredients:

- 1 cup French green lentils (Puy lentils)
- 1 small red onion, finely chopped
- 1 carrot, diced
- 1/4 cup parsley, chopped
- 3 tbsp olive oil
- 1 tbsp Dijon mustard
- 1 tbsp red wine vinegar
- Salt and pepper to taste

Instructions:

1. Cook lentils in boiling water until tender yet firm (about 20-25 minutes). Drain and cool.
2. In a large bowl, combine cooled lentils, red onion, carrot, and parsley.
3. In a small bowl, whisk together olive oil, Dijon mustard, red wine vinegar, salt, and pepper.
4. Pour the dressing over the lentil mixture and toss to coat.
5. Chill before serving to allow flavors to blend.

Benefits for Diabetics:

French lentils are especially good for blood sugar control due to their high fiber content and lower glycemic index. The salad is nutrient-dense, offering a variety of vitamins and minerals.

Per Serving:

Calories: 290 | Fat: 12g | Carbs: 34g | Fiber: 17g | Protein: 14g

Indonesian Gado-Gado

Serves: 2

Prep time: 20 minutes / Cook time: 10 minutes

Ingredients:

- 2 cups mixed vegetables (such as cabbage, bean sprouts, and carrots)
- 1/2 cup boiled potatoes, cubed
- 1/2 cup tofu, fried or boiled
- 1/4 cup peanut butter (unsweetened)
- 1 clove garlic, minced
- 1 tbsp soy sauce
- Juice of 1 lime
- 1 tsp brown sugar or a suitable diabetic-friendly sweetener
- 1/2 cup warm water
- Boiled eggs, halved (optional)

Instructions:

1. Blanch or steam the mixed vegetables until tender-crisp. Arrange on a plate along with potatoes and tofu.
2. For the peanut sauce, mix peanut butter, garlic, soy sauce, lime juice, sweetener, and warm water until smooth and creamy.
3. Drizzle the peanut sauce over the arranged vegetables, potatoes, and tofu.
4. Garnish with boiled eggs if using, and serve.

Benefits for Diabetics:

The dish is rich in vegetables, providing essential nutrients and fiber. The peanut sauce, when made with unsweetened peanut butter and minimal sweetener, offers healthy fats and flavor without excessive sugar.

Per Serving:

Calories: 320 | Fat: 18g | Carbs: 28g | Fiber: 8g | Protein: 16g

Caribbean Chickpea and Sweet Potato Curry

Serves: 2

Prep time: 10 minutes / Cook time: 30 minutes

Ingredients:

- 1 can (15 oz) chickpeas, drained and rinsed
- 1 large sweet potato, peeled and cubed
- 1 onion, chopped   • 2 cloves garlic, minced
- 1 tbsp curry powder   • 1/2 tsp thyme
- 1 can (14 oz) coconut milk
- Salt and pepper to taste
- 1 tbsp vegetable oil
- Fresh cilantro for garnish

Instructions:

1. In a large pot, heat oil over medium heat and sauté onion and garlic until soft.
2. Add curry powder and thyme, stirring for about 1 minute.
3. Add sweet potatoes, chickpeas, and coconut milk. Bring to a boil, then reduce heat and simmer until sweet potatoes are tender.
4. Season with salt and pepper to taste.
5. Garnish with fresh cilantro before serving.

Benefits for Diabetics:

Chickpeas and sweet potatoes are good sources of fiber, aiding in blood sugar control. The coconut milk adds creaminess without the need for heavy creams or sugars.

Per Serving:
Calories: 370 | Fat: 19g | Carbs: 45g | Fiber: 11g | Protein: 10g

Mediterranean Chickpea and Eggplant Stew

Serves: 2
Prep time: 10 minutes / Cook time: 40 minutes

Ingredients:
- 1 medium eggplant, cubed
- 1 can (15 oz) chickpeas, drained and rinsed
- 1 can (14 oz) diced tomatoes
- 1 onion, chopped   • 2 cloves garlic, minced
- 1 tsp dried basil   • 1 tsp dried oregano
- 2 tbsp olive oil
- Salt and pepper to taste
- Fresh parsley for garnish

Instructions:
1. In a large pot, heat olive oil and sauté onion and garlic until soft.
2. Add eggplant and cook until slightly softened.
3. Stir in chickpeas, diced tomatoes, basil, and oregano.
4. Bring to a boil, then reduce heat and simmer for about 30 minutes.
5. Season with salt and pepper to taste.
6. Garnish with fresh parsley before serving.

Benefits for Diabetics:
Eggplant and chickpeas are low in glycemic index and high in fiber, making them excellent choices for blood sugar management. The stew is filling and provides a variety of nutrients without added sugars.

Per Serving:
Calories: 280 | Fat: 10g | Carbs: 40g | Fiber: 15g | Protein: 11g

Japanese Adzuki Bean Porridge (Zenzai)

Serves: 2
Prep time: 8 hours (soaking) / Cook time: 1 hour

Ingredients:
- 1/2 cup adzuki beans, soaked overnight
- 4 cups water
- 1 piece dried kombu (optional for umami flavor)
- 1-2 tbsp erythritol or suitable diabetic-friendly sweetener
- Pinch of salt
- Optional: Shiratama dango or mochi pieces

Instructions:
1. Rinse the soaked adzuki beans and place them in a pot with water and kombu, if using.
2. Bring to a boil, then reduce the heat and simmer until beans are soft and cooked through, about 1 hour.
3. Remove kombu and add a diabetic-friendly sweetener, stirring until dissolved.
4. Add a pinch of salt to enhance the sweetness.
5. Serve warm, optionally with shiratama dango or mochi pieces for a traditional touch.

Benefits for Diabetics:
Adzuki beans are a great source of fiber and nutrients with a low glycemic index, making them suitable for blood sugar management. The natural sweetness allows for less or no added sweetener.

Per Serving:
Calories: 150 | Fat: 0.5g | Carbs: 28g | Fiber: 7g | Protein: 9g

Greek Fava Bean Dip (Fava)

Serves: 2
Prep time: 10 minutes / Cook time: 50 minutes

Ingredients:
- 1 cup yellow split peas, rinsed
- 3 cups water   • 1 onion, quartered
- 2 cloves garlic   • 1 bay leaf
- 1/4 cup olive oil   • Juice of 1 lemon
- Salt and pepper to taste
- Chopped parsley and red onion for garnish

Instructions:
1. In a pot, add split peas, water, onion, garlic, and bay leaf. Bring to a boil, then simmer for about 45-50 minutes until peas are very soft and the mixture is thick.
2. Remove from heat, discard onion, garlic, and bay leaf.
3. Blend the mixture with olive oil and lemon juice until smooth.
4. Season with salt and pepper to taste.
5. Serve warm or at room temperature, garnished with parsley and red onion.

Benefits for Diabetics:
Yellow split peas are a low-fat source of protein and high in fiber, making them ideal for stable blood sugar levels. Olive oil adds heart-healthy fats, enhancing the dish's nutritional profile.

Per Serving:
Calories: 330 | Fat: 14g | Carbs: 40g | Fiber: 15g | Protein: 14g

African Peanut Stew

Serves: 2
Prep time: 15 minutes / Cook time: 30 minutes

Ingredients:
- 1 cup cooked chickpeas
- 1 sweet potato, cubed
- 1 can (14 oz) diced tomatoes
- 2 cups vegetable broth • 1 onion, diced
- 2 cloves garlic, minced
- 1/4 cup natural peanut butter
- 1 tsp ginger, grated
- 1/2 tsp cayenne pepper (adjust to taste)
- 1/2 tsp cumin   • Salt to taste
- 1 tbsp vegetable oil   • Fresh cilantro for garnish

Instructions:
1. In a large pot, heat oil over medium heat and sauté onion, garlic, and ginger until soft.
2. Add sweet potato, chickpeas, diced tomatoes, vegetable broth, peanut butter, cayenne, and cumin.
3. Bring to a boil, then reduce heat and simmer for about

25 minutes until sweet potatoes are tender.
4. Adjust seasoning with salt and additional cayenne if desired.
5. Serve hot, garnished with fresh cilantro.

Benefits for Diabetics:
Chickpeas and sweet potatoes are excellent sources of dietary fiber, aiding in blood sugar control. The natural fats from peanut butter provide satiety and flavor without unhealthy additives.

Per Serving:
Calories: 360 | Fat: 16g | Carbs: 45g | Fiber: 10g | Protein: 13g

Colombian Bean and Plantain Stew (Frijoles con Plátano)

Serves: 2
Prep time: 10 minutes / Cook time: 2 hours (for beans)

Ingredients:
- 1 cup dried red beans, soaked overnight
- 1 green plantain, peeled and sliced
- 4 cups water
- 1 onion, chopped
- 2 cloves garlic, minced
- 1 carrot, diced
- 1 bell pepper, chopped
- 1 tsp cumin
- Salt and pepper to taste
- 1 tbsp olive oil
- Fresh cilantro for garnish

Instructions:
1. Drain and rinse the soaked beans. In a large pot, combine beans with water and bring to a boil. Reduce heat and simmer until beans are tender, about 1.5 to 2 hours.
2. In a separate pan, heat olive oil and sauté onion, garlic, carrot, and bell pepper until soft.
3. Add the sautéed vegetables, plantain slices, and cumin to the cooked beans. Simmer for an additional 20 minutes.
4. Season with salt and pepper to taste.
5. Serve hot, garnished with fresh cilantro.

Benefits for Diabetics:
Red beans are a great source of protein and fiber, supporting stable blood sugar levels. Plantains provide complex carbohydrates and nutrients, making this dish filling and nutritious.

Per Serving:
Calories: 330 | Fat: 5g | Carbs: 60g | Fiber: 15g | Protein: 18g

Middle Eastern Lentil Koftas

Serves: 2
Prep time: 15 minutes / Cook time: 20 minutes

Ingredients:
- 1 cup red lentils, cooked and drained
- 1/2 onion, finely chopped
- 2 cloves garlic, minced
- 1 tsp cumin
- 1/2 tsp coriander
- 1/2 tsp paprika
- 2 tbsp fresh parsley, chopped
- Salt and pepper to taste
- Olive oil for frying

Instructions:
1. In a food processor, combine cooked lentils, onion, garlic, cumin, coriander, paprika, and parsley. Pulse until mixture is well combined but still has some texture.
2. Shape the mixture into small, oval koftas.
3. Heat a small amount of olive oil in a frying pan over medium heat. Fry the koftas until golden brown on all sides.
4. Season with salt and pepper to taste.
5. Serve warm with a side of salad or yogurt sauce.

Benefits for Diabetics:
Red lentils are an excellent source of plant-based protein and fiber, aiding in blood sugar control. The herbs and spices add antioxidants and flavor without the need for added sugars.

Per Serving:
Calories: 240 | Fat: 7g | Carbs: 32g | Fiber: 15g | Protein: 14g

Spanish Chickpea and Spinach Stew (Espinacas con Garbanzos)

Serves: 2
Prep time: 10 minutes / Cook time: 20 minutes

Ingredients:
- 1 can (15 oz) chickpeas, drained and rinsed
- 2 cups fresh spinach, washed and chopped
- 1 can (14 oz) diced tomatoes
- 1 onion, chopped
- 2 cloves garlic, minced
- 1 tsp smoked paprika
- 1/2 tsp cumin
- Salt and pepper to taste
- 2 tbsp olive oil
- Toasted bread for serving (optional)

Instructions:
1. In a large pot, heat olive oil and sauté onion and garlic until soft.
2. Add diced tomatoes, smoked paprika, and cumin. Cook for a few minutes until tomatoes are soft.
3. Add chickpeas and spinach, cooking until spinach is wilted and chickpeas are heated through.
4. Season with salt and pepper to taste.
5. Serve hot, optionally with toasted bread on the side.

Benefits for Diabetics:
Chickpeas are a good source of fiber and protein, offering sustained energy and aiding in blood sugar control. Spinach is low in carbohydrates and high in vitamins and minerals.

Per Serving:
Calories: 280 | Fat: 10g | Carbs: 38g | Fiber: 11g | Protein: 12g

Vietnamese Mung Bean Crepes (Bánh Xèo)

Serves: 2
Prep time: 2 hours (soaking) / Cook time: 30 minutes

Ingredients:
- 1/2 cup mung beans, soaked for 2 hours
- 1 cup rice flour
- 1 1/2 cups water
- 1/2 tsp turmeric
- Salt to taste
- 1 cup bean sprouts
- 1/2 cup sliced mushrooms
- 1/2 cup thinly sliced bell pepper
- Fresh herbs (mint, basil) for serving
- 1 tbsp vegetable oil

Instructions:
1. Drain and rinse the soaked mung beans. Blend with rice flour, water, turmeric, and salt to create a smooth batter.
2. Heat a non-stick pan over medium heat and brush with vegetable oil.
3. Pour a thin layer of batter into the pan, swirling to cover the bottom. Add bean sprouts, mushrooms, and bell pepper on one half of the crepe.
4. Cook until the edges are crispy and the bottom is golden. Fold over to cover the filling.
5. Serve hot with fresh herbs and dipping sauce.

Benefits for Diabetics:
Mung beans are low in fat and high in fiber and protein, making them an excellent choice for blood sugar management. The crepes are a light yet satisfying meal with plenty of nutrients.

Per Serving:
Calories: 220 | Fat: 5g | Carbs: 35g | Fiber: 5g | Protein: 8g

Caribbean Pigeon Pea Rice (Arroz con Gandules)

Serves: 2
Prep time: 10 minutes / Cook time: 30 minutes

Ingredients:
- 1/2 cup pigeon peas, drained and rinsed
- 1 cup long-grain brown rice
- 2 cups low-sodium chicken or vegetable broth
- 1 small onion, diced
- 1 bell pepper, diced
- 2 cloves garlic, minced
- 1/2 tsp turmeric
- 1/2 tsp cumin
- 1 tbsp olive oil
- Salt and pepper to taste
- Fresh cilantro for garnish

Instructions:
1. In a pot, heat olive oil over medium heat and sauté onion, bell pepper, and garlic until softened.
2. Stir in rice, pigeon peas, turmeric, and cumin until well mixed.

3. Add broth and bring the mixture to a boil. Reduce heat, cover, and simmer until rice is tender and liquid is absorbed, about 20 minutes.
4. Season with salt and pepper to taste.
5. Fluff with a fork and garnish with fresh cilantro before serving.

Benefits for Diabetics:
Pigeon peas are a good source of protein and fiber, aiding in blood sugar management. Brown rice provides a whole grain, complex carbohydrate option, better for sustained energy.

Per Serving:
Calories: 350 | Fat: 7g | Carbs: 60g | Fiber: 7g | Protein: 12g

Persian Lentil Patties (Adas Polo)

Serves: 2
Prep time: 15 minutes / Cook time: 20 minutes

Ingredients:
- 1 cup cooked green lentils
- 1/2 onion, finely grated
- 1 garlic clove, minced
- 1 tsp cumin
- 1/2 tsp cinnamon
- 1/4 cup whole wheat breadcrumbs
- Salt and pepper to taste
- Olive oil for frying
- Fresh parsley for garnish

Instructions:
1. In a bowl, mash the cooked lentils with a fork or potato masher.
2. Mix in grated onion, garlic, cumin, cinnamon, and breadcrumbs until well combined. Season with salt and pepper.
3. Shape the mixture into small patties.
4. Heat a small amount of olive oil in a pan over medium heat. Fry patties until golden brown on both sides.
5. Serve hot, garnished with fresh parsley.

Benefits for Diabetics:
Lentils are an excellent source of fiber and plant-based protein, helping to maintain stable blood sugar levels. The spices provide flavor without the need for added sugars.

Per Serving:
Calories: 280 | Fat: 6g | Carbs: 44g | Fiber: 18g | Protein: 16g

Italian Cannellini Bean and Kale Soup

Serves: 2
Prep time: 10 minutes / Cook time: 30 minutes

Ingredients:
- 1 can (15 oz) cannellini beans, drained and rinsed
- 4 cups low-sodium vegetable broth
- 2 cups kale, chopped
- 1 onion, diced
- 2 cloves garlic, minced
- 1/2 tsp dried thyme
- Salt and pepper to taste
- 1 tbsp olive oil
- Parmesan cheese for garnish (optional)

Instructions:

1. In a large pot, heat olive oil and sauté onion and garlic until translucent.
2. Add cannellini beans, vegetable broth, and thyme. Bring to a boil, then reduce heat and simmer for about 20 minutes.
3. Add kale and continue to simmer until the kale is tender.
4. Season with salt and pepper to taste.
5. Serve hot, garnished with grated Parmesan cheese if desired.

Benefits for Diabetics:

Cannellini beans are a low glycemic index food, providing steady energy and fiber. Kale is a superfood, packed with vitamins and minerals beneficial for overall health.

Per Serving:

Calories: 260 | Fat: 7g | Carbs: 38g | Fiber: 10g | Protein: 14g

Moroccan Harira Soup

Serves: 2

Prep time: 15 minutes / Cook time: 45 minutes

Ingredients:

- 1/2 cup lentils, rinsed
- 1/2 cup chickpeas, soaked overnight and drained
- 4 cups low-sodium vegetable broth
- 1 can (14 oz) diced tomatoes
- 1 onion, chopped
- 2 celery stalks, chopped
- 1 carrot, diced
- 1 tsp ginger, grated
- 1 tsp turmeric
- 1 tsp cumin
- 1/2 tsp cinnamon
- Salt and pepper to taste
- 2 tbsp parsley, chopped
- 2 tbsp cilantro, chopped
- 1 tbsp olive oil

Instructions:

1. In a large pot, heat olive oil over medium heat. Add onion, celery, and carrot, sautéing until softened.
2. Add lentils, chickpeas, vegetable broth, diced tomatoes, ginger, turmeric, cumin, and cinnamon.
3. Bring to a boil, then reduce heat and simmer for about 45 minutes until lentils and chickpeas are tender.
4. Stir in parsley and cilantro, and season with salt and pepper to taste.
5. Serve hot, offering a comforting and aromatic experience.

Benefits for Diabetics:

Both lentils and chickpeas are excellent for blood sugar control due to their high fiber and protein content. The variety of spices in Harira provides anti-inflammatory benefits and enhances flavor naturally.

Per Serving:

Calories: 310 | Fat: 8g | Carbs: 45g | Fiber: 14g | Protein: 17g

Chinese Mung Bean Noodles with Veggies

Serves: 2

Prep time: 15 minutes / Cook time: 10 minutes

Ingredients:

- 200g mung bean noodles
- 1 bell pepper, julienned
- 1 carrot, julienned
- 1/2 cucumber, julienned
- 2 green onions, sliced
- 1 tbsp soy sauce (low sodium)
- 1 tsp sesame oil
- 1 garlic clove, minced
- 1 tsp grated ginger
- 1 tsp rice vinegar
- 1/2 tsp chili flakes (optional)
- Sesame seeds for garnish

Instructions:

1. Cook mung bean noodles according to package instructions, then rinse under cold water and drain.
2. In a large bowl, combine noodles with bell pepper, carrot, and cucumber.
3. In a small bowl, whisk together soy sauce, sesame oil, garlic, ginger, rice vinegar, and chili flakes if using.
4. Pour the dressing over the noodles and vegetables, tossing to coat evenly.
5. Garnish with green onions and sesame seeds before serving.

Benefits for Diabetics:

Mung bean noodles are a great alternative to traditional pasta, offering lower glycemic impact. The assortment of vegetables adds fiber and nutrients, while the dressing flavors the dish without added sugar.

Per Serving:

Calories: 220 | Fat: 4g | Carbs: 40g | Fiber: 3g | Protein: 8g

Brazilian Feijoada (Black Bean Stew)

Serves: 2

Prep time: 10 minutes (plus soaking) / Cook time: 2 hours

Ingredients:

- 1 cup black beans, soaked overnight
- 4 cups water
- 1 onion, chopped
- 2 cloves garlic, minced
- 1 bay leaf
- 1/2 tsp smoked paprika
- Salt and pepper to taste
- 1 tbsp olive oil
- Orange slices for serving (traditional garnish)
- Fresh parsley for garnish

Instructions:

1. Drain and rinse the soaked black beans. In a large pot, combine beans, water, onion, garlic, and bay leaf.
2. Bring to a boil, then reduce heat and simmer until beans are very tender, about 2 hours.
3. In the last 30 minutes of cooking, add smoked paprika and continue to simmer.
4. Season with salt and pepper to taste.

5. Serve hot, garnished with orange slices and fresh parsley.

Benefits for Diabetics:

Black beans are an excellent source of dietary fiber and protein, helping to keep blood sugar levels steady. The stew is nutrient-dense and filling, making it a satisfying meal option.

Per Serving:

Calories: 310 | Fat: 5g | Carbs: 50g | Fiber: 15g | Protein: 18g

Middle Eastern Falafel with Tahini Sauce

Serves: 2

Prep time: 15 minutes / Cook time: 10 minutes

Ingredients:

- 1 cup chickpeas, soaked overnight and drained
- 1 small onion, chopped
- 2 cloves garlic, minced
- 1/4 cup parsley, chopped
- 1 tsp cumin
- 1/2 tsp coriander
- Salt and pepper to taste
- 1/4 cup tahini
- Juice of 1 lemon
- Water as needed for sauce consistency
- Olive oil for frying

Instructions:

1. In a food processor, blend chickpeas, onion, garlic, parsley, cumin, and coriander until a coarse mixture forms.
2. Shape the mixture into small patties or balls.
3. Heat olive oil in a pan and fry the falafel until golden brown on all sides.
4. For the tahini sauce, whisk together tahini, lemon juice, and water until smooth.
5. Serve falafel with tahini sauce drizzled on top or on the side for dipping.

Benefits for Diabetics:

Chickpeas are rich in fiber and protein, promoting blood sugar control and satiety. The tahini provides healthy fats, and the overall dish is high in nutrients and flavor.

Per Serving:

Calories: 330 | Fat: 18g | Carbs: 34g | Fiber: 9g | Protein: 13g

Jamaican Rice and Peas

Serves: 2

Prep time: 10 minutes / Cook time: 25 minutes

Ingredients:

- 1/2 cup kidney beans or pigeon peas, drained and rinsed
- 1 cup brown rice
- 2 cups water
- 1/2 cup light coconut milk
- 1 small onion, chopped
- 2 cloves garlic, minced
- 1 scotch bonnet pepper (optional for heat)
- 1 tsp thyme
- 1 green onion, chopped
- Salt and pepper to taste

Instructions:

1. In a pot, combine water, coconut milk, onion, garlic, and scotch bonnet pepper. Bring to a boil.
2. Add rice, beans or peas, thyme, and green onion. Reduce heat to a simmer.
3. Cover and cook until rice is tender and all liquid is absorbed, about 20-25 minutes.
4. Remove scotch bonnet pepper before serving. Season with salt and pepper to taste.
5. Serve hot as a flavorful side or main dish.

Benefits for Diabetics:

Kidney beans and pigeon peas are high in fiber and protein, aiding in blood sugar control. Brown rice is a whole grain with a lower glycemic index compared to white rice, making it a healthier choice.

Per Serving:

Calories: 320 | Fat: 5g | Carbs: 60g | Fiber: 8g | Protein: 10g

Tunisian Chickpea and Vegetable Tagine

Serves: 2

Prep time: 15 minutes / Cook time: 40 minutes

Ingredients:

- 1 can (15 oz) chickpeas, drained and rinsed
- 1 small eggplant, cubed
- 1 zucchini, cubed
- 1 bell pepper, chopped
- 1 onion, chopped
- 2 cloves garlic, minced
- 1 can (14 oz) diced tomatoes
- 1 tsp cumin
- 1 tsp paprika
- 1/2 tsp cinnamon
- 2 tbsp olive oil
- Salt and pepper to taste
- Fresh cilantro or parsley for garnish

Instructions:

1. In a large pot or tagine, heat olive oil over medium heat. Add onion and garlic, sautéing until soft.
2. Add eggplant, zucchini, bell pepper, and spices. Cook for a few minutes until vegetables start to soften.
3. Stir in chickpeas and diced tomatoes. Bring to a simmer.
4. Cover and cook on low heat for about 30 minutes until vegetables are tender.
5. Season with salt and pepper to taste.
6. Garnish with fresh cilantro or parsley before serving.

Benefits for Diabetics:

Chickpeas are an excellent source of fiber and protein, essential for stable blood sugar levels. The variety of vegetables provides nutrients and antioxidants with minimal impact on blood sugar.

Per Serving:

Calories: 330 | Fat: 10g | Carbs: 50g | Fiber: 14g | Protein: 13g

Ethiopian Yellow Split Pea Stew (Kik Alicha)

Serves: 2
Prep time: 10 minutes / Cook time: 1 hour

Ingredients:
- 1 cup yellow split peas, rinsed and soaked for 1 hour
- 4 cups water
- 1 onion, finely chopped
- 2 cloves garlic, minced
- 1 tsp ginger, minced
- 1 tsp turmeric
- 1/2 tsp cumin
- Salt to taste
- 2 tbsp olive oil
- Fresh parsley for garnish

Instructions:
1. Drain and rinse the soaked split peas. In a pot, combine split peas with water and bring to a boil. Reduce heat and simmer until peas are tender, about 45-50 minutes.
2. In a separate pan, heat olive oil over medium heat. Add onion, garlic, and ginger, cooking until onion is translucent.
3. Add cooked onion mixture to the split peas along with turmeric, cumin, and salt. Continue to simmer for an additional 10 minutes.
4. Adjust seasoning as needed and garnish with fresh parsley before serving.

Benefits for Diabetics:
Yellow split peas are a great low-glycemic food, rich in fiber and protein which help regulate blood sugar levels. The spices used provide anti-inflammatory benefits and enhance the dish's flavor.

Per Serving:
Calories: 310 | Fat: 8g | Carbs: 45g | Fiber: 18g | Protein: 18g

Korean Mung Bean Pancakes (Bindaetteok)

Serves: 2
Prep time: 2 hours (soaking) / Cook time: 20 minutes

Ingredients:
- 1 cup mung beans, soaked for 2 hours
- 1/2 cup water
- 1/2 cup kimchi, chopped
- 1/4 cup mung bean sprouts
- 2 green onions, chopped
- 1 carrot, shredded
- 1 tsp sesame oil
- Salt to taste
- Vegetable oil for frying

Instructions:
1. Drain and rinse the soaked mung beans. Blend with water in a food processor until a smooth batter forms.
2. Transfer the batter to a bowl and mix in kimchi, mung bean sprouts, green onions, carrot, and sesame oil. Season with salt.

3. Heat a little vegetable oil in a non-stick pan over medium heat. Pour batter to form small pancakes, cooking until golden brown on both sides.
4. Serve hot, accompanied by soy sauce or a dipping sauce of choice.

Benefits for Diabetics:
Mung beans are low in fat and high in fiber and protein, beneficial for blood sugar control. The addition of vegetables increases the nutritional content without significantly impacting carbohydrate count.

Per Serving:
Calories: 270 | Fat: 10g | Carbs: 35g | Fiber: 8g | Protein: 13g

Mexican Lentil Ceviche

Serves: 2
Prep time: 15 minutes (plus marinating) / Cook time: 20 minutes

Ingredients:
- 1 cup cooked green lentils
- Juice of 2 limes
- Juice of 1 lemon
- 1 tomato, diced
- 1/2 cucumber, diced
- 1/4 red onion, finely chopped
- 1 jalapeño, seeded and minced
- 1/4 cup cilantro, chopped
- Salt and pepper to taste
- Avocado slices for garnish

Instructions:
1. In a bowl, combine cooked lentils with lime and lemon juice. Let marinate for at least 30 minutes.
2. Add tomato, cucumber, red onion, jalapeño, and cilantro to the lentils. Mix well.
3. Season with salt and pepper to taste.
4. Serve chilled, garnished with avocado slices.

Benefits for Diabetics:
Lentils are an excellent source of protein and fiber, helping stabilize blood sugar levels. The citrus juices provide vitamin C, and the overall dish is low in fat and calories.

Per Serving:
Calories: 220 | Fat: 3g | Carbs: 35g | Fiber: 15g | Protein: 12g

Nigerian Bean Pudding (Moi Moi)

Serves: 2
Prep time: 1 hour (for soaking beans) / Cook time: 1 hour

Ingredients:
- 1 cup black-eyed peas, soaked for 1 hour
- 1 onion, chopped
- 1 red bell pepper, chopped
- 1 scotch bonnet pepper (optional for heat)
- 2 cloves garlic, minced
- 1/2 tsp thyme
- 1/2 tsp curry powder
- Salt to taste
- 2 tbsp vegetable oil

Instructions:

1. Drain and rinse the soaked beans. Remove skins by rubbing the beans between your hands and rinsing away the skins.
2. Blend the beans with onion, bell pepper, scotch bonnet pepper, and garlic until smooth.
3. Stir in thyme, curry powder, salt, and vegetable oil.
4. Pour the mixture into greased ramekins or a mold suitable for steaming.
5. Steam for about 1 hour or until the pudding is set and cooked through.
6. Allow to cool slightly before unmolding and serving.

Benefits for Diabetics:

Black-eyed peas are a low glycemic index food, rich in fiber and protein. Moi Moi provides a satisfying meal with minimal impact on blood sugar levels.

Per Serving:

Calories: 330 | Fat: 7g | Carbs: 50g | Fiber: 10g | Protein: 18g

Roasted Beet Hummus

Serves: 2

Prep time: 15 minutes / Cook time: 60 minutes (for roasting beets)

Ingredients:

- 1 medium beet, roasted and peeled
- 1 can (15 oz) chickpeas, drained and rinsed
- 2 tbsp tahini
- 2 cloves garlic, minced
- Juice of 1 lemon
- 2 tbsp olive oil
- Salt and pepper to taste

Instructions:

1. Wrap the beet in foil and roast in a preheated 400°F oven until tender, about 60 minutes. Once cooled, peel and chop.
2. In a food processor, blend roasted beet, chickpeas, tahini, garlic, and lemon juice until smooth.
3. While blending, slowly drizzle in olive oil until fully incorporated.
4. Season with salt and pepper to taste.
5. Serve with a drizzle of olive oil and garnish as desired.

Benefits for Diabetics:

Beets are low in calories and high in nutrients, including fiber, which can help manage blood sugar levels. Chickpeas provide a good source of protein and fiber, essential for diabetic diets.

Per Serving:

Calories: 220 | Fat: 10g | Carbs: 28g | Fiber: 8g | Protein: 8g

Spicy Black Bean Hummus

Serves: 2

Prep time: 10 minutes / Cook time: 0 minutes

Ingredients:

- 1 can (15 oz) black beans, drained and rinsed
- 2 tbsp tahini
- 1 small jalapeño, seeded and chopped
- 1 clove garlic, minced
- Juice of 1 lime
- 2 tbsp olive oil
- 1 tsp cumin
- Salt and chili powder to taste

Instructions:

1. In a food processor, combine black beans, tahini, jalapeño, garlic, lime juice, and cumin.
2. Process until smooth, gradually adding olive oil to reach desired consistency.
3. Season with salt and chili powder to taste.
4. Serve with a sprinkle of chili powder or chopped cilantro.

Benefits for Diabetics:

Black beans are an excellent source of protein and fiber, helping maintain stable blood sugar levels. The addition of jalapeño can boost metabolism without adding sugars.

Per Serving:

Calories: 230 | Fat: 11g | Carbs: 27g | Fiber: 10g | Protein: 9g

Sun-Dried Tomato and Basil Hummus

Serves: 2

Prep time: 10 minutes / Cook time: 0 minutes

Ingredients:

- 1 can (15 oz) chickpeas, drained and rinsed
- 1/4 cup sun-dried tomatoes (not in oil), chopped
- 1/4 cup fresh basil leaves
- 2 tbsp tahini
- 2 cloves garlic, minced
- Juice of 1 lemon
- 2 tbsp olive oil
- Salt and pepper to taste

Instructions:

1. In a food processor, blend chickpeas, sun-dried tomatoes, basil, tahini, garlic, and lemon juice until smooth.
2. Gradually add in olive oil until the hummus reaches your desired consistency.
3. Season with salt and pepper to taste.
4. Serve garnished with additional basil or sun-dried tomatoes if desired.

Benefits for Diabetics:

Chickpeas are a low glycemic index food, beneficial for blood sugar control. Sun-dried tomatoes provide lycopene and basil adds antioxidants without added sugar.

Per Serving:

Calories: 240 | Fat: 12g | Carbs: 28g | Fiber: 7g | Protein: 8g

Chapter 8 : Desserts

Welcome to a sweet journey through delightful diabetic-friendly desserts!

In this chapter, we explore an array of treats that bring joy to the palate while being mindful of dietary needs.

These recipes are crafted with love and care, ensuring that each bite is not only delicious but also suitable for those managing diabetes or looking for healthier dessert options.

Our collection showcases the versatility and creativity possible within diabetic-friendly cooking, featuring a wide range of ingredients from succulent fruits to rich nuts, spices, and alternative sweeteners.

Each recipe is designed to delight the senses and provide satisfaction without the typical sugar rush or guilt.

Whether you crave something creamy, crunchy, tangy, or sweet, these desserts are here to fulfill your desires with health-conscious ingredients and innovative twists.

From the warm spices of autumn to the refreshing zests of summer, there's a dessert for every season and occasion.

Embrace these culinary creations that consider nutritional balance, glycemic impact, and the universal love for something sweet at the end of a meal or as a treat. These desserts aren't just about being "less" — less sugar, less carbs, less guilt. Instead, they are about offering "more" — more flavor, more variety, more joy. So, preheat your ovens, gather your mixing bowls, and prepare to indulge in the art of diabetic-friendly desserts that promise to be a treat for both the body and the soul.

Welcome to guilt-free indulgence!

Almond and Berry Delight

Serves: 2

Prep time: 10 minutes / Cook time: 0 minutes

Ingredients:
- 1 cup mixed berries (strawberries, blueberries, raspberries)
- 1/2 cup unsweetened almond milk
- 2 tbsp chopped almonds • 1 tsp vanilla extract
- 2 tbsp chia seeds • Mint leaves for garnish

Instructions:
1. In a bowl, mix the berries, almond milk, chia seeds, and vanilla extract.
2. Refrigerate the mixture for at least 1 hour until it thickens, preferably overnight.
3. Serve in dessert cups, topped with chopped almonds and garnish with mint leaves.

Benefits for Diabetics:
This dessert is low in carbohydrates and high in fiber, which is beneficial for blood sugar control. Berries are a low-glycemic food, meaning they have a minimal impact on blood sugar levels. Almonds add healthy fats and proteins, making this a well-rounded, nutritious choice for those managing diabetes.

Per Serving:
Calories: 180 | Fat: 9g | Carbs: 18g | Fiber: 7g | Protein: 6g

Cinnamon-Spiced Baked Apples

Serves: 2

Prep time: 10 minutes / Cook time: 30 minutes

Ingredients:
- 2 large apples, cored
- 1/4 cup chopped walnuts or pecans
- 2 tbsp sugar-free sweetener
- 1 tsp ground cinnamon
- 1/4 tsp nutmeg
- 1/2 cup water

Instructions:
1. Preheat your oven to 350°F (175°C).
2. Mix the chopped nuts, sugar-free sweetener, cinnamon, and nutmeg in a bowl.
3. Place the apples in a baking dish and stuff each apple with the nut mixture.
4. Pour water into the bottom of the dish and bake for 30 minutes or until apples are tender.
5. Serve warm, optionally with a dollop of sugar-free whipped cream or Greek yogurt.

Benefits for Diabetics:
Apples are a fiber-rich fruit, which can help with blood sugar control. The combination of cinnamon and nuts provides additional health benefits, including helping to regulate blood sugar levels and adding healthy fats and protein to the dish, all while keeping it diabetes-friendly.

Per Serving:
Calories: 190 | Fat: 8g | Carbs: 31g | Fiber: 5g | Protein: 2g

Cinnamon-Spiced Baked Apples

Serves: 2

Prep time: 15 minutes / Chill time: 30 minutes

Ingredients:
- 1/2 cup unsweetened shredded coconut
- 1/4 cup natural peanut butter
- 1 tbsp sugar-free sweetener
- 1 tsp vanilla extract

Instructions:
1. In a bowl, mix together the peanut butter, shredded coconut, sugar-free sweetener, and vanilla extract until well combined.
2. Form the mixture into small balls and place them on a baking sheet lined with parchment paper.
3. Refrigerate for at least 30 minutes until firm.
4. Serve chilled.

Benefits for Diabetics:
Peanut butter is a great source of healthy fats and protein, which are important for blood sugar stabilization. The unsweetened coconut adds texture and nutrients without the added sugar, making these balls a smart choice for those looking to manage their diabetes.

Per Serving:
Calories: 210 | Fat: 18g | Carbs: 8g | Fiber: 3g | Protein: 6g

Avocado Chocolate Mousse

Serves: 2
Prep time: 10 minutes / Chill time: 1 hour

Ingredients:
- 1 ripe avocado, peeled and pitted
- 2 tbsp unsweetened cocoa powder
- 2 tbsp sugar-free sweetener
- 1/2 tsp vanilla extract • Pinch of salt

Instructions:
1. Combine the avocado, cocoa powder, sugar-free sweetener, vanilla extract, and salt in a blender or food processor.
2. Blend until smooth and creamy, scraping down the sides as needed.
3. Divide the mousse into two serving dishes and refrigerate for at least 1 hour until chilled.
4. Serve with a sprinkle of sugar-free chocolate shavings or fresh berries.

Benefits for Diabetics:
Avocados provide healthy fats and fiber, both of which are beneficial for blood sugar control. The cocoa adds antioxidants without adding sugar, making this dessert not only indulgent but also a healthy choice for individuals managing diabetes.

Per Serving:
Calories: 240 | Fat: 20g | Carbs: 12g | Fiber: 7g | Protein: 3g

Lemon Ricotta Pancakes

Serves: 2
Prep time: 10 minutes / Cook time: 10 minutes

Ingredients:
- 1/2 cup almond flour • 1/4 cup ricotta cheese
- 2 eggs • 1 tbsp sugar-free sweetener
- 1/2 lemon, juice and zest
- 1/2 tsp baking powder
- Butter or oil for cooking

Instructions:
1. In a bowl, mix together the almond flour, baking powder, and sugar-free sweetener.
2. In another bowl, whisk together the eggs, ricotta cheese, lemon juice, and zest.
3. Combine the wet and dry ingredients until a batter forms.
4. Heat a non-stick pan over medium heat and lightly grease with butter or oil.
5. Pour small amounts of batter onto the pan to form pancakes. Cook until bubbles form on the surface, then flip and cook the other side until golden.
6. Serve warm with a dollop of sugar-free yogurt or fresh berries.

Benefits for Diabetics:
Almond flour provides a low-carb alternative to traditional flour, making these pancakes suitable for blood sugar management. Ricotta cheese adds creaminess and protein, and the lemon provides a refreshing flavor and vitamin C.

Per Serving:
Calories: 280 | Fat: 22g | Carbs: 8g | Fiber: 3g | Protein: 15g

Ginger Spice Cookies

Serves: 2
Prep time: 15 minutes / Cook time: 12 minutes

Ingredients:
- 1/2 cup almond flour • 1/4 cup coconut flour
- 1 tsp ground ginger • 1/2 tsp cinnamon
- 1/4 tsp nutmeg • 1/4 cup butter, softened
- 1 egg • 2 tbsp sugar-free sweetener
- 1/4 tsp baking soda

Instructions:
1. Preheat your oven to 350°F (175°C) and line a baking sheet with parchment paper.
2. In a bowl, mix together the almond flour, coconut flour, ginger, cinnamon, nutmeg, and baking soda.
3. In another bowl, beat the butter and sugar-free sweetener until creamy. Add the egg and mix well.
4. Gradually mix the dry ingredients into the wet ingredients until a dough forms.
5. Roll the dough into small balls and place them on the prepared baking sheet, flattening slightly.
6. Bake for 10-12 minutes or until golden and set.
7. Allow to cool before serving.

Benefits for Diabetics:
These cookies are designed with blood sugar control in mind, using low-carb flours and spices known for their anti-inflammatory properties. They offer a guilt-free way to enjoy a sweet treat, providing flavor and satisfaction without the spike in blood sugar.

Per Serving:
Calories: 220 | Fat: 18g | Carbs: 10g | Fiber: 4g | Protein: 6g

Chia Seed Vanilla Pudding

Serves: 2
Prep time: 5 minutes / Chill time: 2 hours

Ingredients:
- 1/4 cup chia seeds
- 1 cup unsweetened almond milk
- 1 tbsp sugar-free sweetener
- 1 tsp vanilla extract

Instructions:
1. In a bowl, mix the chia seeds, almond milk, sugar-free sweetener, and vanilla extract.
2. Stir well to combine and let sit for 5 minutes.
3. Stir again, cover, and refrigerate for at least 2 hours, or until it reaches a pudding-like consistency.
4. Stir before serving and add more almond milk if needed for desired consistency.
5. Serve chilled, topped with fresh berries or a sprinkle of cinnamon.

Benefits for Diabetics:
Chia seeds are rich in fiber, omega-3 fatty acids, and protein, all of which are beneficial for blood sugar control and overall health. This pudding is low in carbs and can be sweetened to taste with a sugar-free sweetener, making it a safe and satisfying dessert option for diabetics.

Per Serving:
Calories: 150 | Fat: 8g | Carbs: 10g | Fiber: 8g | Protein: 5g

Coconut Almond Bark

Serves: 2

Prep time: 5 minutes / Chill time: 30 minutes

Ingredients:
- 1/2 cup sugar-free dark chocolate chips
- 1/4 cup unsweetened shredded coconut
- 1/4 cup slivered almonds

Instructions:
1. Melt the dark chocolate chips in a microwave or double boiler until smooth.
2. Spread the melted chocolate onto a parchment-lined baking sheet into a thin layer.
3. Sprinkle the shredded coconut and slivered almonds over the chocolate.
4. Refrigerate until firm, about 30 minutes.
5. Break into pieces and serve.

Benefits for Diabetics:
Dark chocolate is known for its antioxidant properties and, when sugar-free, can be a good option for those managing diabetes. The addition of almonds and coconut provides healthy fats and fiber, contributing to a more stable blood sugar level.

Per Serving:
Calories: 200 | Fat: 15g | Carbs: 10g | Fiber: 3g | Protein: 4g

Pumpkin Spice Smoothie

Serves: 2

Prep time: 5 minutes / Cook time: 0 minutes

Ingredients:
- 1/2 cup pumpkin puree (canned or fresh)
- 1 cup unsweetened almond milk
- 1/2 tsp pumpkin pie spice
- 1 tbsp sugar-free sweetener
- 1/2 banana (optional for added sweetness)
- Ice cubes

Instructions:
1. Place the pumpkin puree, almond milk, pumpkin pie spice, sugar-free sweetener, banana (if using), and ice cubes in a blender.
2. Blend until smooth and creamy.
3. Taste and adjust sweetener or spices as needed.
4. Serve immediately, sprinkled with a little extra pumpkin pie spice or cinnamon on top.

Benefits for Diabetics:
Pumpkin is low in calories and rich in vitamins and fiber, making it a great choice for blood sugar management. This smoothie uses sugar-free sweeteners and nutrient-rich ingredients to create a satisfying treat without the blood sugar spike.

Per Serving:
Calories: 80 | Fat: 1.5g | Carbs: 15g | Fiber: 4g | Protein: 2g

Zesty Lemon Coconut Bars

Serves: 2

Prep time: 15 minutes / Cook time: 25 minutes

Ingredients:
- For the crust:

- 1/2 cup coconut flour   • 1/4 cup melted coconut oil
- 1 tbsp sugar-free sweetener
- For the filling:
- 2 eggs   • 1/2 cup sugar-free sweetener
- 1/2 cup fresh lemon juice
- 2 tsp lemon zest   • 1/4 cup coconut flour

Instructions:
1. Preheat your oven to 350°F (175°C) and line an 8x8 inch baking dish with parchment paper.
2. Mix coconut flour, melted coconut oil, and sugar-free sweetener to form the crust. Press it evenly into the bottom of the prepared dish.
3. Bake the crust for 10 minutes until just golden.
4. While the crust is baking, whisk together the eggs, sugar-free sweetener, lemon juice, lemon zest, and coconut flour until smooth for the filling.
5. Pour the filling over the baked crust and return to the oven for 15 minutes or until the filling is set.
6. Cool completely before cutting into bars.

Benefits for Diabetics:
Lemon and coconut are both low in carbs and high in flavor, making these bars a great choice for those managing their blood sugar levels. The coconut flour provides a gluten-free, low-carb base, while the lemon adds a refreshing zest without additional sugar.

Per Serving:
Calories: 210 | Fat: 15g | Carbs: 10g | Fiber: 5g | Protein: 6g

Walnut Brownie Bites

Serves: 2

Prep time: 15 minutes / Cook time: 15 minutes

Ingredients:
- 1/2 cup almond flour
- 1/4 cup unsweetened cocoa powder
- 1/4 cup sugar-free sweetener
- 1/4 cup melted butter or coconut oil
- 1 egg   • 1 tsp vanilla extract
- 1/4 cup chopped walnuts

Instructions:
1. Preheat your oven to 350°F (175°C) and line a mini muffin pan with paper liners.
2. Mix together the almond flour, cocoa powder, and sugar-free sweetener.
3. Add the melted butter, egg, and vanilla extract to the dry ingredients and mix until well combined.
4. Fold in the chopped walnuts.
5. Spoon the batter into the mini muffin pan, filling each cup about three-quarters full.
6. Bake for 15 minutes or until a toothpick inserted into the center comes out clean.
7. Let cool before serving.

Benefits for Diabetics:
These brownie bites are low in carbs and sugar, making them a safe choice for those monitoring their blood sugar. Almond flour provides a gluten-free, low-carb base, while walnuts add healthy fats and texture.

Per Serving:
Calories: 220 | Fat: 20g | Carbs: 8g | Fiber: 3g | Protein: 5g

Spiced Carrot Cake Muffins

Serves: 2
Prep time: 15 minutes / Cook time: 20 minutes

Ingredients:
- 1 cup almond flour
- 1/4 cup grated carrot
- 1/4 cup chopped walnuts
- 2 tbsp sugar-free sweetener
- 1 tsp baking powder
- 1/2 tsp cinnamon
- 1/4 tsp nutmeg
- 1 egg
- 1/4 cup unsweetened almond milk

Instructions:
1. Preheat your oven to 350°F (175°C) and line a muffin tin with paper liners.
2. In a bowl, mix together the almond flour, sweetener, baking powder, cinnamon, and nutmeg.
3. Stir in the grated carrot and chopped walnuts.
4. In a separate bowl, whisk together the egg and almond milk, then add to the dry ingredients, stirring until just combined.
5. Divide the batter among the muffin cups and bake for 20 minutes or until a toothpick inserted into the center comes out clean.
6. Let cool before serving.

Benefits for Diabetics:
Carrots are a good source of fiber and beta-carotene, and when used in moderation, provide sweetness without a significant impact on blood sugar. The almond flour and nuts add healthy fats and protein, contributing to the overall low glycemic index of these muffins.

Per Serving:
Calories: 270 | Fat: 20g | Carbs: 15g | Fiber: 4g | Protein: 9g

Berry Swirl Cheesecake Squares

Serves: 2
Prep time: 20 minutes / Cook time: 25 minutes / Chill time: 2 hours

Ingredients:
- 1/2 cup almond flour (for crust)
- 1 tbsp coconut oil (for crust)
- 1 tbsp sugar-free sweetener (for crust)
- 1/2 cup cream cheese, softened
- 1/4 cup Greek yogurt
- 1 egg
- 2 tbsp sugar-free sweetener (for filling)
- 1/2 tsp vanilla extract
- 1/4 cup mixed berries, pureed

Instructions:
1. Preheat your oven to 350°F (175°C) and line a small baking dish with parchment paper.
2. Mix almond flour, coconut oil, and 1 tbsp sweetener to form a crust; press it into the bottom of the dish.
3. Beat the cream cheese, Greek yogurt, egg, 2 tbsp sweetener, and vanilla extract until smooth for the filling.
4. Pour the filling over the crust, then dollop the berry puree on top and use a toothpick to create a swirl pattern.
5. Bake for 25 minutes or until set. Cool completely, then refrigerate for at least 2 hours before cutting into squares and serving.

Benefits for Diabetics:
The combination of cream cheese and Greek yogurt offers a high-protein, low-carb base, while the almond flour crust provides a gluten-free, low-glycemic alternative to traditional crusts. Berries add natural sweetness and antioxidants without significantly impacting blood sugar.

Per Serving:
Calories: 310 | Fat: 26g | Carbs: 12g | Fiber: 3g | Protein: 9g

Creamy Key Lime Parfait

Serves: 2
Prep time: 15 minutes / Chill time: 1 hour

Ingredients:
- 1/2 cup Greek yogurt
- 2 tbsp key lime juice
- 1 tbsp sugar-free sweetener
- 1 tsp lime zest
- 1/4 cup whipped cream
- 1 tbsp crushed nuts or almond flour (for layering)

Instructions:
1. Mix Greek yogurt with key lime juice, sugar-free sweetener, and lime zest until well combined.
2. In serving glasses, layer the key lime mixture with whipped cream and crushed nuts or almond flour, creating alternate layers.
3. Refrigerate for at least 1 hour to allow the flavors to meld.
4. Garnish with additional lime zest or a thin slice of lime before serving.

Benefits for Diabetics:
Greek yogurt provides a creamy base high in protein and low in carbs. The use of key lime juice and zest offers a flavorful experience without added sugar, and the layer of nuts or almond flour adds a satisfying crunch and healthy fats.

Per Serving:
Calories: 150 | Fat: 8g | Carbs: 9g | Fiber: 0g | Protein: 9g

Rustic Pear and Almond Tart

Serves: 2
Prep time: 20 minutes / Cook time: 25 minutes

Ingredients:
- 1/2 cup almond flour
- 2 tbsp coconut oil (for crust)
- 1 tbsp sugar-free sweetener (for crust)
- 1 ripe pear, thinly sliced
- 1/4 tsp cinnamon
- 1/4 cup sliced almonds (for topping)

Instructions:
1. Preheat your oven to 350°F (175°C) and line a small baking sheet with parchment paper.
2. Mix almond flour, coconut oil, and sweetener to form the crust dough; press it into a tart shape on the baking sheet.
3. Arrange the thinly sliced pear on top of the crust, slightly overlapping.
4. Sprinkle with cinnamon and sliced almonds.
5. Bake for 25 minutes or until the crust is golden and the pears are tender.
6. Cool slightly before serving.

Benefits for Diabetics:
Pears are a good source of fiber and provide natural

sweetness without a high glycemic load. Almond flour offers a low-carb crust alternative, and the addition of almonds provides healthy fats and a satisfying crunch.

Per Serving:
Calories: 320 | Fat: 24g | Carbs: 22g | Fiber: 5g | Protein: 8g

Chocolate Avocado Truffles

Serves: 2
Prep time: 15 minutes / Chill time: 1 hour

Ingredients:
- 1 ripe avocado • 1/4 cup unsweetened cocoa powder
- 2 tbsp sugar-free sweetener
- 1/2 tsp vanilla extract
- Cocoa powder or crushed nuts for coating

Instructions:
1. Puree the ripe avocado until smooth.
2. Mix in the cocoa powder, sugar-free sweetener, and vanilla extract until well combined.
3. Chill the mixture for about 30 minutes until it's firm enough to handle.
4. Form the mixture into small balls and roll them in cocoa powder or crushed nuts to coat.
5. Refrigerate the truffles for an additional 30 minutes or until firm.
6. Serve chilled.

Benefits for Diabetics:
Avocados provide healthy fats and a creamy texture without added sugars. Cocoa powder offers the indulgence of chocolate without the high sugar content, making these truffles a luxurious yet health-conscious treat.

Per Serving:
Calories: 230 | Fat: 17g | Carbs: 18g | Fiber: 7g | Protein: 4g

Mango Coconut Frozen Yogurt

Serves: 2
Prep time: 10 minutes / Freeze time: 4 hours

Ingredients:
- 1 cup Greek yogurt
- 1/2 cup diced mango (fresh or frozen)
- 1/4 cup shredded unsweetened coconut
- 2 tbsp sugar-free sweetener

Instructions:
1. Blend Greek yogurt, diced mango, shredded coconut, and sugar-free sweetener until smooth.
2. Pour the mixture into a shallow dish and freeze for at least 4 hours, stirring every hour to break up ice crystals.
3. Once frozen to a creamy consistency, scoop and serve.

Benefits for Diabetics:
Greek yogurt is high in protein and low in carbohydrates, making it a suitable base for frozen desserts. Mango adds a natural sweetness and is a good source of vitamins, while coconut provides healthy fats, all contributing to a balanced treat.

Per Serving:
Calories: 180 | Fat: 6g | Carbs: 19g | Fiber: 2g | Protein: 10g

Cinnamon Apple Chips

Serves: 2
Prep time: 10 minutes / Cook time: 2 hours

Ingredients:
- 2 large apples, thinly sliced • 1/2 tsp cinnamon
- Optional: 1 tbsp sugar-free sweetener

Instructions:
1. Preheat your oven to 200°F (93°C) and line a baking sheet with parchment paper.
2. Arrange the thinly sliced apples in a single layer on the baking sheet.
3. Sprinkle with cinnamon and optional sugar-free sweetener.
4. Bake for 1-2 hours, flipping halfway through until the apple slices are dried and crispy.
5. Let cool completely before serving.

Benefits for Diabetics:
Apples are a good source of fiber and vitamin C, with a natural sweetness that makes them a great snack for diabetics when consumed in moderation. The addition of cinnamon not only adds flavor but also has been shown to help regulate blood sugar levels.

Per Serving:
Calories: 95 | Fat: 0g | Carbs: 25g | Fiber: 5g | Protein: 0.5g

Vanilla Almond Flaxseed Pudding

Serves: 2
Prep time: 5 minutes / Chill time: 2 hours

Ingredients:
- 1/4 cup ground flaxseeds
- 1 cup unsweetened almond milk
- 1 tbsp sugar-free sweetener
- 1/2 tsp vanilla extract
- Sliced almonds for garnish

Instructions:
1. In a bowl, whisk together ground flaxseeds, almond milk, sugar-free sweetener, and vanilla extract until well combined.
2. Let the mixture sit for 5 minutes, then whisk again to prevent clumping.
3. Cover and refrigerate for at least 2 hours or until it achieves a pudding-like consistency.
4. Before serving, give it a good stir and garnish with sliced almonds.

Benefits for Diabetics:
Flaxseeds are a powerhouse of nutrients, including omega-3 fatty acids and fiber, which are essential for blood sugar management and overall health. Almond milk provides a low-carb, dairy-free base, making this pudding both nutritious and accommodating for various dietary needs.

Per Serving:
Calories: 140 | Fat: 9g | Carbs: 8g | Fiber: 7g | Protein: 5g

Peach Basil Sorbet

Serves: 2
Prep time: 10 minutes / Freeze time: 4 hours

Ingredients:
- 2 ripe peaches, peeled and diced • 1/4 cup water
- 1/4 cup fresh basil leaves
- 2 tbsp sugar-free sweetener

Instructions:
1. In a blender, puree the peaches, water, basil leaves, and

sugar-free sweetener until smooth.

2. Pour the mixture into a shallow dish and freeze for 4 hours, stirring every hour to break up ice crystals.

3. Once it's frozen to the desired consistency, use a fork to scrape and fluff the sorbet.

4. Serve immediately, garnished with additional basil leaves if desired.

Benefits for Diabetics:

Peaches are a low glycemic fruit that provides natural sweetness along with a good dose of vitamins and fiber. Basil adds a unique flavor twist and contains antioxidants, contributing to the overall health benefits of this delightful sorbet.

Per Serving:

Calories: 60 | Fat: 0g | Carbs: 15g | Fiber: 2g | Protein: 1g

Espresso Walnut Brownies

Serves: 2

Prep time: 15 minutes / Cook time: 20 minutes

Ingredients:

- 1/2 cup almond flour
- 1/4 cup unsweetened cocoa powder
- 1/4 cup sugar-free sweetener
- 1 shot of espresso or 2 tsp instant coffee powder
- 1/4 cup chopped walnuts
- 1/4 cup melted butter or coconut oil
- 1 egg
- 1/2 tsp vanilla extract

Instructions:

1. Preheat your oven to 350°F (175°C) and line a small baking pan with parchment paper.

2. Mix together the almond flour, cocoa powder, and sugar-free sweetener.

3. Stir in the espresso or coffee powder, chopped walnuts, melted butter, egg, and vanilla extract until well combined.

4. Pour the batter into the prepared pan and spread evenly.

5. Bake for 20 minutes or until a toothpick inserted into the center comes out clean.

6. Cool completely before slicing and serving.

Benefits for Diabetics:

Almond flour provides a low-carb alternative to regular flour, making these brownies suitable for a diabetic diet. Walnuts add healthy fats and a satisfying crunch, while the natural stimulant properties of espresso give a delightful depth of flavor without adding sugar.

Per Serving:

Calories: 280 | Fat: 25g | Carbs: 10g | Fiber: 3g | Protein: 7g

Tropical Fruit Salad with Lime

Serves: 2

Prep time: 15 minutes / Chill time: 30 minutes

Ingredients:

- 1/2 cup diced pineapple
- 1/2 cup diced mango
- 1/2 banana, sliced
- Zest of 1 lime
- 1/2 cup sliced kiwi
- Juice of 1 lime
- Fresh mint leaves for garnish

Instructions:

1. In a large bowl, combine the diced pineapple, mango,

sliced kiwi, and banana.

2. Drizzle with lime juice and sprinkle lime zest over the top, tossing gently to coat all the fruit.

3. Refrigerate for 30 minutes to allow the flavors to meld.

4. Serve chilled, garnished with fresh mint leaves.

Benefits for Diabetics:

This fruit salad contains a variety of tropical fruits that are high in vitamins, minerals, and fiber. The natural sweetness of the fruits makes this salad a delightful treat without the need for added sugars. The lime juice adds a refreshing twist and can help with the digestion of the fruit sugars.

Per Serving:

Calories: 120 | Fat: 0.5g | Carbs: 30g | Fiber: 4g | Protein: 1g

No-Bake Coconut Lime Energy Bites

Serves: 2

Prep time: 10 minutes / Chill time: 30 minutes

Ingredients:

- 1/2 cup shredded unsweetened coconut
- 1/4 cup ground almonds or almond flour
- 1/4 cup pumpkin seeds or sunflower seeds
- 2 tbsp sugar-free sweetener
- Zest of 1 lime
- Juice of 1 lime
- 1 tbsp coconut oil

Instructions:

1. In a bowl, mix together the shredded coconut, ground almonds, seeds, sugar-free sweetener, lime zest, and lime juice.

2. Melt the coconut oil and add to the mixture, stirring until well combined.

3. Form the mixture into small balls and place on a tray lined with parchment paper.

4. Refrigerate for at least 30 minutes until firm.

5. Serve chilled, storing any leftovers in the refrigerator.

Benefits for Diabetics:

These energy bites are low in carbs and high in healthy fats and protein, providing sustained energy without spiking blood sugar levels. The coconut and lime offer a dose of tropical flavor while keeping the recipe fresh and light.

Per Serving:

Calories: 200 | Fat: 15g | Carbs: 10g | Fiber: 4g | Protein: 6g

Savory Spinach and Feta Crepes

Serves: 2

Prep time: 20 minutes / Cook time: 10 minutes

Ingredients:

- 1/2 cup almond flour
- 1/4 cup water
- 1 tbsp olive oil
- 1/4 cup feta cheese, crumbled
- Fresh herbs for garnish
- 2 eggs
- Pinch of salt
- 1 cup fresh spinach, chopped

Instructions:

1. In a bowl, whisk together the almond flour, eggs, water, and a pinch of salt until smooth to create the crepe batter.

2. Heat a non-stick skillet over medium heat and lightly grease with olive oil.

3. Pour a small amount of batter into the skillet, swirling to cover the bottom. Cook until edges lift, then flip and cook the other side. Repeat with remaining batter.
4. For the filling, sauté the spinach in a separate pan until wilted, then mix in the crumbled feta cheese.
5. Fill each crepe with the spinach and feta mixture, folding into quarters.
6. Serve warm, garnished with fresh herbs.

Benefits for Diabetics:
Almond flour crepes are a low-carb alternative to traditional wheat flour crepes, making them a suitable choice for those with diabetes. Spinach is rich in nutrients and low in carbs, while feta adds a tangy flavor without adding too much fat or sugar.

Per Serving:
Calories: 280 | Fat: 22g | Carbs: 8g | Fiber: 3g | Protein: 14g

Rosemary and Orange Infused Olive Oil Cake

Serves: 2
Prep time: 15 minutes / Cook time: 30 minutes

Ingredients:
- 1 cup almond flour
- 1/4 cup sugar-free sweetener
- 1/4 cup olive oil   • 2 eggs
- Zest of 1 orange
- 1 tbsp fresh rosemary, finely chopped
- 1 tsp baking powder   • Pinch of salt

Instructions:
1. Preheat your oven to 350°F (175°C) and grease a small round cake pan.
2. In a bowl, mix together the almond flour, sugar-free sweetener, baking powder, and salt.
3. Stir in the olive oil, eggs, orange zest, and rosemary until well combined.
4. Pour the batter into the prepared cake pan and smooth the top.
5. Bake for 30 minutes or until a toothpick inserted into the center comes out clean.
6. Let cool before slicing and serving.

Benefits for Diabetics:
This cake uses almond flour and sugar-free sweetener to keep it low in carbohydrates. Olive oil provides healthy fats, while the natural flavors of rosemary and orange zest offer a delightful taste without additional sugar.

Per Serving:
Calories: 320 | Fat: 28g | Carbs: 12g | Fiber: 3g | Protein: 8g

Blueberry Lemon Chia Seed Pudding

Serves: 2
Prep time: 10 minutes / Chill time: 2 hours

Ingredients:
- 1/4 cup chia seeds
- 1 cup unsweetened almond milk
- 1/2 cup fresh blueberries
- 1 tbsp sugar-free sweetener
- Zest of 1 lemon

- 1/2 tsp vanilla extract

Instructions:
1. In a bowl, whisk together the chia seeds, almond milk, sugar-free sweetener, lemon zest, and vanilla extract.
2. Gently fold in the blueberries, reserving a few for garnish.
3. Let the mixture sit for 5 minutes, then stir again to prevent clumping.
4. Cover and refrigerate for at least 2 hours, or until it achieves a pudding-like consistency.
5. Serve chilled, garnished with the reserved blueberries.

Benefits for Diabetics:
Chia seeds are a fantastic source of fiber and omega-3 fatty acids, which are beneficial for maintaining blood sugar levels. Blueberries and lemon provide antioxidants and vitamins without adding a significant amount of sugar.

Per Serving:
Calories: 150 | Fat: 8g | Carbs: 15g | Fiber: 10g | Protein: 5g

Spiced Poached Pears in Red Wine

Serves: 2
Prep time: 10 minutes / Cook time: 30 minutes

Ingredients:
- 2 ripe pears, peeled, halved, and cored
- 1 cup dry red wine   • 1/4 cup water
- 2 tbsp sugar-free sweetener
- 1 cinnamon stick   • 2 cloves
- 1 star anise

Instructions:
1. In a saucepan, combine the red wine, water, sugar-free sweetener, cinnamon stick, cloves, and star anise. Bring to a simmer.
2. Add the pear halves to the saucepan, ensuring they are covered by the wine mixture.
3. Simmer gently for 25-30 minutes, or until the pears are tender but still hold their shape.
4. Remove the pears and set aside. Continue to simmer the wine mixture until it reduces to a syrupy consistency.
5. Serve the pears with a drizzle of the reduced wine syrup.

Benefits for Diabetics:
Pears are a fiber-rich fruit that can have a modest impact on blood sugar levels. The red wine and spices infuse the pears with rich flavors without the need for added sugars, making this a luxurious yet diabetic-friendly dessert.

Per Serving:
Calories: 210 | Fat: 0g | Carbs: 28g | Fiber: 5g | Protein: 1g

Ricotta and Berry Compote Stuffed Crepes

Serves: 2
Prep time: 20 minutes / Cook time: 10 minutes

Ingredients:
- 2 low-carb, high-fiber crepes
- 1/2 cup ricotta cheese
- 1 cup mixed berries (strawberries, blueberries, raspberries)
- 1 tbsp sugar-free sweetener
- Zest of 1 lemon

Instructions:
1. Prepare the berry compote by simmering the mixed

berries with sugar-free sweetener and lemon zest until the berries break down and the mixture thickens. Let cool.

2. Spread a layer of ricotta cheese over half of each crepe.
3. Spoon the cooled berry compote over the ricotta.
4. Fold the crepes in half or roll them up.
5. Serve immediately, garnished with a sprinkle of lemon zest or a few fresh berries.

Benefits for Diabetics:
The combination of high-fiber crepes and ricotta cheese provides a balanced mix of nutrients, including protein and healthy fats, which are important for blood sugar control. The berry compote offers a natural sweetness and antioxidant benefits without the need for added sugars.

Per Serving:
Calories: 240 | Fat: 12g | Carbs: 18g | Fiber: 4g | Protein: 14g

Cashew Butter and Chocolate Swirl Fudge

Serves: 2
Prep time: 10 minutes / Chill time: 2 hours

Ingredients:
- 1/2 cup cashew butter • 1/4 cup coconut oil
- 1/4 cup unsweetened cocoa powder
- 2 tbsp sugar-free sweetener
- 1 tsp vanilla extract

Instructions:
1. Melt the coconut oil and mix with cashew butter, sugar-free sweetener, and vanilla extract until smooth.
2. Pour half of the mixture into a small parchment-lined dish.
3. Mix the unsweetened cocoa powder into the remaining half of the mixture.
4. Dollop the chocolate mixture over the cashew layer and use a knife or toothpick to create a swirl pattern.
5. Refrigerate for at least 2 hours or until firm.
6. Cut into squares and serve chilled.

Benefits for Diabetics:
Cashew butter provides a source of healthy fats and protein, helping to slow down sugar absorption and manage blood sugar levels. The use of sugar-free sweetener and dark chocolate keeps this dessert low in sugar while still satisfying your sweet tooth.

Per Serving:
Calories: 300 | Fat: 25g | Carbs: 12g | Fiber: 2g | Protein: 7g

Ginger Peach Yogurt Popsicles

Serves: 2
Prep time: 10 minutes / Freeze time: 4 hours

Ingredients:
- 1 cup Greek yogurt • 1 ripe peach, diced
- 1 tbsp grated fresh ginger
- 2 tbsp sugar-free sweetener

Instructions:
1. Blend the Greek yogurt, diced peach, fresh ginger, and sugar-free sweetener until smooth.
2. Pour the mixture into popsicle molds.
3. Freeze for at least 4 hours or until solid.
4. To serve, run the mold under warm water for a few seconds to release the popsicles.

Benefits for Diabetics:
Greek yogurt is high in protein and low in sugar, making it an excellent base for healthy desserts. Peaches add natural sweetness and ginger provides a spicy kick along with digestive benefits, creating a treat that's flavorful and beneficial for blood sugar control.

Per Serving:
Calories: 120 | Fat: 3g | Carbs: 15g | Fiber: 2g | Protein: 10g

Cardamom-Scented Apricot Compote

Serves: 2
Prep time: 5 minutes / Cook time: 20 minutes

Ingredients:
- 1 cup fresh apricots, halved and pitted
- 1/4 cup water   • 2 tbsp sugar-free sweetener
- 1/2 tsp ground cardamom
- A strip of lemon zest

Instructions:
1. In a saucepan, combine the apricots, water, sugar-free sweetener, cardamom, and lemon zest.
2. Bring to a simmer over medium heat and cook until the apricots are soft and the liquid has thickened into a syrup, about 20 minutes.
3. Remove from heat and let cool slightly. Remove the lemon zest before serving.
4. Serve warm or chilled, as desired.

Benefits for Diabetics:
Apricots are a low glycemic fruit that provide natural sweetness along with fiber and nutrients. Cardamom adds a layer of complex flavor and potential digestive benefits, while keeping the dish free of added sugars.

Per Serving:
Calories: 80 | Fat: 0.5g | Carbs: 18g | Fiber: 3g | Protein: 1g

Matcha Green Tea Mousse

Serves: 2
Prep time: 15 minutes / Chill time: 2 hours

Ingredients:
- 1 cup heavy whipping cream
- 1 tbsp matcha green tea powder
- 2 tbsp sugar-free sweetener
- 1/2 tsp vanilla extract

Instructions:
1. In a bowl, whip the heavy cream until it forms soft peaks.
2. Sift in the matcha green tea powder and sugar-free sweetener, then add the vanilla extract.
3. Gently fold the matcha and sweetener into the whipped cream until fully incorporated and smooth.
4. Spoon the mousse into serving dishes and refrigerate for at least 2 hours until set.
5. Serve chilled, garnished with a dusting of matcha powder or a few fresh berries.

Benefits for Diabetics:
Matcha is known for its high antioxidant content, particularly EGCG, which has been linked to various health benefits. The use of sugar-free sweetener makes this dessert suitable for those managing their blood sugar levels, while the cream provides a satisfying richness.

Per Serving:
Calories: 250 | Fat: 25g | Carbs: 4g | Fiber: 0g | Protein: 3g

Hazelnut Chocolate Chip Biscotti

Serves: 2

Prep time: 15 minutes / Cook time: 40 minutes

Ingredients:
- 1 cup almond flour   • 1/4 cup chopped hazelnuts
- 1/4 cup sugar-free chocolate chips
- 2 tbsp sugar-free sweetener   • 1 egg
- 1/2 tsp vanilla extract • 1/2 tsp baking powder

Instructions:
1. Preheat your oven to 350°F (175°C) and line a baking sheet with parchment paper.
2. In a bowl, mix together almond flour, chopped hazelnuts, sugar-free chocolate chips, sweetener, and baking powder.
3. Beat in the egg and vanilla extract until a dough forms.
4. Shape the dough into a log on the prepared baking sheet and flatten slightly.
5. Bake for 20 minutes, then remove from the oven and let cool for a few minutes.
6. Slice the log diagonally into 1/2-inch thick slices and place them cut side down on the baking sheet.
7. Bake for an additional 20 minutes or until golden and crisp.
8. Cool on a wire rack before serving.

Benefits for Diabetics:
Almond flour provides a low-carb base for these biscotti, making them a better option for blood sugar management. Hazelnuts and sugar-free chocolate chips add flavor and texture without the added sugars typically found in cookies.

Per Serving:
Calories: 280 | Fat: 22g | Carbs: 12g | Fiber: 4g | Protein: 8g

Coconut Mango Rice Pudding

Serves: 2

Prep time: 5 minutes / Cook time: 25 minutes

Ingredients:
- 1/2 cup cooked brown rice   • 1 cup coconut milk
- 1/2 cup diced mango   • 2 tbsp sugar-free sweetener
- 1/4 tsp vanilla extract • Pinch of cinnamon

Instructions:
1. In a saucepan, combine the cooked brown rice, coconut milk, and sugar-free sweetener.
2. Bring to a simmer over medium heat, stirring occasionally, until the mixture thickens, about 20 minutes.
3. Remove from heat and stir in the vanilla extract and cinnamon.
4. Let the pudding cool slightly, then fold in the diced mango.
5. Serve warm or chilled, garnished with a sprinkle of cinnamon or extra mango pieces.

Benefits for Diabetics:
Brown rice is a whole grain that offers more nutrients and fiber than white rice, contributing to a slower digestion and better blood sugar control. Coconut milk provides a creamy texture and healthy fats, while mango adds natural sweetness and a burst of tropical flavor.

Per Serving:
Calories: 260 | Fat: 18g | Carbs: 25g | Fiber: 2g | Protein: 3g

Baked Cinnamon Grapefruit

Serves: 2

Prep time: 5 minutes / Cook time: 15 minutes

Ingredients:
- 1 large grapefruit, halved • 1 tbsp sugar-free sweetener
- 1/2 tsp ground cinnamon

Instructions:
1. Preheat your oven to 375°F (190°C).
2. Sprinkle each grapefruit half evenly with sugar-free sweetener and cinnamon.
3. Place the grapefruit halves, cut side up, on a baking sheet or in a baking dish.
4. Bake for 15 minutes or until the tops are caramelized and slightly golden.
5. Serve warm, optionally with a dollop of sugar-free yogurt or whipped cream.

Benefits for Diabetics:
Grapefruit is a low glycemic fruit that offers vitamin C and other nutrients while being relatively low in sugar. The addition of cinnamon not only enhances flavor but may also have beneficial effects on blood sugar levels.

Per Serving:
Calories: 60 | Fat: 0g | Carbs: 15g | Fiber: 2g | Protein: 1g

Pear and Walnut Crumble

Serves: 2

Prep time: 15 minutes / Cook time: 25 minutes

Ingredients:
- 2 ripe pears, cored and sliced
- 1/4 cup walnuts, chopped
- 1/2 cup almond flour
- 2 tbsp sugar-free sweetener
- 1/2 tsp ground cinnamon
- 1/4 tsp ground nutmeg
- 2 tbsp unsalted butter, cold and cubed

Instructions:
1. Preheat your oven to 375°F (190°C) and lightly grease a small baking dish.
2. Arrange the sliced pears in the bottom of the dish.
3. In a bowl, combine the chopped walnuts, almond flour, sugar-free sweetener, cinnamon, and nutmeg.
4. Add the cold, cubed butter to the flour mixture and use your fingers to mix until it resembles coarse crumbs.
5. Sprinkle the crumble mixture evenly over the pears.
6. Bake for 25 minutes or until the topping is golden and the pears are tender.
7. Serve warm, optionally with a dollop of sugar-free whipped cream or yogurt.

Benefits for Diabetics:
Pears provide natural sweetness and fiber, making them a good choice for a low glycemic impact. Walnuts and almond flour add healthy fats and protein to the crumble topping, contributing to satiety and a slower release of sugars.

Per Serving:
Calories: 350 | Fat: 24g | Carbs: 28g | Fiber: 6g | Protein: 7g

Chapter 9: Staples, Sauces, Dips, and Dressings - Elevating Every Meal

Welcome to Chapter 9, a treasure trove of culinary secrets that will transform your everyday meals into extraordinary experiences.

In this chapter, we focus on staples, sauces, dips, and dressings, the essential elements that add flavor, texture, and nutritional value to your dishes. These components are particularly crucial in a diabetic-friendly diet, where balancing taste and health is paramount.

Here, you'll learn to master the art of creating versatile staples that serve as the foundation for countless recipes. We'll explore how to prepare whole grains, noodles, and other basic elements in ways that enhance their natural goodness while keeping your blood sugar levels in check.

Moving beyond the basics, this chapter delves into the world of sauces, dips, and dressings. Each recipe is designed to add a burst of flavor to your meals without adding unnecessary sugars or unhealthy fats.

From zesty vinaigrettes to creamy dips and robust sauces, these condiments will bring life to salads, main dishes, and snacks in a healthy, diabetes-friendly way.

As you journey through this chapter, you'll discover that a little creativity and knowledge can go a long way in making nutritious meals that delight the senses. Whether you're dressing a salad, topping a grilled fish, or dipping your favorite vegetables, the possibilities are endless. Welcome to the flavorful world of staples, sauces, dips, and dressings!

Smoky Chipotle Tomato Salsa

erves: 2

Prep time: 10 minutes / Cook time: 0 minutes

Ingredients:
- 4 medium ripe tomatoes, diced
- 1 small onion, finely chopped
- 2 chipotle peppers in adobo sauce, minced
- 1/4 cup fresh cilantro, chopped
- Juice of 1 lime   • Salt and pepper to taste

Instructions:
1. In a bowl, combine the diced tomatoes, chopped onion, minced chipotle peppers, cilantro, and lime juice.
2. Mix well and season with salt and pepper to taste.
3. Let it sit for at least 10 minutes to allow flavors to meld.
4. Serve with diabetic-friendly snacks or as a topping for grilled meats.

Benefits for Diabetics:
Tomatoes are low in carbs and rich in vitamins, while the chipotle peppers offer a smoky taste without added sugars. This salsa is high in antioxidants and vitamins, promoting overall health and blood sugar control.

Per Serving:
Calories: 60 | Fat: 0.5g | Carbs: 14g | Fiber: 4g | Protein: 2g

Creamy Garlic Cauliflower Mash

Serves: 2

Prep time: 10 minutes / Cook time: 15 minutes

Ingredients:
- 1 head of cauliflower, cut into florets
- 2 cloves garlic, minced• 2 tbsp unsalted butter
- 1/4 cup grated Parmesan cheese
- Salt and pepper to taste
- Fresh chives, chopped for garnish

Instructions:
1. Steam the cauliflower florets until very tender.
2. In a pan, sauté garlic in butter until golden and fragrant.
3. In a food processor, blend the steamed cauliflower, garlic butter, and Parmesan until smooth.
4. Season with salt and pepper to taste.
5. Serve hot, garnished with chives.

Benefits for Diabetics:
Cauliflower is an excellent low-carb alternative to potatoes, high in fiber and essential nutrients. This dish provides the comforting texture and taste of a classic staple without the high glycemic impact.

Per Serving:
Calories: 150 | Fat: 12g | Carbs: 10g | Fiber: 4g | Protein: 6g

Spicy Lemon Herb Chicken Skewers

Serves: 2

Prep time: 20 minutes (plus marinating) / Cook time: 10 minutes

Ingredients:
- 2 boneless, skinless chicken breasts, cut into chunks
- Juice of 1 lemon   • 2 tbsp olive oil
- 1 tsp red pepper flakes • Salt and pepper to taste
- 1 tbsp mixed herbs (such as thyme, rosemary, and oregano)

Instructions:
1. In a bowl, whisk together lemon juice, olive oil, red pepper flakes, mixed herbs, salt, and pepper.
2. Add the chicken chunks to the marinade and let sit for at least 30 minutes.
3. Thread the marinated chicken onto skewers.
4. Grill on medium-high heat for about 5 minutes per side or until fully cooked.
5. Serve hot with a side of vegetables or salad.

Benefits for Diabetics:
Chicken is a great source of lean protein, essential for blood sugar regulation. The spicy lemon herb marinade adds flavor without sugar, making these skewers a perfect, balanced choice for diabetics.

Per Serving:
Calories: 250 | Fat: 12g | Carbs: 3g | Fiber: 0g | Protein: 30g

Cucumber and Dill Greek Yogurt Dip

Serves: 2

Prep time: 10 minutes / Cook time: 0 minutes

Ingredients:
- 1 cup Greek yogurt, unsweetened
- 1/2 cucumber, finely diced
- 2 tbsp fresh dill, chopped • 1 clove garlic, minced
- Salt and pepper to taste • Lemon zest for garnish

Instructions:
1. In a bowl, combine Greek yogurt, cucumber, dill, and garlic.
2. Season with salt and pepper to taste.
3. Chill for at least 30 minutes to allow flavors to blend.
4. Serve garnished with lemon zest.

Benefits for Diabetics:
Greek yogurt provides a good source of protein and probiotics, while cucumber adds hydration and fiber. This dip is low in carbohydrates and high in flavor, ideal for blood sugar management.

Per Serving:
Calories: 90 | Fat: 2g | Carbs: 10g | Fiber: 1g | Protein: 9g

Toasted Almond and Garlic Green Beans

Serves: 2

Prep time: 5 minutes / Cook time: 10 minutes

Ingredients:
- 2 cups fresh green beans, trimmed
- 1/4 cup sliced almonds • 2 cloves garlic, minced
- 1 tbsp olive oil • Salt and pepper to taste

Instructions:
1. In a skillet, heat olive oil over medium heat.
2. Add the green beans and cook, stirring occasionally, until they start to soften.
3. Add garlic and almonds, continue to cook until beans are tender and almonds are golden.
4. Season with salt and pepper to taste.
5. Serve warm.

Benefits for Diabetics:
Green beans are low in carbohydrates and high in fiber, making them an excellent choice for blood sugar management. Almonds add healthy fats and a satisfying crunch, enhancing both nutrition and taste.

Per Serving:
Calories: 160 | Fat: 12g | Carbs: 12g | Fiber: 5g | Protein: 5g

Spiced Pumpkin Seed Crunch

Serves: 2

Prep time: 5 minutes / Cook time: 15 minutes

Ingredients:
- 1 cup raw pumpkin seeds • 1 tsp olive oil
- 1/2 tsp smoked paprika • 1/4 tsp cumin
- 1/4 tsp garlic powder • Salt to taste

Instructions:
1. Preheat oven to 350°F (175°C).
2. In a bowl, toss pumpkin seeds with olive oil, smoked paprika, cumin, and garlic powder until well coated.
3. Spread the seeds in a single layer on a baking sheet.
4. Bake for 15 minutes or until golden and crunchy, stirring occasionally.
5. Season with salt while still warm.
6. Let cool and serve as a snack or salad topping.

Benefits for Diabetics:
Pumpkin seeds are a fantastic source of magnesium, zinc, and healthy fats, all beneficial for blood sugar control and overall health. The spices add flavor without the need for sugar or excess salt.

Per Serving:
Calories: 180 | Fat: 15g | Carbs: 4g | Fiber: 2g | Protein: 9g

Tangy Mustard Broccoli Slaw

Serves: 2

Prep time: 15 minutes / Cook time: 0 minutes

Ingredients:
- 2 cups broccoli slaw mix • 2 tbsp Dijon mustard
- 1 tbsp apple cider vinegar
- 1 tsp honey (optional, or use a diabetic-friendly sweetener)
- 2 tbsp olive oil • Salt and pepper to taste

Instructions:
1. In a large bowl, whisk together Dijon mustard, apple cider vinegar, honey (or sweetener), and olive oil until well combined.
2. Add the broccoli slaw mix to the bowl and toss until evenly coated.
3. Season with salt and pepper to taste.
4. Let the slaw sit for at least 10 minutes before serving to allow flavors to meld.

Benefits for Diabetics:
Broccoli is high in fiber and nutrients while being low in calories and carbs, making it an excellent choice for blood sugar management. The tangy mustard dressing adds a burst of flavor without unnecessary sugars.

Per Serving:
Calories: 110 | Fat: 9g | Carbs: 7g | Fiber: 3g | Protein: 2g

Roasted Red Pepper and Walnut Dip

Serves: 2

Prep time: 10 minutes / Cook time: 5 minutes

Ingredients:
- 1 cup roasted red peppers, drained
- 1/2 cup walnuts, toasted • 1 garlic clove, minced
- 2 tbsp olive oil • 1 tsp cumin
- Salt and pepper to taste

Instructions:
1. In a food processor, blend the roasted red peppers, toasted walnuts, garlic, and cumin until smooth.
2. While blending, slowly add the olive oil until the mixture is creamy.
3. Season with salt and pepper to taste.
4. Serve as a dip or spread on sandwiches or wraps.

Benefits for Diabetics:
Rich in healthy fats from walnuts and olive oil, this dip offers essential nutrients without high carbs. Red peppers provide a good dose of vitamin C and antioxidants, supporting overall health.

Per Serving:
Calories: 220 | Fat: 20g | Carbs: 8g | Fiber: 2g | Protein: 4g

Cool Cilantro Lime Yogurt Sauce

Serves: 2

Prep time: 5 minutes / Cook time: 0 minutes

Ingredients:
- 1 cup Greek yogurt, unsweetened
- 1/4 cup fresh cilantro, chopped
- Juice of 1 lime   • 1 tsp lime zest
- 1 garlic clove, minced   • Salt to taste

Instructions:
1. In a bowl, mix together Greek yogurt, chopped cilantro, lime juice, lime zest, and minced garlic.
2. Season with salt to taste.
3. Chill in the refrigerator for at least 30 minutes before serving to let flavors meld.
4. Serve as a sauce or dressing as desired.

Benefits for Diabetics:
Greek yogurt is a fantastic source of protein and calcium, while being low in sugar. The addition of lime and cilantro offers a boost of flavor and antioxidants without adding carbohydrates.

Per Serving:
Calories: 90 | Fat: 4g | Carbs: 7g | Fiber: 0g | Protein: 9g

Spicy Black Bean Dip

Serves: 2

Prep time: 10 minutes / Cook time: 0 minutes

Ingredients:
- 1 cup cooked black beans, drained and rinsed
- 1 small jalapeño, seeded and chopped
- 2 tbsp onion, finely chopped
- 1 garlic clove, minced   • 1 tsp ground cumin
- Juice of 1 lime   • Salt and pepper to taste

Instructions:
1. In a food processor, blend black beans, jalapeño, onion, garlic, cumin, and lime juice until smooth.
2. Season with salt and pepper to taste.
3. Serve with diabetic-friendly vegetables or whole grain crackers.

Benefits for Diabetics:
Black beans are an excellent source of fiber and protein, helping to manage blood sugar levels. The spices and lime juice add flavor without sugar, making this a hearty and healthy choice.

Per Serving:
Calories: 120 | Fat: 1g | Carbs: 20g | Fiber: 8g | Protein: 8g

Tangy Tarragon Mustard Sauce

Serves: 2

Prep time: 5 minutes / Cook time: 0 minutes

Ingredients:
- 1/4 cup Dijon mustard
- 2 tbsp fresh tarragon, finely chopped
- 1 tbsp apple cider vinegar
- 1 tsp honey (optional, or use a diabetic-friendly sweetener)
- Salt and pepper to taste

Instructions:
1. In a small bowl, combine Dijon mustard, chopped tarragon, apple cider vinegar, and honey or sweetener.
2. Whisk together until smooth and well blended.
3. Season with salt and pepper to taste.
4. Serve as a condiment with grilled or roasted meats and vegetables.

Benefits for Diabetics:
Mustard is a low-calorie, high-flavor condiment, while tarragon adds a unique herbaceous note. This sauce provides bold flavor without added sugars, making it a diabetic-friendly choice.

Per Serving:
Calories: 30 | Fat: 1g | Carbs: 4g | Fiber: 1g | Protein: 1g

Mediterranean Olive Tapenade

Serves: 2

Prep time: 10 minutes / Cook time: 0 minutes

Ingredients:
- 1 cup mixed olives, pitted • 1 tbsp capers, drained
- 1 garlic clove, minced   • 2 tbsp fresh parsley, chopped
- 1 tbsp lemon juice   • 2 tbsp olive oil
- Salt and pepper to taste

Instructions:
1. In a food processor, combine olives, capers, garlic, parsley, and lemon juice.
2. Pulse until coarsely chopped.
3. While pulsing, slowly drizzle in olive oil until the mixture is slightly chunky or smooth, as preferred.
4. Season with salt and pepper to taste.
5. Serve as a dip or spread on bread or crackers.

Benefits for Diabetics:
Olives are a great source of healthy fats and low in carbohydrates, making this tapenade a smart choice for maintaining blood sugar levels. It's rich in flavor and nutrients, offering a heart-healthy option for snacking or enhancing meals.

Per Serving:
Calories: 180 | Fat: 18g | Carbs: 4g | Fiber: 2g | Protein: 1g

Zesty Horseradish and Dill Sauce

Serves: 2

Prep time: 5 minutes / Cook time: 0 minutes

Ingredients:
- 1/4 cup horseradish, drained • 1/2 cup sour cream
- 2 tbsp fresh dill, chopped   • 1 tsp lemon juice
- Salt and pepper to taste

Instructions:
1. In a bowl, combine horseradish, sour cream, chopped dill, and lemon juice.
2. Mix until well combined and creamy.
3. Season with salt and pepper to taste.
4. Chill for at least 30 minutes before serving to allow flavors to develop.
5. Serve with meats or as a dip for vegetables.

Benefits for Diabetics:
Horseradish is naturally low in carbohydrates and adds a significant flavor punch without sugar. Combined with the probiotics in sour cream, this sauce is not only flavorful but also beneficial for digestion.

Per Serving:
Calories: 120 | Fat: 10g | Carbs: 6g | Fiber: 1g | Protein: 2g

Sweet and Smoky BBQ Sauce

Serves: 2

Prep time: 5 minutes / Cook time: 20 minutes

Ingredients:
- 1 cup tomato sauce, no added sugar
- 2 tbsp apple cider vinegar
- 1 tbsp Worcestershire sauce
- 2 tsp smoked paprika • 1/2 tsp garlic powder
- 1/2 tsp onion powder
- Sweetener equivalent to 2 tbsp sugar
- Salt and pepper to taste

Instructions:
1. In a saucepan, combine all ingredients and whisk together.
2. Bring to a simmer over medium heat, then reduce to low and cook for 20 minutes, stirring occasionally.
3. Adjust seasonings to taste and add sweetener as needed.
4. Cool and use as a sauce for grilling or as a condiment.

Benefits for Diabetics:
By using a sugar substitute and natural tomato sauce, this BBQ sauce minimizes sugar intake while maximizing flavor. It's a great way to enjoy the taste of barbecue without the worry of blood sugar spikes.

Per Serving:
Calories: 45 | Fat: 0.5g | Carbs: 10g | Fiber: 2g | Protein: 2g

Creamy Tahini and Lemon Dressing

Serves: 2

Prep time: 5 minutes / Cook time: 0 minutes

Ingredients:
- 1/4 cup tahini   • Juice of 1 lemon
- 1 garlic clove, minced
- 2-3 tbsp water (for desired consistency)
- Salt and pepper to taste

Instructions:
1. In a bowl, whisk together tahini, lemon juice, and minced garlic.
2. Gradually add water until you reach your desired consistency.
3. Season with salt and pepper to taste.
4. Serve as a dressing or dip as desired.

Benefits for Diabetics:
Tahini is a great source of healthy fats and minerals, supporting overall health and blood sugar control. Lemon adds a fresh, tangy flavor without the need for sugars or artificial ingredients.

Per Serving:
Calories: 180 | Fat: 16g | Carbs: 8g | Fiber: 3g | Protein: 5g

Ginger Sesame Soy Dressing

Serves: 2

Prep time: 5 minutes / Cook time: 0 minutes

Ingredients:
- 2 tbsp soy sauce (low sodium)
- 1 tbsp sesame oil   • 1 tbsp rice vinegar
- 1 tsp fresh ginger, grated   • 1 garlic clove, minced
- 1 tsp sugar substitute   • 1 tsp sesame seeds

Instructions:
1. In a bowl, whisk together soy sauce, sesame oil, rice vinegar, ginger, garlic, and sugar substitute until well combined.
2. Stir in sesame seeds.
3. Serve immediately or store in the refrigerator for up to a week.
4. Shake well before using as a dressing or marinade.

Benefits for Diabetics:
This dressing is low in carbohydrates and high in flavor, utilizing natural ingredients like ginger and garlic to boost taste without adding sugar. Sesame oil provides healthy fats, beneficial for overall health.

Per Serving:
Calories: 70 | Fat: 7g | Carbs: 2g | Fiber: 0g | Protein: 1g

Fiery Chipotle Avocado Sauce

Serves: 2

Prep time: 10 minutes / Cook time: 0 minutes

Ingredients:
- 1 ripe avocado
- 1 chipotle pepper in adobo sauce
- 1/4 cup cilantro leaves • Juice of 1 lime
- 1 garlic clove   • Salt to taste
- Water for thinning

Instructions:
1. In a blender or food processor, combine avocado, chipotle pepper, cilantro, lime juice, and garlic.
2. Blend until smooth, adding water as necessary to reach desired consistency.
3. Season with salt to taste.
4. Serve immediately or store in an airtight container in the refrigerator.

Benefits for Diabetics:
Avocados are an excellent source of healthy fats and fiber, aiding in blood sugar control. The chipotle pepper adds a smoky heat without relying on sugary condiments, making this sauce both flavorful and healthful.

Per Serving:
Calories: 160 | Fat: 15g | Carbs: 9g | Fiber: 7g | Protein: 2g

Herbed Greek Feta Dip

Serves: 2

Prep time: 10 minutes / Cook time: 0 minutes

Ingredients:
- 1/2 cup feta cheese, crumbled
- 1/4 cup Greek yogurt, unsweetened
- 1 tbsp olive oil
- 1 tbsp fresh dill, chopped
- 1 tbsp fresh mint, chopped
- 1 garlic clove, minced
- Salt and pepper to taste

Instructions:
1. In a bowl, combine crumbled feta, Greek yogurt, olive oil, dill, mint, and minced garlic.
2. Mash and mix until well combined and slightly creamy.
3. Season with salt and pepper to taste.

4. Serve chilled as a dip with vegetables or spread on bread.

Benefits for Diabetics:
Feta cheese provides a flavorful base with fewer calories and carbs, while Greek yogurt adds a creamy texture and good dose of protein. The fresh herbs bring a burst of flavor without adding sugar or fat.

Per Serving:
Calories: 150 | Fat: 12g | Carbs: 4g | Fiber: 0g | Protein: 8g

Sun-Dried Tomato and Basil Pesto

Serves: 2
Prep time: 10 minutes / Cook time: 0 minutes

Ingredients:
- 1/2 cup sun-dried tomatoes, drained and chopped
- 1 cup fresh basil leaves
- 1/4 cup grated Parmesan cheese
- 1/4 cup pine nuts or walnuts
- 2 garlic cloves   • 1/4 cup olive oil
- Salt and pepper to taste

Instructions:
1. In a food processor, combine sun-dried tomatoes, basil, Parmesan, nuts, and garlic.
2. Pulse while gradually adding olive oil until a smooth paste forms.
3. Season with salt and pepper to taste.
4. Serve or store in an airtight container in the refrigerator.

Benefits for Diabetics:
This pesto offers a good balance of healthy fats, protein, and antioxidants while keeping carbohydrates in check. Sun-dried tomatoes add a natural sweetness and intense flavor without the need for added sugars.

Per Serving:
Calories: 190 | Fat: 18g | Carbs: 6g | Fiber: 2g | Protein: 5g

Creamy Beet and Horseradish Spread

Serves: 2
Prep time: 10 minutes / Cook time: 0 minutes

Ingredients:
- 1 medium beet, cooked and peeled
- 2 tbsp prepared horseradish
- 1/4 cup Greek yogurt, unsweetened
- 1 tsp apple cider vinegar
- Salt and pepper to taste

Instructions:
1. In a food processor, blend the cooked beet, horseradish, Greek yogurt, and apple cider vinegar until smooth.
2. Season with salt and pepper to taste.
3. Chill in the refrigerator for at least 1 hour before serving.
4. Serve as a spread on sandwiches or as a colorful dip.

Benefits for Diabetics:
Beets are low in calories and high in nutrients, offering a sweet taste naturally. Horseradish adds a spicy kick without the need for sugar, while Greek yogurt provides a creamy base and extra protein.

Per Serving:
Calories: 90 | Fat: 1g | Carbs: 15g | Fiber: 3g | Protein: 6g

Roasted Garlic and White Bean Hummus

Serves: 2
Prep time: 15 minutes / Cook time: 30 minutes

Ingredients:
- 1 cup cooked white beans
- 1 whole head of garlic, roasted
- 2 tbsp olive oil   • 1 tbsp lemon juice
- Salt and pepper to taste   • 1 tsp paprika (for garnish)

Instructions:
1. Squeeze the roasted garlic cloves out of their skins and into a food processor.
2. Add white beans, olive oil, and lemon juice to the roasted garlic.
3. Blend until smooth, adding a little water if necessary for consistency.
4. Season with salt and pepper to taste.
5. Garnish with a sprinkle of paprika before serving.
6. Serve with fresh vegetables or whole-grain crackers.

Benefits for Diabetics:
White beans are an excellent source of fiber and protein, aiding in blood sugar stability. Roasted garlic adds depth of flavor without the need for additional sugars or unhealthy fats.

Per Serving:
Calories: 200 | Fat: 7g | Carbs: 25g | Fiber: 6g | Protein: 10g

Smoky Eggplant Baba Ganoush

Serves: 2
Prep time: 15 minutes / Cook time: 40 minutes (for roasting eggplant)

Ingredients:
- 1 large eggplant   • 2 tbsp tahini
- 1 garlic clove, minced • Juice of 1 lemon
- 1 tsp smoked paprika   • Salt and pepper to taste
- Olive oil for drizzling

Instructions:
1. Roast the eggplant over an open flame or in the oven until the skin is charred and the inside is tender.
2. Peel the skin off the cooled eggplant and place the flesh in a food processor.
3. Add tahini, garlic, lemon juice, and smoked paprika.
4. Blend until smooth, drizzling in olive oil as needed for consistency.
5. Season with salt and pepper to taste.
6. Serve with a drizzle of olive oil and a sprinkle of paprika.

Benefits for Diabetics:
Eggplant is a low-carb vegetable, high in fiber and nutrients. Combined with tahini, a source of healthy fats, this dish is not only flavorful but also beneficial for blood sugar control and overall health.

Per Serving:
Calories: 140 | Fat: 10g | Carbs: 12g | Fiber: 6g | Protein: 3g

Roasted Red Pepper & Walnut Sauce

Serves: 2
Prep time: 10 minutes / Cook time: 5 minutes

Ingredients:
- 2 large red bell peppers, roasted and peeled
- 1/2 cup walnuts, toasted • 2 cloves garlic, minced
- 1 tbsp olive oil • 1 tsp smoked paprika
- Salt and pepper to taste

Instructions:
1. In a blender or food processor, combine roasted red peppers, walnuts, garlic, olive oil, and smoked paprika.
2. Blend until smooth, adding a little water if necessary to reach desired consistency.
3. Season with salt and pepper to taste.
4. Serve as a sauce for grilled meats, vegetables, or as a unique dip.

Benefits for Diabetics:
This sauce is rich in antioxidants and healthy fats, thanks to the red peppers and walnuts. It's low in carbohydrates and high in flavor, making it a great choice for maintaining blood sugar levels.

Per Serving:
Calories: 190 | Fat: 17g | Carbs: 9g | Fiber: 3g | Protein: 4g

Zesty Cilantro Lime Sauce

Serves: 2

Prep time: 10 minutes / Cook time: 0 minutes

Ingredients:
- 1 cup fresh cilantro leaves
- Juice and zest of 1 lime • 1 clove garlic
- 1/4 cup Greek yogurt, unsweetened
- 2 tbsp olive oil
- Salt and pepper to taste

Instructions:
1. In a blender or food processor, combine cilantro, lime juice and zest, garlic, Greek yogurt, and olive oil.
2. Blend until smooth.
3. Season with salt and pepper to taste.
4. Serve over your favorite grilled meats or vegetables, or use as a dressing for salads.

Benefits for Diabetics:
This sauce is low in carbs and sugars while being high in flavor and nutrients. The Greek yogurt provides a creamy texture and protein, while the cilantro and lime offer a refreshing taste and antioxidants.

Per Serving:
Calories: 120 | Fat: 10g | Carbs: 4g | Fiber: 1g | Protein: 3g

Golden Turmeric Tahini Sauce

Serves: 2

Prep time: 5 minutes / Cook time: 0 minutes

Ingredients:
- 1/4 cup tahini • 1 tsp ground turmeric
- Juice of 1/2 lemon • 1 clove garlic, minced
- Salt and pepper to taste
- Water, as needed for consistency

Instructions:
1. In a bowl, whisk together tahini, turmeric, lemon juice, and minced garlic.
2. Gradually add water until you reach a pourable consistency.
3. Season with salt and pepper to taste.

4. Drizzle over your favorite dishes for a boost of flavor and color.

Benefits for Diabetics:
Turmeric is known for its anti-inflammatory properties and may help in blood sugar control. Tahini is a good source of healthy fats and protein, making this sauce not only delicious but also beneficial for blood sugar management.

Per Serving:
Calories: 180 | Fat: 16g | Carbs: 6g | Fiber: 2g | Protein: 5g

Balsamic Thyme Reduction

Serves: 2

Prep time: 2 minutes / Cook time: 20 minutes

Ingredients:
- 1 cup balsamic vinegar • 2 sprigs fresh thyme
- 1 clove garlic, crushed • Salt and pepper to taste

Instructions:
1. In a small saucepan, combine balsamic vinegar, thyme, and crushed garlic.
2. Bring to a boil, then reduce heat and simmer until the vinegar is reduced by half and thickened.
3. Season with salt and pepper to taste.
4. Strain out the thyme and garlic, then drizzle the reduction over your desired dish.

Benefits for Diabetics:
Balsamic vinegar has a low glycemic index, meaning it doesn't cause a rapid spike in blood glucose levels. This reduction offers a flavorful alternative to sugary sauces, complementing a variety of dishes without the added sugar.

Per Serving:
Calories: 70 | Fat: 0g | Carbs: 14g | Fiber: 0g | Protein: 1

Spicy Ginger Peanut Sauce

Serves: 2

Prep time: 10 minutes / Cook time: 0 minutes

Ingredients:
- 1/4 cup natural peanut butter
- 1 tbsp soy sauce (low sodium)
- 1 tbsp rice vinegar
- 1 tsp grated ginger
- 1 small garlic clove, minced
- 1/2 tsp chili flakes (adjust to taste)
- Warm water to thin

Instructions:
1. In a bowl, whisk together peanut butter, soy sauce, rice vinegar, ginger, garlic, and chili flakes.
2. Gradually add warm water until the sauce reaches your desired consistency.
3. Adjust chili flakes to reach your preferred level of heat.
4. Serve as a dipping sauce or drizzle over your favorite Asian-inspired dishes.

Benefits for Diabetics:
Peanut butter provides healthy fats and protein, making this sauce a hearty and satisfying option that's low in carbs. Ginger and garlic add a boost of flavor and potential blood sugar-regulating properties.

Per Serving:
Calories: 160 | Fat: 12g | Carbs: 8g | Fiber: 2g | Protein: 7g

Minty Avocado Green Sauce

Serves: 2
Prep time: 10 minutes / Cook time: 0 minutes

Ingredients:
- 1 ripe avocado
- Juice of 1 lime
- Salt and pepper to taste
- Water, as needed for consistency
- 1/4 cup fresh mint leaves
- 1 clove garlic

Instructions:
1. In a blender, combine avocado, mint leaves, lime juice, and garlic.
2. Blend until smooth, adding water as needed to reach desired consistency.
3. Season with salt and pepper to taste.
4. Serve as a fresh dressing or dip to add a burst of flavor to any dish.

Benefits for Diabetics:
Avocado is a great source of healthy fats and fiber, promoting heart health and blood sugar stability. Mint and lime add a fresh zest without additional sugars, making this sauce a delightful addition to a diabetic-friendly diet.

Per Serving:
Calories: 160 | Fat: 14g | Carbs: 10g | Fiber: 7g | Protein: 2g

Smoky Tomato Aioli

Serves: 2
Prep time: 10 minutes / Cook time: 0 minutes

Ingredients:
- 1/2 cup mayonnaise (preferably low-fat)
- 1/4 cup sun-dried tomatoes, finely chopped
- 1 tsp smoked paprika
- 1 clove garlic, minced
- Salt and pepper to taste

Instructions:
1. In a bowl, combine mayonnaise, sun-dried tomatoes, smoked paprika, and minced garlic.
2. Mix until well combined and smooth.
3. Season with salt and pepper to taste.
4. Refrigerate for at least 30 minutes before serving to allow flavors to meld.
5. Use as a spread for sandwiches or as a dipping sauce.

Benefits for Diabetics:
The smoky tomato aioli is low in carbohydrates and offers a flavorful alternative to sugary or high-carb sauces. The sun-dried tomatoes provide antioxidants and a concentrated flavor without the need for added sugars.

Per Serving:
Calories: 200 | Fat: 20g | Carbs: 4g | Fiber: 1g | Protein: 1g

Roasted Red Pepper and Walnut Pesto

Serves: 2
Prep time: 10 minutes / Cook time: 0 minutes

Ingredients:
- 1 cup roasted red peppers, drained and chopped
- 1/2 cup walnuts, toasted
- 2 cloves garlic, minced
- 1/4 cup grated Parmesan cheese
- 2 tbsp olive oil
- Salt and pepper to taste

Instructions:
1. In a food processor, blend roasted red peppers, walnuts, garlic, and Parmesan until smooth.
2. While blending, slowly add in olive oil until well combined.
3. Season with salt and pepper to taste.
4. Serve over grilled vegetables, chicken, or fish.

Benefits for Diabetics:
Walnuts are rich in omega-3 fatty acids and antioxidants, supporting heart health. Roasted red peppers provide a good source of vitamins A and C, all with minimal impact on blood sugar levels.

Per Serving:
Calories: 220 | Fat: 20g | Carbs: 6g | Fiber: 2g | Protein: 6g

Tangy Herb Greek Yogurt Dip

Serves: 2
Prep time: 5 minutes / Cook time: 0 minutes

Ingredients:
- 1 cup unsweetened Greek yogurt
- 2 tbsp fresh dill, chopped
- 1 tbsp fresh parsley, chopped
- 1 clove garlic, minced
- Juice of 1/2 lemon
- Salt and pepper to taste

Instructions:
1. In a bowl, mix together Greek yogurt, dill, parsley, garlic, and lemon juice.
2. Season with salt and pepper to taste.
3. Chill for at least 1 hour before serving to allow flavors to develop.
4. Serve with vegetable sticks or as a dressing for salads.

Benefits for Diabetics:
Greek yogurt provides a healthy dose of protein and probiotics, aiding in digestion and blood sugar control. The addition of fresh herbs offers antioxidant benefits without added sugars.

Per Serving:
Calories: 90 | Fat: 2g | Carbs: 5g | Fiber: 0g | Protein: 14g

Balsamic & Garlic Vinaigrette

Serves: 2
Prep time: 5 minutes / Cook time: 0 minutes

Ingredients:
- 1/4 cup balsamic vinegar
- 1/2 tsp Dijon mustard
- Salt and pepper to taste
- 1 clove garlic, minced
- 1/2 cup olive oil

Instructions:
1. In a bowl, whisk together balsamic vinegar, garlic, and Dijon mustard.
2. Gradually whisk in olive oil until the mixture is well combined and emulsified.
3. Season with salt and pepper to taste.
4. Drizzle over salads or use as a marinade for meats.

Benefits for Diabetics:
Balsamic vinegar offers a natural sweetness without a significant sugar content, making it a diabetic-friendly option. Olive oil provides healthy fats, aiding in blood

sugar regulation and heart health.

Per Serving:
Calories: 250 | Fat: 27g | Carbs: 3g | Fiber: 0g | Protein: 0g

Spicy Avocado Cilantro Sauce

Serves: 2

Prep time: 10 minutes / Cook time: 0 minutes

Ingredients:
- 1 ripe avocado
- 1/4 cup fresh cilantro leaves
- 1 small jalapeño, seeded and chopped
- Juice of 1 lime
- Salt to taste
- 2 tbsp water (or more for desired consistency)

Instructions:
1. In a blender, combine avocado, cilantro, jalapeño, lime juice, and water.
2. Blend until smooth, adding more water if necessary to reach desired consistency.
3. Season with salt to taste.
4. Serve immediately or store in an airtight container in the fridge.

Benefits for Diabetics:
Avocado is known for its healthy fats and fiber, aiding in blood sugar stabilization and heart health. The jalapeño adds a spicy flavor without the need for added sugars or unhealthy fats.

Per Serving:
Calories: 160 | Fat: 15g | Carbs: 9g | Fiber: 7g | Protein: 2g

Lemon Tahini Dressing

Serves: 2

Prep time: 5 minutes / Cook time: 0 minutes

Ingredients:
- 1/4 cup tahini
- Juice of 1 lemon
- 1 clove garlic, minced
- Salt to taste
- 2-4 tbsp water (for desired consistency)

Instructions:
1. In a small bowl, whisk together tahini, lemon juice, and garlic.
2. Gradually add water until you reach a pourable consistency.
3. Season with salt to taste.
4. Drizzle over salads, steamed vegetables, or use as a dip.

Benefits for Diabetics:
Tahini is a great source of healthy fats and protein, helping to maintain stable blood sugar levels. Lemon adds a dose of vitamin C and freshness without adding sugar.

Per Serving:
Calories: 180 | Fat: 16g | Carbs: 8g | Fiber: 2g | Protein: 5g

Fresh Mint Chutney

Serves: 2

Prep time: 10 minutes / Cook time: 0 minutes

Ingredients:
- 1 cup fresh mint leaves
- 1/2 cup fresh cilantro leaves
- 1 small green chili, chopped
- 1/2 inch ginger, chopped
- Juice of 1 lime
- Salt to taste
- 1-2 tbsp water (for blending)

Instructions:
1. In a blender, combine mint, cilantro, green chili, ginger, lime juice, and a little water.
2. Blend until smooth, adding more water if necessary for a pourable consistency.
3. Season with salt to taste.
4. Serve as a dip or drizzle over grilled meats and vegetables.

Benefits for Diabetics:
Mint and cilantro are known for their digestive benefits and very low impact on blood sugar. The addition of lime and ginger provides a boost of flavor without added sugars.

Per Serving:
Calories: 25 | Fat: 0g | Carbs: 6g | Fiber: 2g | Protein: 1g

Sesame Ginger Soy Sauce

Serves: 2

Prep time: 5 minutes / Cook time: 0 minutes

Ingredients:
- 1/4 cup low sodium soy sauce
- 1 tbsp sesame oil
- 1 tbsp grated fresh ginger
- 1 clove garlic, minced
- 1 tsp rice vinegar
- 1/2 tsp black sesame seeds (for garnish)

Instructions:
1. In a bowl, whisk together soy sauce, sesame oil, ginger, garlic, and rice vinegar.
2. Let the mixture sit for a few minutes to allow flavors to meld.
3. Sprinkle with black sesame seeds before serving.
4. Use as a dipping sauce, dressing, or marinade.

Benefits for Diabetics:
The low sodium soy sauce offers a deep umami flavor without the sugar or high salt content. Sesame oil and ginger add healthful properties, including anti-inflammatory effects and aiding in blood sugar control.

Per Serving:
Calories: 70 | Fat: 7g | Carbs: 1g | Fiber: 0g | Protein: 1g

Smoky Paprika Almond Sauce

Serves: 2

Prep time: 10 minutes / Cook time: 0 minutes

Ingredients:
- 1/2 cup raw almonds, soaked and drained
- 1 tsp smoked paprika
- 1 clove garlic, minced
- 2 tbsp olive oil
- Juice of 1/2 lemon
- Salt to taste
- Water for blending

Instructions:
1. In a blender, combine soaked almonds, smoked paprika, garlic, olive oil, and lemon juice.
2. Blend until smooth, adding water as needed to reach desired consistency.
3. Season with salt to taste.
4. Serve as a spread on sandwiches or a dip for vegetables.

Benefits for Diabetics:
Almonds are a great source of healthy fats, protein, and fiber, aiding in blood sugar control. Smoked paprika adds a flavor boost without the need for sugar or excess salt.

Per Serving:
Calories: 210 | Fat: 19g | Carbs: 7g | Fiber: 4g | Protein: 6g

30-Day Meal Plan

	Breakfast	Lunch	Dinner	Snack/Dessert
Day 1	Spinach and Mushroom Egg Muffins	Mediterranean Chicken and Vegetable Casserole	Lemon Garlic Baked Cod	Almond and Berry Delight
Day 2	Avocado and Salmon Lettuce Wrap	Slow-Cooked Beef and Broccoli	Rosemary Garlic Grilled Lamb Chops	Cinnamon-Spiced Baked Apples
Day 3	Chia and Coconut Yogurt Parfait	Turkey and Sweet Potato Skillet Casserole	Herb-Crusted Salmon with Spinach Salad	Cinnamon-Spiced Baked Apples
Day 4	Turkey and Veggie Breakfast Skillet	Lemon-Thyme Chicken & Quinoa	Herb-Crusted Pork Tenderloin	Avocado Chocolate Mousse
Day 5	Blueberry Almond Overnight Oats	Nordic Salmon with Dill Mustard Sauce	Blackened Catfish with Avocado Slaw	Lemon Ricotta Pancakes
Day 6	Cinnamon Flaxseed Pancakes	Swedish Turkey Meatballs with Lingonberry	Mediterranean Beef Kabobs	Ginger Spice Cookies
Day 7	Greek Yogurt and Nuts Breakfast Bowl	Finnish Mushroom Soup	Seared Scallops with Asparagus	Chia Seed Vanilla Pudding
Day 8	Savory Quinoa Breakfast Bowl	Rye Bread Open Sandwich (Smørrebrød)	Spicy Lamb Meatballs with Yogurt Sauce	Coconut Almond Bark
Day 9	Tomato Basil Omelet	Norwegian Cod with Root Vegetables	Coconut Curry Shrimp	Pumpkin Spice Smoothie
Day 10	Vegan Tofu Scramble	Icelandic Barley and Lamb Stew	Balsamic Glazed Pork Chops	Zesty Lemon Coconut Bars
Day 11	Spinach and Feta Breakfast Wrap	Maple Glazed Salmon	Honey Soy Glazed Salmon	Walnut Brownie Bites
Day 12	Apple Cinnamon Oatmeal	Poutine with Oven-Baked Fries	Lemon and Herb Roast Beef	Spiced Carrot Cake Muffins
Day 13	Berry Smoothie Bowl	Wild Rice and Chicken Casserole	Mediterranean Grilled Swordfish	Berry Swirl Cheesecake Squares
Day 14	Southwestern Tofu Scramble	Roasted Beet and Goat Cheese Salad	Garlic Butter Beef Tips	Creamy Key Lime Parfait
Day 15	Cottage Cheese and Peach Breakfast Bowl	Lentil Shepherd's Pie	Chili Lime Fish Tacos	Rustic Pear and Almond Tart

	Breakfast	**Lunch**	**Dinner**	**Snack/Dessert**
Day 16	Low-Carb Breakfast Burrito	Baked Cod with Maple Balsamic Brussels Sprouts	Spiced Lamb Shank Stew	Chocolate Avocado Truffles
Day 17	Pumpkin Seed and Oat Granola	Crockpot Turkey Chili	Garlic Butter Scallops with Herbs	Mango Coconut Frozen Yogurt
Day 18	Zucchini and Herb Breakfast Fritters	Beef Stew with Root Vegetables	Spicy Beef Stir-Fry with Broccoli	Cinnamon Apple Chips
Day 19	Pear and Walnut Baked Oatmeal	Slow-Cooked Pulled Pork	Asian-Style Steamed Mussels	Vanilla Almond Flaxseed Pudding
Day 20	Mediterranean Veggie Breakfast Skillet	Crockpot Chicken Cacciatore	Herbed Pork Tenderloin with Zucchini	Peach Basil Sorbet
Day 21	Hearty Veggie Breakfast Hash	Slow-Cooker Salsa Verde Chicken	Poached Salmon in Tomato Basil Sauce	Espresso Walnut Brownies
Day 22	Lemon Ricotta Pancakes	Crockpot Beef and Broccoli	Beef and Mushroom Stuffed Peppers	Tropical Fruit Salad with Lime
Day 23	Pumpkin Spice Protein Oats	Whole Wheat Spaghetti with Grilled Vegetables	Lamb and Feta Burgers	No-Bake Coconut Lime Energy Bites
Day 24	Southwestern Tofu Scramble Wrap	Chicken and Mushroom Risotto	Baked Tilapia with Dill Sauce	Savory Spinach and Feta Crepes
Day 25	Mediterranean Frittata	Shrimp and Zucchini Noodles	Pork Loin with Ginger-Peach Glaze	Rosemary and Orange Infused Olive Oil Cake
Day 26	Zucchini and Carrot Pancakes	Eggplant Parmesan with Almond Flour	Spicy Grilled Shrimp	Blueberry Lemon Chia Seed Pudding
Day 27	Pear and Walnut Baked Oatmeal	Italian Sausage and Peppers over Cauliflower Rice	Seared Beef Steak with Cauliflower Mash	Spiced Poached Pears in Red Wine
Day 28	Savory Breakfast Salad	Lean Beef Bolognese over Spaghetti Squash	Pan-Seared Scallops with Lemon Butter Sauce	Ricotta and Berry Compote Stuffed Crepes
Day 29	Broccoli and Cheese Breakfast Muffins	Grilled Chicken Caprese	Citrus-Herb Marinated Pork Tenderloin	Cashew Butter and Chocolate Swirl Fudge
Day 30	Smoked Salmon and Avocado Toast	Tuscan Bean Soup	Grilled Tuna Steaks with Avocado Salsa	Ginger Peach Yogurt Popsicles

INDEX